SMASH REVIEWS FOR THE PLAYS OF TERRENCE McNALLY

The Lisbon Traviata:

"I don't know when I have heard such scaldingly intimate dialogue in the New York theater."
—Rex Reed, *New York Post*

"A savagely amusing and empathetic study of two men whose lives have been lost in opera."
—Frank Rich, *The New York Times*

"A highly entertaining, amusing, touching, compelling play."
—*New York Observer*

Frankie and Johnnie in the Clair de Lune:

"A very sweet, extraordinarily funny, romantic, ribald comedy."
—Clive Barnes, *New York Post*

"Fresh, illuminating . . . the most serious play yet about intimacy in the age of AIDS."
—Frank Rich, *The New York Times*

"Among the best plays he has written."
—Edith Oliver, *The New Yorker*

It's Only a Play:

"Charged with an energy that leaps and zigzags from the merely frantic to the hysterical."
—Brendan Gill, *The New Yorker*

"Frequently uproarious!"
—Frank Rich, *The New York Times*

TERRENCE McNALLY is the author of numerous plays, including the book for the musical *The Rink* and the smash Broadway hit *The Ritz*. He has received two Guggenheim Fellowships, a Rockefeller grant, and a citation from the American Academy of Arts and Letters. He lives in New York City.

THREE PLAYS BY TERRENCE McNALLY

The Lisbon Traviata

Frankie and Johnny in the Clair de Lune

It's Only a Play

Terrence McNally

A PLUME BOOK

PLUME
Published by the Penguin Group
Penguin Books USA Inc., 375 Hudson Street,
New York, New York 10014, U.S.A.
Penguin Books Ltd, 27 Wrights Lane,
London W8 5TZ, England
Penguin Books Australia Ltd, Ringwood,
Victoria, Australia
Penguin Books Canada Ltd, 2801 John Street,
Markham, Ontario, Canada L3R 1B4
Penguin Books (N.Z.) Ltd, 182–190 Wairau Road,
Auckland 10, New Zealand

Penguin Books Ltd, Registered Offices:
Harmondsworth, Middlesex, England

First published by Plume, an imprint of Penguin Books USA Inc.
Published simultaneously in Canada.

First Printing, August, 1990
10 9 8 7 6 5 4 3 2 1

REGISTERED TRADEMARK—MARCA REGISTRADA

LIBRARY OF CONGRESS CATALOGING-IN-PUBLICATION DATA

McNally, Terrence.
  [Plays. Selections]
  Three plays / by Terrence McNally.
    p.   cm.
  Contents: The Lisbon traviata—Frankie and Johnny in the Clair
de Lune—It's only a play.
  ISBN 0-452-26425-1
  I. Title.
PS3563.A323A6   1990
812'.54—dc20
                                          90-31360
                                          CIP

Printed in the United States of America
Set in Times Roman
Designed by Julian Hamer

For Lynne Meadow

A Few Words
of Introduction

The three plays in this volume are my most recently produced plays in New York City, where I live, sometimes happily, and work, always happily.

New York can be a difficult and terrible place to be, but if you write plays it is the only place to be if you want to work with the best directors, actors, and designers in the American theater. I realize this is a provincial point of view (it's certainly an unfashionable one), but it's mine, and the only one I have after more than twenty-five years of working in the American theater. I dread being mugged or spoken to rudely as much as the next person, but I dread working with weak actors, unspecific directors, and copycat designers even more. The quality of my life goes hand in hand with the quality of the people I get to work with when we put on one of my plays. The people who brought these plays so stunningly to life all live on the isle of Manhattan. And as far as I know, none of them was done bodily harm in the process. If indeed the best actors, directors, and designers all live in New York City, maybe these same folks figure the best playwrights probably live here, too. At least I'm pretty sure they're thinking something pretty much like that as *they* endure the daily indignities of being part of the Big Apple.

The three plays in this collection are inextricably linked with the Manhattan Theatre Club, a not-for-profit subscription theater that produces a season of new plays on two stages at City Center on West 55th Street. Manhattan Theatre Club is my artistic home. I was something of a theatrical orphan before they took me in, wandering script in hand from one production to another. Some were successful, some weren't, but there was never any continuity between them. Playwrights need a home where they are fed, nourished, and challenged. I am lucky to have found one at MTC. Those were lonely streets in Manhattan before MTC took me in.

When *Broadway, Broadway* (the original title for *It's Only a Play*) closed in Philadelphia en route to its Broadway opening at the Eugene O'Neill Theatre, I felt many things, and none of them was good. I certainly didn't feel like writing another play, and so I didn't. Looking back, I wonder, if it weren't for the enthusiasm of director John Tillinger for the play, just how many years would have passed before my appetite for the theater was restored. Tillinger brought me and the play to Lynne Meadow and the Manhattan Theatre Club. The production was a success, and my appetite, instead of being merely restored, became voracious. I haven't stopped wanting to write plays since.

It's Only a Play is a comedy, but it's one of the most serious plays I have ever written. It's my attempt to describe exactly what it was like to work in the Broadway theater in the 1980s. It is probably the closest thing I will ever write to a documentary. Because it is a comedy, people think I am exaggerating the truth. I am not. It is a true play. The truth as I know it. Why the truth is not supposed to be funny is one of those rules someone must have come up with somewhere along the line and everyone believed him (or her). I doubt it was Aristotle. Whoever he or she was, I would like to thank him or her for making my life very difficult. Everyone agrees that comedy is supposed to be truthful. But hardly anyone agrees that the truth can be treated humorously. In this case, I agree with myself 100 percent. *It's Only a Play* is a result of that handshake.

It was during one of the previews of *It's Only a Play* that Lynne Meadow said she would produce my next play sight unseen. It was the best Christmas present any playwright ever got. Almost at once, I sat down and wrote *Frankie and Johnny in the Clair de Lune*. Some plays and productions come easily. *Frankie and Johnny* is one of those blessed ones. The writing was accomplished in less than two months. I wrote it for a great actress, Kathy Bates, and she said yes. Paul Benedict agreed to direct. The miracle that is Kenneth Welsh came into our lives as Johnny at an old-fashioned audition. I changed perhaps ten lines in rehearsal and previews. Audiences seemed to like the play from the dress rehearsal on. The play has been seen virtually around the world. It looks like there will be a motion picture.

I still don't quite know where *Frankie and Johnny* came from. I do know I began it shortly after I had lost my two best friends and dearest collaborators in the theater, Robert Drivas and James Coco. Friends seemed especially precious and life unbelievably fragile. I had always thought they would be in my personal and professional life forever. But if *It's Only a Play* was born of a painful personal experience, *Frankie and Johnny* is more a poem about feelings than a true story about anyone I know. I missed Bobby and Jimmy a lot. I still do, I always will, but I missed them less while I was writing *Frankie and Johnny*.

I do know I felt I was Johnny while I was writing it. I identified with him completely. I kept thinking he had his hands full with that Frankie, poor guy. About a year later I was watching a production of the play at the Mark Taper Forum in Los Angeles when I realized I was Frankie. Johnny suddenly sounded and acted like a Martian to me, but that Frankie was someone I could really identify with.

Obviously, I had to be a little bit of both of them to have written the play, but I've only begun to realize how emotionally autobiographical my plays are. Just about the only true facts of my own life I have put in my plays are Frankie's speech about her Nana in *Frankie and Johnny* and Peter's memory (in *It's Only a Play*) of his belief that George and Ira Gershwin were happily married songwriters. Growing up in a smallish town in Texas as I did has its distinct cultural liabilities. There are no men named Ira in Corpus Christi, Texas.

The Lisbon Traviata was never an easy play. It was hard to write, hard to cast, hard to rehearse, hard to perform, hard to get the critics to see what I was driving at. As I write these words it is running at the Promenade Theatre in what I consider a definitive production. Anthony Heald and Nathan Lane are the kind of actors I was talking about in the first paragraph. You simply don't find their equals in Cleveland. That is not a knock at Cleveland. It is the reason I choose to live in New York.

The same John Tillinger has been passionate in his devotion to and protection of *Lisbon* since he read the first act. We are both aware that the first act is "funny" and the second act "serious." The critics have spilled a lot of ink in telling us that. It is clearly not a well-made play in which the first act prepares us for everything that happens in the second. Yesterday did not prepare me for what happened today. Life is a lousy playwright that way. I was merely trying to reflect that in *The Lisbon Traviata*.

Fortunately, the play has its ardent admirers among the press, so it looks like we shall have a good run with it. Unfortunately, we New Yorkers live in a city where the press has too much influence on what people choose to see when they go to the theater. That is our fault. Instead of working diligently to lower the costs of producing a play (and, consequently, the price of tickets), we spend prodigious amounts of money advertising our plays in the pages of the very newspapers or on the airwaves of the very television networks that often mock and attack us. I dream of a city in which people go to the theater because they love it, because they can't live without it, not because they have been intimidated into attendance by over-advertising. The Broadway theater is the Age of Hype's most pathetic victim. That is a knock at New York and is one of the reasons I sometimes wish I lived and worked in Cleveland.

At first glance, *It's Only a Play*, *Frankie and Johnny in the Clair de Lune*, and *The Lisbon Traviata* might seem like three very different plays. In many ways, they are. The first is a fairly sophisticated drawing-room comedy; the second, a romantic drama with fairy-tale overtones; and the third, an opera buffa that ends up verismo tragedy. And yet I recognize that they are very much the work of the same author. In each play, the unattainable is pursued at great length and at great risk. The people in these plays aren't fooling around. I think passion is what connects them. Mendy and Stephen in *The Lisbon Traviata* are as surely Johnny's brothers in *Frankie and Johnny* as they are Virginia's or Julia's or Peter's or James's or any of the "theater folk" in *It's Only a Play*. The milieu of these three plays is what distinguishes them. The heartbeat that informs each of them is my own.

The
Lisbon Traviata

For Dominic Cuskern

The Lisbon Traviata was produced at the Promenade Theatre in New York City by the Manhattan Theatre Club. It opened on October 31, 1989, with the following cast:

STEPHEN .... Anthony Heald
MENDY.................... Nathan Lane
MIKE .... Dan Butler
PAUL.................... John Slattery

It was directed by John Tillinger. Set designed by Philipp Jung. Lighting designed by Ken Billington. Costumes designed by Jane Greenwood. Sound designed by Gary and Timmy Harris. Fight staged by B.H. Barry. The production stage manager was Pamela Singer.

An earlier version of *The Lisbon Traviata* was produced at Theatre Off Park in New York City. It was produced by Sherwin M. Goldman, Westport Productions, and Theatre Off Park Inc. It opened on June 4, 1985, with the following cast:

STEPHEN .... Benjamin Hendrickson
MENDY.................... Seth Allen
MIKE .... Stephen Schnetzer
PAUL.................... Steven Culp

It was directed by John Tillinger. Set designed by Philipp Jung. Lighting designed by Michael Orriss Watson. Costumes designed by C. L. Hundley. Sound designed by Gary Harris. The production stage manager was John M. Atherlay, and the stage manager was Charlie Eisenberg.

THE CHARACTERS

MENDY—Middle-aged, appealing, somewhat out of shape. Wears good clothes well. Intelligent. His manner can be excessive (it often is) and may take some getting used to.

STEPHEN—Ten years younger than Mendy but looks even younger. Good looking. Fair. In trim. Somewhat closed and guarded in his manner.

MIKE—Several years younger than Stephen. Handsome, sexual. Dark coloring. Moves well. Direct manner.

PAUL—Mid-twenties. Good looking. Appealing, friendly, open manner. Likes himself.

The time of the play is now.
The place of the play is New York City.

A word about the settings:

Mendy's apartment is warm, romantic, crowded with good antiques. It is a floor-through in a brownstone in the West Village. One would be hard pressed to imagine a lovelier cocoon. The windows are heavily draped. There is a fire in the fireplace.

Stephen and Mike's apartment, by comparison, is lean and modern. It is a one-bedroom in a newish high-rise in the same neighborhood. There is at least one abstract painting on the wall. A large leather sofa dominates the living room.

The one thing both apartments have in common are lots and lots of phonograph records, cassettes, and reel-to-reel tapes, and the elaborate equipment for playing them. Mendy's records and tapes are strewn all over the place. Those in Stephen and Mike's place are alphabetically arranged in a large, hi-tech cabinet and many built-in shelves. Mendy's hi-fi equipment is probably out-of-date. Stephen and Mike's is the latest thing.

ACT I
(Mendy & Stephen)

Mendy's. After dinner. There are dessert plates and coffee cups about. Phonograph records are strewn everywhere. A general, but genial, clutter.

STEPHEN *is seated on the end of a chaise, not lying back in it. His shoes are off.* MENDY *is at the hi-fi, trying to find a certain groove on a well-worn record. He has the volume up quite high, so that the noise of the needle scratching against the record is quite loud and painful.*

STEPHEN: Jesus, Mendy!

MENDY: Damnit!

STEPHEN: Be careful!

MENDY: I can't wait for you to hear this.

STEPHEN: Just put it on at the beginning.

MENDY: She's not in the beginning.

STEPHEN: I can wait for her. Anything but that.

MENDY: I've been playing it all day.

STEPHEN: I'm sure you have. Mendy, please!

MENDY: Here we are!

STEPHEN: I don't—

MENDY: Sshh.

STEPHEN: I—

MENDY: Sshh!

(The needle has found the groove MENDY *was looking for and begun to track the record. Unfortunately, and almost at*

once, we hear a steady clunk, clunk, clunk. Not only is the record badly scratched, but the needle is stuck.)

STEPHEN: I don't believe you.

MENDY: I just bought it!

STEPHEN: All it takes you is one playing to ruin a brand new record.

MENDY: Ssshh! Listen.

(He gives the tone arm a push.)

STEPHEN: I told you to put everything on tape.

MENDY: You're not listening. Sshh!

STEPHEN: Though God knows you'd probably find a way to scratch a tape, too.

MENDY: Will you listen?

STEPHEN: I'm sure even a CD wouldn't survive you.

MENDY: *Ascolta!*

(The needle is tracking now. What we are listening to is a "pirated" recording of Maria Callas. The sound is appropriately dim and distant, and decidedly low-fidelity. The music is Violetta's recitative "È strano . . . è strano," preceding the aria "Ah forsè lui" from the first act of Verdi's La Traviata.)

MENDY: It's to die.

STEPHEN: *La Traviata.*

MENDY: I can just see her. Jet black hair parted in the middle, a chignon in the back, flashing eyes, that white dress with the red carnation, the use of the fan.

STEPHEN: *(Eyes closed, concentrating)* Just a minute.

MENDY: And the gloves. Long white kid gloves over the elbow. God, she was so beautiful. The glory, the glory.

STEPHEN: Okay! I think I've got it. *Traviata,* London, June 20, 1958 with Cesare Valletti and Mario Zanasi. The conductor was Nicola Rescigno. Am I right?

MENDY: You've heard it?

STEPHEN: Of course I've heard it. I have it. Just turn it off. Those scratches are worse than chalk on a chalkboard. I thought you were going to put on something I hadn't heard.

MENDY: When did you buy it?

STEPHEN: I don't know. A month ago, six weeks. May I see the album cover, please?

MENDY: They told me it just came out.

STEPHEN: Where was that? The album, Mendy.

MENDY: Music Masters.

(HE hands STEPHEN the album.)

STEPHEN: *(Looking at the album)* Music Masters! Well no wonder. They haven't even gotten in the Lisbon *Traviata* yet. I told you to go to Discophile.

MENDY: What Lisbon *Traviata?*

STEPHEN: The *Traviata* she sang in Lisbon, March 27, 1958. What do you mean, "What Lisbon *Traviata?"*

MENDY: Stephen!

STEPHEN: "June 21." I could have sworn it was June 20. I think this is a mistake.

(He will find a book among a pile on the floor and start looking for the information he requires.)

MENDY: Stephen!

STEPHEN: What?

MENDY: There's a Lisbon *Traviata?*

STEPHEN: Kraus is the Alfredo.

MENDY: Alfredo Kraus is the Alfredo?

STEPHEN: No, his sister, Lily Kraus. What do you care? You don't like Alfredo Kraus.

MENDY: I do if he sings with Maria.

STEPHEN: *(Finding the date)* "June 20." When I'm wrong, I'm wrong. But when I'm right, I'm right. Have you heard Nilsson's *Frau Ohne Schatten* from Munich?

MENDY: Stephen, this isn't funny. How is she?

STEPHEN: Loud, louder, and loudest. She runs the gamut. But Rysanek is spectacular.

MENDY: Stephen, how is she?

STEPHEN: Who she? What she? I don't even know what you're talking about.

MENDY: Maria!

STEPHEN: Oh, that she!

MENDY: On the Lisbon *Traviata!*

STEPHEN: She's fantastic. Did you get the new *Masked Ball* on Philips?

MENDY: I can't believe you didn't bring it.

STEPHEN: I assumed you had it. Save your money. Caballè and Carreras have their moments but Colin Davis's conducting is so non-echt Italian, you know?

MENDY: Stephen, I'm talking about the Lisbon *Traviata*.

STEPHEN: So was I. Then I changed the subject to the new *Masked Ball*.

MENDY: Fuck the new *Masked Ball*.

STEPHEN: I don't know why you hate Caballè so much.

MENDY: She can't sing.

STEPHEN: Oh, come on, Mendy. She has a beautiful voice.

MENDY: It's not enough.

STEPHEN: You've got to admit she's trying. I mean, she has improved.

MENDY: Not enough. She'll never catch up to Callas. To Tebaldi, maybe. To Maria, never. Is Discophile still open?

STEPHEN: What do I look like? Information Please?

MENDY: What's their number?

STEPHEN: What am I supposed to do while you run over there?

MENDY: You haven't heard Sutherland's *Merry Widow*, I bet.

STEPHEN: I hate Sutherland. So do you. You'd buy anything.

MENDY: What's their number?

STEPHEN: It's after nine.

MENDY: What is their number, will you?

STEPHEN: How should I know?

MENDY: Be that way!

(MENDY *has gone to the phone and punch dialed the number for information.*)

STEPHEN: It's not that good a performance. The London is better.

MENDY: You just said it was fantastic.

STEPHEN: It is, but not that fantastic.

MENDY: *(Into the phone)* Information?

STEPHEN: You know they charge you a quarter for that?

MENDY: *(Into the phone)* Do you have the number for a Discophile on West 8th St. in the Village?

STEPHEN: Michael does the same thing.

MENDY: *(Into the phone)* Yes, it's in Manhattan. *(Covers phone, groans)* Oy! All this talk about the Third World. New York *is* the Third World.

STEPHEN: If you think I'm going to sit here all by myself listening to scratchy records while you go over to—

MENDY: *(Into the phone)* Discophile! It's a record shop. That's "D" as in . . . as in what? . . . you've got me so rattled . . . !

STEPHEN: "D" as in David.

MENDY: *(Into phone)* As in De Los Angeles. Not the town. The singer. Victoria De Los Angeles. All right, Information, have it your way: "D" as in David then. *(Covers phone)* Do you believe this?

STEPHEN: WAtkins 9–8818.

MENDY: What?

STEPHEN: WAtkins 9–8818.

MENDY: Are you sure?

STEPHEN: *(Pointing)* It's right on their shopping bag.

MENDY: *(Into phone)* Never mind, Information, and never was an organization less-aptly named. And don't charge me for this! I'm going to check next month's statement to see if you did.

(HE hangs up.)

STEPHEN: You're incredible.

MENDY: In this day and age in this particular *ville*, one can't afford not to be.

(HE punch dials another number.)

WAtkins 9–8818, was it?

STEPHEN: Have you heard Sills's last *Thais?*

MENDY: Unfortunately, I heard her first *Thais.*

STEPHEN: Anyone who never heard her early *Manons* never heard Sills.

MENDY: I heard her *Manon*.

STEPHEN: You heard her middle and late *Manons*. I said her first *Manons*.

MENDY: I heard her *Manon* in 1971 at the New York State Theatre and it was one big wobble.

STEPHEN: 1971 was already her middle *Manons*. I'm talking about 68/69.

MENDY: *(Into the phone)* Hello? Discophile? You don't sound familiar. Are you new? *(Covers phone)* He's new. Be still my beating heart. *(Into phone)* Do you have a copy of the Callas Lisbon *Traviata?* The Callas Lisbon *Traviata*. It's a pirate. Thank you. *(Covers phone)* No wonder he didn't sound familiar. They're playing Dame Janet Baker.

STEPHEN: Who else?

MENDY: *(Listening)* She's singing the *Nuits d'été*.

STEPHEN: They'll never beat Eleanor Steber's recording of that. Mike turned me on to that.

MENDY: *(Still listening)* No, wait. It's not Baker. It's too fruity . . . it's Crespin! Or is it?

(HE listens hard.)

STEPHEN: *(Trying to take the phone)* Here, let me.

MENDY: *(Pulling away with phone)* Just a minute. Did Christa Ludwig ever record it?

STEPHEN: I hope not. Will you let me?

MENDY: Don't grab!

(STEPHEN takes the phone from MENDY and listens)

Suzanne Danco? Hildegard Behrens? Josephine Veasey? This is driving me crazy.

STEPHEN: *(Listening)* Number one, it's not *Nuits d'été*. It's *L'Invitation au Voyage*. Number two, it's Jessye Norman.

MENDY: Number three, fuck you.

STEPHEN: *(Into phone)* Hello? *(HE covers phone.)* They're out of the Lisbon *Traviata*. They have Dallas and London and he thinks La Scala if you want him to check.

MENDY: Give me that! *(HE takes the phone.)* You're sure you don't have the Lisbon? Did you try the shelf under the Angel and RCA cut-outs? Sometimes Franz puts them there. He isn't around by any chance? When do you expect it back in again? How many have you sold so far? Thirty? You've sold thirty Lisbon *Traviatas*? *(To* STEPHEN*)* They've sold thirty Lisbon *Traviatas! (Back into phone)* You wouldn't by any chance know offhand who you might have sold some of them to? Couldn't you look? I mean, you must keep receipts, some sort of record. I'm calling for Mme. Scotto. I'm her secretary and she asked me to track down a copy before she leaves town in the morning. Renatta Scotto, who else?

STEPHEN: Absolutely incredible!

MENDY: She's doing her first Violetta in years and everybody's told her to listen to the Lisbon *Traviata* first. Mme. Scotto never sings anything without listening to Callas first. I know she'd really appreciate it if you could make some effort to track one down. Yes, tonight. I told you, she's leaving in the morning, first thing. But couldn't you at least—! We've tried Music Masters. They're the ones who stuck me with this London *Traviata* everybody else seems to have already heard. Besides, they're closed. They don't work their staff like coolies. I don't think I've communicated the urgency of this call to you. Thank you for nothing. *(HE hangs up.* STEPHEN *is glancing at his watch.)* Stephen?

STEPHEN: No. I'd love to hear some Flagstad.

MENDY: What do you mean, no? You don't even know what I was going to say.

STEPHEN: Mendy, I always know what you're going to say.

MENDY: Please.

STEPHEN: I said no.

MENDY: It's only eight blocks.

STEPHEN: I'm not going eight blocks and back in this weather for a record album.

MENDY: Who said anything about coming back? We'll go there and stay. This was a dinner invitation, not a slumber party. I'll pay for the cab.

STEPHEN: No!

MENDY: You're going to have to go home eventually. We'll just do it now.

STEPHEN: I'm not going home tonight.

MENDY: Where are you going?

STEPHEN: None of your business.

MENDY: Are you tricking with that guy I saw you with at *Parsifal?*

STEPHEN: Don't be ridiculous.

MENDY: You are!

STEPHEN: I am not.

MENDY: I can see it in your face!

STEPHEN: You think everyone's a trick.

MENDY: He lives just down the street. I've seen him walking his dog. He's cute. Larry Daimlett had him at the Pines last summer.

STEPHEN: So?

MENDY: He's very into drugs.

STEPHEN: He is not.

MENDY: Larry thinks he took cash from his wallet. Close to a hundred dollars. He knows he took his lime-green cashmere cable-knit sweater from Paul Stuart.

STEPHEN: I don't believe you.

MENDY: The question is: do you believe Larry Daimlett?

STEPHEN: I believe Larry Daimlett would have liked to sleep with Hal at the Pines last summer.

MENDY: Hal? Is that his name? Hal what?

STEPHEN: Never mind. Koerner. Hal Koerner.

MENDY: That's the one. He's a writer and he waits on tables at The Front Porch.

STEPHEN: Just three nights a week.

MENDY: But not enough to keep him in cashmere sweaters and out of other people's wallets.

STEPHEN: That's really a vicious story.

MENDY: Don't say I didn't warn you.

STEPHEN: We've had drinks a couple of times. That's it. He likes to talk about literature.

MENDY: He looks like a real highbrow.

STEPHEN: He writes extremely well, as a matter of fact.

MENDY: What does he write?

STEPHEN: What do you mean, what does he write?

MENDY: What genre?

STEPHEN: Poetry.

MENDY: I'm biting my tongue.

STEPHEN: It's not what you're thinking.

MENDY: I don't suppose he knows you're an editor with a lot of influence at a major publishing house? No, he couldn't possibly.

STEPHEN: He's not like that. I'm not dating the guy. We may have a drink together after he gets off work tonight. I thought you had some new things to play for me.

MENDY: I thought I did, too. But it seems you've already heard them. Listen, why don't you put Mme. Flagstad on the phonograph, make yourself comfortable, and let me run over to your place and get it?

STEPHEN: Mike's there.

MENDY: I'll just be a second. All he has to do is hand it to me. I don't want to neck with him.

STEPHEN: He's got someone there with him.

MENDY: A trick?

STEPHEN: I didn't ask.

MENDY: Well, if it's not a trick I'm sure he wouldn't mind if I popped over and got it.

STEPHEN: I'll bring it over tomorrow.

MENDY: I'd like to hear it tonight.

STEPHEN: I'm sorry. How's this new *Tosca?*

MENDY: Terrible.

STEPHEN: Why did you buy it then?

MENDY: Because I didn't know it was terrible until I had listened to it. Couldn't you just call Mike and ask him if it would be okay for me to pop over?

STEPHEN: I can tell you it wouldn't be. *(Looking at the back of a record album)* I wish Maria had recorded some of these arias. Maria should have recorded everything.

MENDY: If it was worth recording, she did.

STEPHEN: Callas sings Mussorgsky. Callas sings the Beatles. Callas sings I'm Bad.

MENDY: Maybe I could call Mike, even though I'm not officially speaking to him this week.

STEPHEN: Why not?

MENDY: I don't remember.

STEPHEN: I'm sure Michael does.

MENDY: I'm sure it was something I said or did. It usually is. I'm too much for most people. I can't help it. It's genetic. Stephen, please, please, please!

STEPHEN: It's just a record.

MENDY: That's easy for you to say. You've already heard it. Is it good?

STEPHEN: I told you, it's fantastic.

MENDY: I'll give you a thousand dollars.

STEPHEN: It's not that fantastic. The London is better. Lisbon is just another *Traviata*.

MENDY: Maria never sang "just another *Traviata*" in her life. She wasn't capable of "just another *Traviata*." The whole point of Maria is that she never sang "just another" anything. It's what killed her.

STEPHEN: What about those last La Scala *Medea*s?

MENDY: They were different. She was sick. She had a temperature, her blood pressure had fallen alarmingly. Her doctors told her not to appear. And if you'd listen to those recordings carefully, you'd hear that she brought a lot of new insights to the role.

STEPHEN: New insights but no voice.

MENDY: What about the way she does *Lontan! Lontan! Serpenti, via da me!?*

STEPHEn: You're going to hurt your voice doing that.

MENDY: I bet those little kids playing her children shit in their diapers when she said to them, *Lontan! Lontan! Serpenti, via da me!*

STEPHEN: All right, certain phrases were better, I grant you.

MENDY: And what about that high C at the end of the second act? Don't worry, I'm not going to attempt it.

STEPHEN: It's not a high C. It's a B flat and it's a fluke. She only took the high C in the Dallas performances.

MENDY: Are you sure it's not a C?

STEPHEN: Have you got it?

MENDY: Somewhere. I always thought she took the C in the La Scala performances with Schippers, too.

STEPHEN: The last time she took the C at the end of the second act of *Medea* was in Epidaurus.

MENDY: There's no recording of those two *Medea*s in Epidaurus.

STEPHEN: I was there.

MENDY: You never told me that.

STEPHEN: Well, I was.

MENDY: You heard Maria sing *Medea* in the ancient Greek theater of Dionysus at Epidaurus?

STEPHEN: And the *Norma*s there, two years later.

MENDY: I don't believe you.

STEPHEN: Why not?

MENDY: Well how come you never mentioned it?

STEPHEN: I just did. It's not exactly the kind of thing you go around mentioning all the time. "Hi, I'm Steve. I heard Maria Callas sing *Medea* in Epidaurus, Greece. You live around here?"

MENDY: You think you would have mentioned it to me at least.

STEPHEN: You heard her concert at the Acropolis.

MENDY: August 5th! There was a full moon, as if she needed one!

STEPHEN: Well, if you heard her in Athens why can't I have heard her in Epidaurus?

MENDY: Who was the Pollione?

STEPHEN: Jon Vickers.

MENDY: Vickers never sang *Norma* with her. It was the tragedy of his career and hers.

STEPHEN: Well, it was someone like Jon Vickers.

MENDY: The day Flaviano Labò is anything like John Vickers is the day Joan Sutherland does her first *Lulu*.

STEPHEN: Flaviano Labò, my God, that's right.

MENDY: The Adalgisa was what's-her-name . . . ? You know!

STEPHEN: That Greek mezzo with hair on her chest. What's-her-name? Paleo-something.

MENDY: Irene Paleolithic. All right, your final question, who sang the Clotilde?

STEPHEN: I don't remember. Nobody ever remembers who sang Clotilde. I doubt if even Maria would remember who sang Clotilde with her in Epidaurus.

MENDY: I bet she remembered who sang Clotilde with her in London on November 8th, 1952.

STEPHEN: The whole world remembers who sang Clotilde with her in London in 1952: big Joan Sutherland herself, The Beast From Down Under.

MENDY: Maria said Sutherland didn't have the legato to sing a good Clotilde.

STEPHEN: The rhythm to sing it is what Maria said.

MENDY: I read "legato."

STEPHEN: Well, you read wrong. Besides, Sutherland has legato. Even I would grant her that. But she always sings behind the beat. That's why Maria said Sutherland didn't have the rhythm to sing even a decent Clotilde. God knows what she thought of her *Norma*.

MENDY: You're too butch to know so much about opera.

STEPHEN: I'm not butch. Rise Stevens is butch. Are you still looking for that *Medea?*

MENDY: Here's Dallas, the first La Scalas with Lenny, Covent Garden, the night she met Onassis, *O notte tremenda, notte d'orrore*, but where's the last La Scalas?

STEPHEN: Mendy, I don't want to hear *Medea*. Any of them. I hate *Medea*. I loathe *Medea*. I despise *Medea*.

MENDY: Even with Maria?

STEPHEN: Even with Ethel Merman. It's boring music.

MENDY: Maria was never boring.

STEPHEN: She was in *Medea*.

MENDY: You're going to go to hell for that.

STEPHEN: I already have. I'm just here on a pass.

MENDY: I just can't believe you were there.

STEPHEN: We didn't speak to one another for five years, remember. It was probably during that period. Didn't I send you a postcard from Epidaurus?

MENDY: No.

STEPHEN: I must have really been mad at you.

MENDY: It was mutual.

STEPHEN: Do you remember what it was about?

MENDY: Perfectly.

STEPHEN: You took Peter Wingate to a performance of *Tristan* I would have given my right nut to see, just because I met Michael at your annual Callas birthday party.

MENDY: You didn't just meet Michael here, you left with him.

STEPHEN: Mendy, Michael wasn't interested in you.

MENDY: That's no excuse. He should have been. And so should you. Not inviting you to *Tristan* was my only revenge.

STEPHEN: I could have killed you. Nilsson and Vickers never sang *Tristan* together again. They were calling it the coupling of the century.

MENDY: I thought that was you and Mike.

STEPHEN: I guess we were sort of the Liz and Dick of Sheridan Square. I didn't know he was married. He didn't know I was still involved with Jimmy Marks. What a mess.

MENDY: I was so in love with you.

STEPHEN: You just thought you were in love with me.

MENDY: That's not true. When you two left together—I remember I was standing right over there listening to Bobby Staub hold forth about his dinner with Susan Sontag (thank God they never made a movie out of that)—and when I saw that door close on you two, I wanted to die. I knew you'd be making love within the hour.

STEPHEN: It was more like ten minutes. I kissed him in your hallway.

MENDY: Thanks a lot.

STEPHEN: I've never been that way with anyone. Usually I wait for them to make the first move. "Does it have to be tonight?" he asked. "If you ever want to see me again, it does." I couldn't believe myself.

MENDY: And here I was on the other side of the door feeling like a combination of the Marschallin—all gentle resignation, *ja, ja, ja,* age deferring to beauty and all that shit—and the second act of *Tosca*—stab the son of a bitch in the heart.

(MENDY *seizes a knife from a fruit bowl and raises it dramatically.*)

STEPHEN: Careful, Mendy.

MENDY: *Questo è il baccio di Tosca!*

(HE *"stabs"* STEPHEN, *who reacts melodramatically.*)

STEPHEN: *Aiuto . . . aiuto . . . muoio . . .*

MENDY: *E ucciso da una donna . . .* Killed by a woman! *Guardami! . . . Son Tosca, o Scarpia!*

STEPHEN: *Soccorso!*

MENDY: *Tu suffoco il sangue? . . . Muori! muori!! muori!!! Ah e morto! . . . Or gli perdono!*

(STEPHEN starts to get up.)

Just a minute! I'm not finished. *E avanti a lui tremava tutta Roma.*

(HE lets the knife drop and waits for the proper ovation. Instead,)

STEPHEN: You want to hear something funny?

MENDY: I thought I just had. I don't know why I bother!

STEPHEN: The first time I saw Mike, I wasn't even sure he was gay.

MENDY: On these premises? Darling, I've been raided.

STEPHEN: He was so . . . I want to say masculine but that's not the word. There's something beyond masculine.

MENDY: I know. Me.

STEPHEN: The moment I saw him, even before he'd seen me, before we were introduced, I knew he was going to be the one. He was my destiny and I was his. I saw my future flash before me and it was all with him. It was like the first act of *Carmen*. Don José sees her, she throws him the acacia flower, and his fate is sealed.

MENDY: Carmen isn't gay.

STEPHEN: She is when a certain mezzo's singing her.

MENDY: What did Mike throw you?

STEPHEN: Wouldn't you like to know?

MENDY: I love your choice of role models. Carmen and Don José. They were a fun couple.

STEPHEN: We're turning into . . . who? I can't think of anyone who ends happily in opera.

MENDY: Hansel and Gretel.

STEPHEN: There you go! That's us. You know what I feel like? The Rosa Ponselle *Vestale* arias.

MENDY: The way you feel about *Medea* is the way I feel about *Vestale*. A whole opera about a fucking vestal virgin.

STEPHEN: What do you want to hear then?

MENDY: The Lisbon *Traviata*.

STEPHEN: You're obsessed with the Lisbon *Traviata*.

MENDY: You knew I would be.

STEPHEN: I thought you had it.

MENDY: I don't care what they're doing over there. I just want them to give me the record. Tell them I'll wear a ski mask. I'll go blindfolded. They can throw it down to me in the street out the window.

STEPHEN: Call them yourself. I'm not doing it.

MENDY: I should have told that cretin with attitude at Discophile I worked for Birgit Nilsson. I'm sure she has much more clout than Renata Scotto. *(Into phone)* Hello, Mike? Who is this? *(Covers phone)* "A friend of his." I bet. *(Into phone)* Would you ask him to call Stephen when he gets back?

STEPHEN: *(Sharply)* Mendy!

MENDY: Tell him I'm at Mendy's. He has the number. Thank you.

(He hangs up.)

STEPHEN: Why did you do that, Mendy? He's going to think I was calling to check up on him.

MENDY: Mike's out getting pizza. They're listening to *Sweeney Todd.*

STEPHEN: I'm going to tell him it was you. And then *you're* going to tell him it was you.

MENDY: The trick sounded cute.

STEPHEN: You reduce everything to tricks.

MENDY: Maybe that's because I haven't had one since 1901.

STEPHEN: All great beauties are finally alone. Look at Maria. That apartment in Paris became her tomb.

MENDY: *(Begins to sing)* "In quelle trine morbide."

STEPHEN: I should have known!

MENDY: *"Sola, abbandonata in questo popoloso deserto che appellano Parigi."*

STEPHEN: I'm going to leave if you keep that up. Couldn't we just talk?

MENDY: Stephen, tell me something: why can't I find someone to love?

STEPHEN: Don't start, Mendy. Please!

MENDY: Is he?

STEPHEN: Is who what?

MENDY: The trick cute?

STEPHEN: He's all right.

MENDY: I thought you didn't know him.

STEPHEN: I said I didn't know if he was a trick.

MENDY: You just said he was.

STEPHEN: Maybe he is. Why don't you call him and ask him? You would, too!

MENDY: All I asked was, is he cute?

STEPHEN: I said he was all right.

MENDY: You've met him?

STEPHEN: No. I saw him. In our lobby. He was going up. I was coming down.

MENDY: Then how did you know it was him?

STEPHEN: He was completely naked except for a big sign around his neck: Mike's trick. I just did! What is this? The Riddle Scene from *Turandot?* Could we put something on?

MENDY: What's his name?

STEPHEN: I don't know. Paul.

MENDY: Paul? Just Paul?

STEPHEN: Paul Della Rovere.

MENDY: Paul Della Rovere! If that's not a trick's name, I'd like to know what is.

STEPHEN: He's a social worker, so I doubt it. You know what they're like: serious and looking for a real commitment.

MENDY: So am I, so am I! Why can't I meet someone like that? Do you want to give him my number? I've got an extra seat for *Daughter of the Regiment.*

STEPHEN: Has anyone ever said anything to you about your scotch?

MENDY: No, why?

STEPHEN: It's terrible.

MENDY: I don't drink.

STEPHEN: Well, your guests do and it's terrible.

MENDY: So tell me a good brand and I'll buy it. So what's going to happen?

STEPHEN: With Mike and I? Nothing.

MENDY: Mike and me. I can't believe you edit for a living.

STEPHEN: For content. I have an assistant for the grammar. That's who I should fix you up with.

MENDY: Does he like opera?

STEPHEN: He's getting there. He's into crossover albums. He just bought Teresa Stratas in *Funny Girl*.

MENDY: I think I'll pass. So what if Mike and this number get serious?

STEPHEN: They won't.

MENDY: Why not?

STEPHEN: They just won't. We have an agreement about this sort of thing. No involvement.

MENDY: So did you and Jimmy Marks when you met Mike.

STEPHEN: Jimmy and I weren't that serious about each other in the first place. We were each other's Pinkerton just pretending to be each other's Butterfly until the real thing came along. No one got hurt.

MENDY: That's not how I remember it.

STEPHEN: He got over it.

MENDY: Sometimes I think he's still in love with you.

STEPHEN: I hope not. I see Jimmy and Donald together and I can't believe we were ever lovers. There's this void. It's like it never happened.

MENDY: As if it never happened.

STEPHEN: Shut up, Mendy.

MENDY: Bad grammar is a knife in my heart, right here.

STEPHEN: You just need to get laid.

MENDY: Lot's of luck in the Fabulous '80s!

STEPHEN: Some people are managing.

MENDY: I don't even care about sex anymore. I'd settle for a hug. Well, maybe not a hug.

STEPHEN: What ever happened to you and that curator at the Modern anyway?

MENDY: I took him to *Pelleas et Melisande* and he fell asleep in the first scene. I had to wake him for intermission.

STEPHEN: *Pelleas?* Give the guy a break. Take him to *Tosca, Trovatore.* Something with balls.

MENDY: Debussy has balls. He just doesn't wear them on his sleeve.

STEPHEN: You're going to die with your secret, Mendy.

MENDY: I don't even know what it is.

STEPHEN: That's why it's your secret. I think you'd rather listen to opera than fuck.

MENDY: Opera doesn't reject me. The real world does. I don't understand love. *"Non capisco amore."*

STEPHEN: I don't think I understand anything but.

MENDY: I don't understand agreements either. I never thought the two of you would last. And when it did, I was a little envious. No, a lot envious. And now that it's sort of over . . .

STEPHEN: It's not over.

MENDY: I feel a little sad.

STEPHEN: I said, it's not over.

MENDY: The part I was jealous of is. The passion.

STEPHEN: Our passion is just fine. Thank you. It's just a little different.

MENDY: That's for sure. If he's with someone else, it sounds like the first act of *Carmen* is turning into the last. The final duet. Only in your production, who's Carmen and who's Don José?

STEPHEN: Wouldn't you like to know? *(Spoken)* *"Frappe-moi donc ou laisse-moi passer!"*

MENDY: You need more chest. Maria does it with more chest. *"Frappe-moi donc ou laisse-moi passer!"*
(STEPHEN "stabs" him and MENDY falls dramatically. "Death" convulsions.)
Can I ask you a personal question?

STEPHEN: No.

MENDY: Do you and Mike still have sex?

STEPHEN: None of your business.

MENDY: So you don't. Do you think he'll move out?

STEPHEN: No. Besides, where would he go? Now *basta*, Mendy. I didn't come over here for this.

MENDY: What did you come over for?

STEPHEN: You invited me. For music, for conversation, for . . . not for this. What about Marilyn Horne's *Tancredi* from Dallas last year?

MENDY: It's in the country.

STEPHEN: Everything good you have is in the country.

MENDY: Everything good you have, like the Lisbon *Traviata,* is only eight blocks from here.

STEPHEN: What's the *Tancredi* like?

MENDY: Terrible. She's sharp.

STEPHEN: Marilyn Horne doesn't sharp. She flats.

MENDY: Well she sure as shit sharped November 5th in Dallas, Texas.

STEPHEN: Really? I'll have to hear it sometime.

MENDY: You'll have to come to Connecticut.

STEPHEN: I wouldn't cross the street to hear Marilyn Horne sing on pitch. She sings like a truck driver.

MENDY: What do you expect? Marilyn Horne was a truck driver. She was discovered singing the Habanera while operating a forklift in a Los Angeles gravel pit.

STEPHEN: Now that's vicious.

MENDY: What's vicious is you not getting the goddamn Lisbon *Traviata.* How long does it take to get a pizza anyway?

STEPHEN: Maria flats on the Lisbon *Traviata.*

MENDY: Where?

STEPHEN: Twice in *"Ah, fors'e lui,"* once in *"Sempre libera,"* and practically the entire *"Dite alla giovine"* is a quarter-tone down.

MENDY: I don't believe you.

STEPHEN: It's on the record.

MENDY: Maria never flatted in her entire life. Sharped, yes; flatted, never.

STEPHEN: Maybe it was something she ate, a rancid paella or something, I don't know, Mendy, but she flatted in Lisbon just like Marilyn Horne sharped in Dallas.

MENDY: Fuck Marilyn Horne.

STEPHEN: I can't help it if I was born with perfect pitch.

MENDY: And fuck your perfect pitch. It's Maria's pitch that you're impugning.

STEPHEN: Who's impugning? I'm stating fact. On the night of March 27th, 1958, Maria Callas sang flat in a performance of *La Traviata* at the Teatro San Marco in Lisbon, Portugal. Nobody's perfect.

MENDY: Maria is.

STEPHEN: Was.

MENDY: And always will be. (HE *is dialing a number.*)

STEPHEN: Mendy, leave them alone!

MENDY: I may not have your ear but I have a pitch pipe I bought in Salzburg at that music shop three doors down from the house Mozart was born in. Herbert Von Karajan was there buying batons.

STEPHEN: What does that have to do with anything?

MENDY: Herbert Von Karajan would hardly be seen buying batons in a music shop that didn't sell excellent pitch pipes. We'll see how flat Maria was. (*Into phone*) Is he back yet? What's-his-name! Your friend whose apartment you're at who's out buying pizza. They've got me so rattled over here I can't even remember his name.

STEPHEN: It's Michael.

MENDY: Thank you. (*Covers phone*) I love this one's voice. Della—what was it?

STEPHEN: Della Rovere.

MENDY: He could be the first Italian hump tenor with that name.

STEPHEN: I thought you thought Franco Corelli was a hump.

MENDY: I never said I thought Franco Corelli was a hump. I said I liked his legs in *Turandot*. He sang like a beast.

STEPHEN: Mike is going to kill you for this.

MENDY: They're playing *Sweeney Todd* so loud over there I don't know how they can think. I'll never understand what people see in musicals. I mean, why settle for *The Sound of Music* when you can have *Dialogue of the Carmelites? (Into phone)* Mike? It's Mendy.

STEPHEN: Tell him it wasn't me who called before.

MENDY: I wonder if I could as you a favor.

STEPHEN: Tell him it wasn't me.

MENDY: Stephen's telling me to tell you it wasn't him, whatever that means. Listen—

STEPHEN: Let me talk to him when you're finished.

MENDY: You've got a record over there, it's Stephen's actually, the Lisbon *Traviata.*

STEPHEN: He won't have a clue what you're talking about.

MENDY: The Lisbon *Traviata!* If you could perhaps turn Mme. Lansbury down for just a moment . . . ? Thank you. *(Covers phone)* He called him "Babe." What's-his-name? The Italian hump. Mike called him "Babe."

STEPHEN: Mike calls everyone "Babe."

MENDY: I bet *Sweeney Todd's* not all they're playing.

STEPHEN: Anyway, he's Portuguese.

MENDY: The Italian hump is Portuguese? Maybe he was there.

STEPHEN: Maybe he was where?

MENDY: The Lisbon *Traviata! (Into phone)* Can you hear me now? Yes, perfectly. Listen, Mike, there's a favor I'd like to ask you. Well, it's two favors actually. *(To STEPHEN)* Would you stop snooping at my desk?

STEPHEN: I'm not snooping. I was looking for *Opera News.*

MENDY: *(Into phone)* Stephen left a record album there I specifically asked him to bring over with him tonight. I was wondering if I stopped by I might pick it up?

STEPHEN: Are these your tickets for *Elektra?* I got fourth row on the aisle.

MENDY: How soon? I could come right now. Couldn't you wait a couple of minutes until I got there? It's only a couple of blocks.

STEPHEN: Eight blocks, Mendy, and it's raining.

MENDY: What if I took a cab? You'll be passing right by here. I could meet you halfway.

STEPHEN: Who's the postcard from?

MENDY: I don't want to be a pest about it, Michael, but really, it's terribly important.

STEPHEN: It looks like Rio.

MENDY: If you just got back with the pizza, I don't understand why you have to go rushing out again to the movies. If you'd returned my call when I asked you to call, just as soon as you got back with it, I could have been over there and gone by now. This is all really very inconsiderate of you, Michael. As a matter of fact, to me it *is* a matter of life and death. I'm sorry I feel this way about it, too.

STEPHEN: Why didn't you tell me Lester was sick?

MENDY: Never mind the second favor. I'm sorry I asked you the first.

STEPHEN: Don't hang up.

MENDY: The next time you're offered a pair of free tickets to the Met, they won't be from me. That's not the point. I offered them. Whether or not you wanted them is immaterial.

STEPHEN: Don't hang up.

MENDY: You're a selfish, self-centered, stereotypical, aging, immature queen. No wonder you don't have any friends. Yes, all that just because you won't bring a goddamn record album over here or let me come over there to get it! Besides, the Maria Callas Lisbon *Traviata* is not just another goddamn record album of Stephen's. Right now, at this particular moment in my not-so-terrific life, it's probably the most goddamn important thing in the world to me, but I wouldn't expect an insensitive faggot who's idea of a good time is sitting around listening to Angela Lansbury shrieking on about "The Worst Pies in London," like yourself, to understand what I'm talking about.

I'm not surprised you don't like opera. People like you don't like life.

STEPHEN: I want to talk to him when you're through.

MENDY: Not a moment too soon! *(Back into phone)* Your lover would like a word with you, Michael, though for the life of me, I can't imagine why. Although after to-night I can understand why he's well on his way to being your ex. There's not one person in this entire city who thought it would last, including David Minton.

STEPHEN: Who is David Minton?

MENDY: *(Into phone)* I will simply never, never understand how Stephen got that way with you in the first place. *(Hands phone to STEPHEN)* Here.

STEPHEN: You could've been over there by now. *(Into phone)* Mike? Hi.

MENDY: Tell him his friend Mr. Della Rovere used to work standing room at the old Met.

STEPHEN: I don't know. Some Callas record.

MENDY: I had him halfway through Flagstad's farewell Isolde.

STEPHEN: That's okay.

MENDY: I know some people who had him during her first.

STEPHEN: Did you know Lester Cantwell has been in a hospital in Rio de Janeiro for the past five weeks with a ruptured spleen?

MENDY: I refuse not to be taken seriously like this!

STEPHEN: Mendy got a postcard from him.

MENDY: Doesn't he think I meant any of it?

STEPHEN: I don't know. *(To MENDY)* How long ago did you get it?

MENDY: After what I just said to him and he has the nerve to ask me about Lester Cantwell's ruptured spleen?

STEPHEN: Mendy, he's one of our best friends and we'd like to know.

MENDY: If he's one of your best friends then why don't you just call him? He's been back for at least three weeks.

STEPHEN: *(Into phone)* Did you hear that? *(To* MENDY*)* How is he?

MENDY: Like he always is: hysterical. Now he thinks he has AIDS. From what? I asked him. Watching *Dynasty* reruns? The spleen business was months ago if you'd just looked at the postmark, and I thought I asked you not to snoop around my desk in the first place anyway.

STEPHEN: *(Into phone)* I guess it has been a while since we spoke to him. What are you two up to anyway?

MENDY: Would you mind not monopolizing that thing? I'm expecting a call.

STEPHEN: It's a dumb movie but the special effects are fantastic. Where are you seeing it? The Greenwich? With their sound system? Lots of luck.

MENDY: I thought they were in such a hurry.

STEPHEN: We're just listening to records. Veal piccata. *(To* MENDY*)* He loves your veal piccata.

MENDY: He's had his last helping.

STEPHEN: *(Into phone)* I don't know. I might have something on later. I'm expecting a call.

MENDY: What am I? Stage door canteen? Some pit stop? Some place to kill time while you wait for a late date to call? Fuck you, too, Stephen.

STEPHEN: The guy I told you about. The writer.

MENDY: What writer? He's a waiter at a second-rate, over-priced gay hamburger stand.

STEPHEN: He wasn't sure if he'd be free after work.

MENDY: His kind never is. Stephen, I told you I was expecting a call.

STEPHEN: You want to hear something funny? I was going to ask you to walk Sammy. Sometimes I completely forget. Two years and sometimes I think he's still with us. Oh, listen, I think we might be low on milk.

MENDY: Listen to you two. You'd think you were married and had kids at Dalton.

STEPHEN: Why can't the two of you go to his place? I told you it wasn't definite. Why does he have to stay over? Forget it. I took a change with me.

MENDY: No wonder she forgot the record. She's carrying tomorrow's wardrobe in there.

STEPHEN: As long as he's out of there by eight. All right, I'll call when I know. But don't change your plans because of me. Maybe you better tell him about that loose floorboard on my side of the bed. We don't want a lawsuit on our hands.

(He laughs at something MIKE *says, then extends phone to* MENDY.*)*

He wants to talk to you.

MENDY: Well, I don't want to talk to him.

STEPHEN: He wants to know what the other favor was, just in case.

MENDY: In case of what?

STEPHEN: In case he might be able to do it.

MENDY: You really don't take me seriously, either one of you!

STEPHEN: Oh, come on.

MENDY: I was only going to ask him, not that it matters now and I certainly wouldn't want to put him out or anything, even if he did spend three summers with me on Fire Island as a permanent, non-paying, non-dishwashing, non-anything but hanging around on the meat rack guest, if his little Portuguese friend had maybe heard Maria's *Traviata* in Lisbon, but if he's so heavily into Stephen Sondheim, I would seriously doubt it!

STEPHEN: *(Into phone)* Did you hear that? *(To* MENDY*)* He's asking him.

MENDY: He's just wasting his time. Six times over and back I could've been.

STEPHEN: Why don't you put on the Berlin *Lucia?*

MENDY: I'm sick of it. Besides, I lent it to Elaine.

STEPHEN: I thought Elaine hated opera.

MENDY: She does, but she likes the Berlin *Lucia*. She was over the other night and loved it.

STEPHEN: That's amazing. I mean, wasn't Callas named in your divorce for alienation of affections?

MENDY: I don't know who I thought I was kidding. Certainly not Elaine.

STEPHEN: You still see her?

MENDY: Of course I do. She's one of my best friends. We had more than a kid together.

STEPHEN: Is she seeing anyone?

MENDY: Some stockbroker, but Jason can't stand him. Neither can I.

STEPHEN: He must be ten by now.

MENDY: Thirteen. What's happening?

STEPHEN: I guess he's still asking. Thirteen! He's one thing I envy you. Remember the time we—

MENDY: What loose board?

STEPHEN: —took him to *Rigoletto?*—Hunh?

MENDY: You said something about a loose board on your side?

STEPHEN: Oh. There's a loose floorboard on my side of the bed and if you don't know about it, you could step on it wrong and it could pop up and you could hurt yourself. I should have let Mr. Della Rovere find out for himself.

MENDY: Then they are sleeping together?

STEPHEN: It would seem so.

MENDY: And in your bed?

STEPHEN: This is the first time he's ever asked that.

MENDY: I knew it. And you're sleeping with Ezra Pound *manqué*.

STEPHEN: Well, we'll see tonight. So far it's my brain he's interested in.

MENDY: The minute I saw you two at *Parsifal* I said to myself, "He's with a trick."

STEPHEN: Knowing you, you probably said it to the people you were with.

MENDY: Well, Stephen, it was kind of obvious: two grown men at a performance of *Parsifal*.

STEPHEN: What's so obvious about two men going to *Parsifal* together?

MENDY: Face it, Stephen, ice hockey at the Garden it's not. *(Indicating phone)* What are they doing over there? Making love?

STEPHEN: Is there anyone or anything you don't reduce to sex?

MENDY: My son, Jason, my Volvo station wagon, and Maria Callas.

STEPHEN: You wonder why you don't have a lover, but have you ever listened to yourself?

MENDY: I have an analyst for that.

STEPHEN: What does he say?

MENDY: She can't find a thing wrong with me.

STEPHEN: Another one! How many have you had?

MENDY: Ten years, six analysts. Elaine says I go through them like Kleenex.

STEPHEN: She should—*(Into phone)* Hello?

MENDY: Know or talk?

STEPHEN: *(To* MENDY*)* It's Paul.

MENDY: For me?

STEPHEN: He doesn't have all night.

MENDY: *(Into phone)* Paul? This is Mendy. Did Mike tell you what I—? Well, that's what I was wondering, but if you're not sure then I'm sure you weren't. Well of course someone sang it. Someone usually does. Otherwise there's no performance or they call it a play.

(Makes face at STEPHEN*)*

STEPHEN: You're wasting your time.

MENDY: *(Covers phone)* Pick up the extension! *(Back into phone)* This would have been in '56 or '57.

STEPHEN: It was 1958. March 25th and 27th.

MENDY: Stephen says it was 1958.

STEPHEN: March 25th and 27th.

MENDY: You were how old then? *(Covers phone)* Don't pick up! You don't want to know. *(Back into phone)* But you remember your grandfather taking you to an opera? This is encouraging. Tell me everything you remember about it. No, the one with bulls in it is *Carmen.* Very inappropriate for a child. *Traviata*'s about a courtesan dying of consumption. A courtesan: what Stephen was before he became the youngest senior editor at Knopf and an avocation to which he will soon be returning if he doesn't come up with another bestseller.

STEPHEN: Mendy! He doesn't have to know that.

MENDY: No, horses and camels are *Aida.* I wish you could remember the singers as well as you do the animals. *Traviata* begins at a party. Everyone is drinking champagne and being very gay. I'll ignore that! And then the tenor's father, the baritone, comes in and ruins everything, as fathers will. And then there's a gambling scene, and in the last act she reads a letter, *"Teneste la promessa,"* and dies. You remember that much? Then you definitely remember *Traviata.* Now try to describe the soprano who was singing Violetta. Violetta is the heroine. You're making me feel like Milton Cross. Skip it. Just tell me about the soprano. Other than the fact that you didn't like her, what can you tell me about her? "Lousy" is a strong word, Paul. So is "stunk." I don't care about your opinion as a matter of fact! It's her name I'm after. I think you heard Maria Callas. That's a good question. I loved her so much. I still do. Everything about her. Anything. I'll take crumbs when it comes to Maria. Her time was so brief. That's why I was hoping maybe you could tell me something about her I didn't know. She's given me so much: pleasure, ecstasy, a certain solace, I suppose; memories that don't stop. This doesn't seem to be such a terrible existence with people like her to illuminate it. We'll never see her like again. How do you describe a miracle to someone who wasn't there? Do yourself a favor. Put on one of her records. *Puritani* or *Sonnambula* or *Norma*. If what you hear doesn't get to you, really speak to you, touch your heart, Paul, the truth of it, the intensity of the feeling . . . well, I can't imagine such a thing. I don't think we could be friends. I know we couldn't. There's a reason we called her "La Divina," but if you don't even remember who sang *Traviata* that night, there's no point in going on with this even if you did hear Callas. For people like you, it might as well have been Zinka Milanov. Skip that one too. Listen, thank you for your trouble. Enjoy the movie. No, I don't care what your grandfather · thought of her either. The two of you heard the greatest singer who ever lived and you don't even remember it. Yes, she's dead, thanks to people like you! Murderer! I hope you hate the movie.

(HE *hangs up*)

God, I loathe the Portuguese.

STEPHEN: Half an hour ago you were in love with the sound of his voice.

MENDY: Half an hour ago I didn't know he was at the Lisbon *Traviata* and doesn't even remember her.

STEPHEN: He remembers the *Traviata*. It's Callas he doesn't remember.

MENDY: They're the same thing. And stop calling her that! Callas! It makes her sound faraway, formidable.

STEPHEN: She was and is. Now what do you want to hear?

MENDY: I don't care anymore! *Einstein on the Beach*.

STEPHEN: The whole thing?

MENDY: Oh, that's right: you're in a rush.

STEPHEN: I'm not in a rush right now. He doesn't get off until after midnight. It's a tentative date anyway. What about this *Andrea Chenier*?

MENDY: I'm not in the mood for Verismo.

STEPHEN: I just want to hear what Marton does with it.

MENDY: She does what she does with everything: screams her way through it.

STEPHEN: I like her *Tosca*.

MENDY: There is only one *Tosca*.

STEPHEN: That's ridiculous. You can't just listen to Maria.

MENDY: Why not?

STEPHEN: I was going to say it's not normal.

MENDY: You? Normal? Your whole life is a mockery of the word.

STEPHEN: What you said about her, just now, on the phone, it was touching.

MENDY: Oh please!

STEPHEN: I mean it. It's true, too. Sometimes I forget how much we owe her. There's my Maria and then there's the woman who changed the face of opera.

MENDY: Maria Callas *is* opera.

STEPHEN: You don't have to convert me, Mendy. If you'll remember, I was into her several years before you.

MENDY: It wasn't a contest.

STEPHEN: No, but it's a fact.

MENDY: Have it your way. You usually do.

STEPHEN: What is that supposed to mean?

MENDY: Nothing. I thought you were going to put something on.

STEPHEN: Everything means something.

MENDY: Well, don't you?

STEPHEN: You know I don't.

MENDY: I wasn't talking about Mike.

STEPHEN: Well, then don't make a remark like that.

MENDY: I was talking about . . . I don't know what I was talking about.

STEPHEN: You usually don't.

MENDY: Thanks a lot. What I meant was, you've always had someone.

STEPHEN: I've always wanted someone.

MENDY: You think I don't want someone?

STEPHEN: You're always looking too hard. It doesn't happen that way.

MENDY: How does it happen?

STEPHEN: I don't know. It just happens. But if you try making it happen, somehow it never does.

MENDY: In other words, I frighten people off with my needs?

STEPHEN: I didn't say that.

MENDY: That's what Elaine thinks.

STEPHEN: Everybody has needs, Mendy.

MENDY: And I guess your needs are more attractive than mine.

STEPHEN: I don't find any needs attractive, especially my own.

MENDY: That sounds ominous.

STEPHEN: It is.

MENDY: What are your needs?

STEPHEN: Mike, Mike, and more Mike. But we're going to be fine. We're going through a phase. I hate phases. I hate change.

MENDY: You and Mike aren't on the verge of breaking up?

STEPHEN: Michael and I are just on the verge of what to do with the rest of our lives.

MENDY: I'm sorry.

STEPHEN: I'm a big boy. What about this *Nabucco?*

MENDY: The last thing I'm in the mood for tonight is a chorus of wailing Hebrews.

STEPHEN: I've spent the whole evening looking for a record I haven't heard and you say no!

MENDY: I've got the new *Adriana* with Caballè and Carreras.

STEPHEN: So do I. It's atrocious.

MENDY: Well, what do you expect from those two? The Spanish Frick and Frack.

STEPHEN: Nine thousand records and we can't find one!

MENDY: There's always Maria.

STEPHEN: I'm sick of Maria. I'm sick of opera. I'm sick of life.

MENDY: I'd hate to be your date tonight.

STEPHEN: You are my date tonight.

MENDY: I meant after.

STEPHEN: He's probably going to break it.

MENDY: Why would you say that?

STEPHEN: Just a hunch.

MENDY: I worry about you, Stephen.

STEPHEN: So do I.

STEPHEN: May I have some more scotch?

MENDY: I thought you didn't like it.

STEPHEN: When did that stop me? Could we put on some Leyla Gencer? She's good for when you're really fucked.

MENDY: I wish you'd tell me what's really going on.

STEPHEN: Nothing. The only thing I care about right now is the phone ringing.

MENDY: I don't believe that.

STEPHEN: You'd better. My self-esteem for the next couple of hours is in the hands of a mildly attractive young man I'm not even sure I approve of. I certainly don't his poetry. If you hear we're publishing him, call the Art Police and have me locked up.

MENDY: What are we going to do about you?

STEPHEN: I just want to feel somebody's arms around me for the next couple of hours.

MENDY: Aren't you worried about—?

STEPHEN: I'm terrified. Okay?

MENDY: Thank God I'm not eighteen. I don't know how they cope. At least we have Maria.

STEPHEN: What about this new *Wozzeck?*

MENDY: No! Absolutely not! I hate twentieth-century opera. So do you.

STEPHEN: Why did you buy it then?

MENDY: I was being pretentious. Give me *bel canto* or give me death.

STEPHEN: You hate the twentieth century.

MENDY: With increasingly good reason.

STEPHEN: (HE *has picked up a magazine.)* Where did you get this?

MENDY: What?

STEPHEN: The new *Blueboy*.

MENDY: I don't know. I think Tom Ewing must have left it here.

STEPHEN: I still only have last month's.

MENDY: You actually read those things?

STEPHEN: No one reads them, Mendy. Are you sure you're gay?

MENDY: Ha ha ha!

STEPHEN: *(Turning pages in the magazine)* God, he's gorgeous. *(MENDY joins him and looks.)*

MENDY: He's all right.

STEPHEN: You wouldn't kick him out of bed.

MENDY: He's too beefy.

STEPHEN: They're called muscles. Good boys who go to the gym get them for Christmas.

MENDY: I would rather be tortured on a rack than exercise. I don't know how you stay so trim.

STEPHEN: Is this more to your liking?

MENDY: He looks like Carlo Bergonzi as Radames.

STEPHEN: Will you look at those legs!

MENDY: My needs are different.

STEPHEN: They're perfect.

MENDY: They're urgent.

STEPHEN: I love legs like that.

MENDY: If I don't get back into a relationship soon, I don't know what I'm going to do.

STEPHEN: I told you: don't fret it. Just lay back and let it happen.

MENDY: You make it sound like something obscene.

STEPHEN: With a little luck, it is.

MENDY: What's the matter?

STEPHEN: For a minute I thought it was Hal.

MENDY: Your waiter friend.

STEPHEN: I wish you'd stop calling him that. He's a writer.

MENDY: He looks like that?

STEPHEN: A little.

MENDY: No wonder you're hoping he'll call.

STEPHEN: I thought you'd seen him walking his dog.

MENDY: I have, but if he'd been dressed like that, believe me, I would never have noticed the dog. If this is what you go for, no wonder you never saw anything in me.

STEPHEN: I'm going to turn the page, all right?

MENDY: Why is it that whenever I say anything serious, you let it pass?

STEPHEN: The only thing we ever saw in one another was Maria Callas.

MENDY: That's not true.

STEPHEN: Think about it. I'm going to turn the page, all right?

MENDY: Like I said: have it your way.

STEPHEN: Like you said: I usually do.

MENDY: That was a very hurtful thing you just said.

STEPHEN: It's true.

(HE *turns the page.*)

If it weren't for Maria, I doubt we'd even be friends.

(HE *turns the page*)

Well, maybe we'd be friends but we wouldn't be—

(HE *turns the page.*)

MENDY: Wouldn't be what?

STEPHEN: Friends like this.

MENDY: I always thought we should have been lovers.

STEPHEN: Oh, come on!

MENDY: Mike doesn't even especially like opera. I don't know how you've stood it. He barely tolerates Maria.

STEPHEN: He doesn't have a choice, living with me. That one has a sexy neck.

MENDY: What do you do with a neck?

MENDY: We could have been lovers, too, if . . .

STEPHEN: Nice and thick.

MENDY: . . . if this had been the best of all possible worlds.

STEPHEN: Michael has a wonderful neck. You know whose neck I've always loved? Alan Bates.

MENDY: You were so cute then.

STEPHEN: Thanks a lot.

MENDY: I had my good points, too.

STEPHEN: You still do.

MENDY: Well then?

STEPHEN: Can you see the two of us in bed together? First we'd get the giggles and then we'd quarrel over which *Puritani* to play.

MENDY: There is only one *Puritani* to play.

STEPHEN: The Mexico City, May 11th, 1952 one.

MENDY: Over her 1954 Chicago performances?

STEPHEN: You see? Besides, they were in 1955. We would have killed one another by now.

MENDY: What are those? They look like want ads.

STEPHEN: They're the personals. Men looking for other men. "Gay white male, 40, non-smoker, seeks same for safe and sane good times."

MENDY: I could never do that.

STEPHEN: Sure you could. Look, here's one for you. He's a 5′10″, hairy weight-lifter who's into rare Renata Tebaldi tapes.

MENDY: Let me see that. Oh my God, he is! Did you put this in?

STEPHEN: It's a big world we live in. Someone for everyone. Why don't you call him? Maybe he's nice.

MENDY: If he likes Tebaldi, I doubt it. They're a mean little bunch. It was a Tebaldi fan who threw those radishes at Maria at the first Saturday matinee *Norma*. Tebaldi fans belong in a soccer stadium.

STEPHEN: You never seem to run into them anymore.

MENDY: It's true. After Renata stopped singing, it was as if they had vanished from the face of the earth. We, on the other hand, are still everywhere. I sometimes think we're increasing. Maria lives through us. We've kept her alive or maybe it's vice-versa. We're some kind of survivors.

STEPHEN: She's the only one who didn't.

MENDY: You didn't tell me: how does she read the letter on it?

STEPHEN: What letter?

MENDY: Maria on the Lisbon *Traviata.*

STEPHEN: It's beautiful.

MENDY: Better than Dallas?

STEPHEN: Different. It's more like Covent Garden.

MENDY: It couldn't be better than Dallas. Nothing will ever be better than Dallas.

(*And he's off!*)

"*Teneste la promessa. La disfida ebbe luogo, il Barone fu ferito, pero migliora. Alfredo e in stranio suolo; il vostro sacrificio io stesso gli ho svelato. Egli a voi tornera pel suo perdono; io pur verro.*"

(*The telephone has begun to ring.* STEPHEN *looks at his watch.*)

STEPHEN: This won't be him. It's too early.

(MENDY *has picked up the phone.*)

MENDY: "*Curatevi: mertate un avvenir migliore. Giorgio Germont. E tardi!*" You've reached Heartbreak House. This is Cio Cio San speaking. Just a moment. (*Covers phone.*) You're going to kill me. It's your waiter friend.

STEPHEN: So soon?

MENDY: Ask him to drop by if he'd like.

STEPHEN: (*Into phone*) Hi. How's it going? Mendy. He was just camping.

MENDY: That's not true. I was doing Maria. I wasn't camping. I never camp.

STEPHEN: We're just sitting around, playing a few records.

MENDY: And looking at his picture in *Blueboy!*

STEPHEN: (*Covers phone*) Mendy!

MENDY: Ask him over.

STEPHEN: (*Into phone*) So listen, are we going to be able to get together tonight or what?

MENDY: He can come here first. There's food, tell him.

STEPHEN: Oh. I understand.

MENDY: He's standing you up? How dare he? Let me speak to that hussy—!

STEPHEN: *(Covers phone)* If you don't shut up, I am going to break your face open! *(Into phone)* Sorry. I could meet you after if it wouldn't be too late. I guess you're right. I was just hoping to see you tonight. I know it wasn't definite. I'm sorry, too. What about tomorrow night?

MENDY: You're supposed to be going to *Meistersinger* with me.

STEPHEN: That's right. I forgot. You know I got seats for Bruce Springsteen next Friday?

MENDY: You're not going to the Albanese recital in Newark?

STEPHEN: Do you think you'll have any free time before then?

MENDY: She's doing two arias from *Rondine!*

STEPHEN: Like I said, I just want to see you sometime. You'd better get back there then. That's one mean maître d'. That's okay. I'll probably just head home. I've got the new Muriel Spark. I like her, too. Did you read—? Okay, okay! Go! Goodbye. Call when you can.

(HE hangs up.)

MENDY: What's the problem?

STEPHEN: Something came up.

MENDY: I'm sorry.

STEPHEN: It wasn't definite. He said this might happen.

MENDY: Join the club. I loathe the younger generation. They have no respect for old farts like us. What do you want me to put on?

STEPHEN: I knew this would happen.

MENDY: I know! Eileen Farrell, *I've Got a Right to Sing the Blues.*

STEPHEN: Shit.

(Doorbell rings)

MENDY: *Quel bon surpris!* Who can this be? Discophile! It's a new policy. They deliver.

STEPHEN: Mendy, I don't want to see any of your friends tonight.

MENDY: What's wrong with my friends? Pete and Timmy said they might stop by.

(HE goes to window and looks out.)

STEPHEN: I think I'm going to take off.

MENDY: There's a cab down there.

(The doorbell rings again; HE goes to intercom.)

Hello?

MIKE'S VOICE: Hello? Mendy?

MENDY: Mike?

MIKE'S VOICE: Mendy? Can I come up?

MENDY: Sure. Second floor.

(MENDY presses the buzzer.)

It's Mike. What do you think he wants?

STEPHEN: He's probably locked himself out. I don't know what he'd do without me. Is he alone?

(MENDY goes to window and looks out.)

MENDY: I can't tell.

(Knock on the door)

You want me to get it?

STEPHEN: It's not my apartment.

(MENDY goes to door and admits MIKE, who is dressed casually underneath an oilskin jacket. He has a record album in a plastic shopping bag with him.)

MIKE: Here.

MENDY: What's that?

MIKE: What do you think?

MENDY: You didn't have to do that.

MIKE: It was on the way. No big deal.

MENDY: I was only kidding. Come in, come in. Stephen's still here.

MIKE: I'm dripping.

MENDY: Darling, these rugs were in the original production of *Kismet* with Otis Skinner.

MIKE: I've got a cab waiting. We're running late.

MENDY: Bring your friend up. A little dessert, coffee.

MIKE: Some other time.

MENDY: He probably thinks I'm a raving lunatic.

MIKE: Stephen?

MENDY: Excuse me.

MIKE: That's okay.

MENDY: My advice is needed in the kitchen. Stephen? It's the Lisbon *Traviata*.

(HE *sets the shopping bag down and goes.*)

STEPHEN: That was nice of you. He's been on me all evening.

MIKE: So what's happening?

STEPHEN: So what's happening?

MIKE: Do you know your plans yet?

STEPHEN: No.

MIKE: How soon will you?

STEPHEN: I don't know! He's a working boy. He doesn't have a nice doctor to bundle him up in a warm taxi to see a movie I told you wasn't that good. Jesus, the new Almodovar is right at the Quad. It's fabulous.

MIKE: He wants to see this one.

(*Taxi begins honking impatiently off.*)

STEPHEN: There's a Chuck Norris retrospective on 42nd Street. Maybe you can make it.

MIKE: I've had a rough day, Stephen. The hospital was a nightmare. Billy Todd died, okay?

STEPHEN: I'm sorry.

MIKE: I'd like to know as soon as possible.

STEPHEN: Does it have to be tonight?

MIKE: You know my schedule. It could be weeks before I'm off again. His sister from Boston is at his place. I don't think she's ready for two men in one bed.

STEPHEN: Okay, okay, I hear you.

MIKE: It's sort of an anniversary. We met six months ago.

STEPHEN: I thought it was three.

MIKE: He's very sentimental about things like this.

STEPHEN: So are you. I'll try to arrange it.

MIKE: I'd really appreciate it.

STEPHEN: That jacket is not warm enough in this.

MIKE: I'll check the machine when we get out of the movie.
(*Awkward moment.* MIKE *hesitates about going to* STEPHEN, *decides to just wave.*)

STEPHEN: Aren't you even wearing a scarf?

MIKE: I'll see you, Mendy!
(HE *goes.* STEPHEN *crosses to window and looks out. Sounds of taxi door opening and closing.* MENDY *returns.*)

MENDY: That was very sweet of him. Every time I swear I'm never going to speak to him, he does something like this. Did you get a look at the chippy?

STEPHEN: No.

MENDY: I can't wait to hear this.
(HE *begins to open* MIKE'*s shopping bag. At the same time,* STEPHEN *goes to phone and dials a number.*)
Who are you calling?

STEPHEN: Our machine. I forgot to tell him something.

MENDY: (*Taking out album*) I don't believe this! He brought the London *Traviata*! It's the same one I have. Do you believe this? I don't. Stephen, it's the wrong *Traviata*.

STEPHEN: London, Lisbon, they're all the same to him.

MENDY: His heart was in the right place. He's basically a wonderful man. I hate him.

STEPHEN: (*Into phone*) Mike? He just called. We're on. Have fun. I plan to. Bye.
(HE *hangs up.*)

MENDY: What was that all about? None of my business?

STEPHEN: I think I really will shove off.
(HE *will start getting ready to go.*)

MENDY: It's early. You just got here. I bet you haven't heard the tapes of the television documentary. It just came out.

STEPHEN: We've got *Meistersingers* tomorrow.

MENDY: Don't you want to hear it? They're all on it. Scotto, Caballè, Tebaldi, Gobbi, all of them. They all talk about how much she meant to them and how she changed the face of opera. Zeffirelli narrates.

STEPHEN: Some other time.

MENDY: It's very moving.

STEPHEN: I saw the program.

MENDY: You know you don't want to go.

STEPHEN: I don't know what I want to do.

MENDY: Then stay. You want some ice cream?

STEPHEN: I'll get the Lisbon *Traviata* to you.

MENDY: Why don't you want to hear the documentary? It brings her all back. It's as if she were in the room with you. You'll cry when you hear parts of it. I do every time.

STEPHEN: I already have it. Thanks for dinner.

MENDY: You already have it? We can listen to it together. Compare things. Where are you going?

STEPHEN: I'll probably go to a bar.

MENDY: You want me to come with you?

STEPHEN: We tried that, remember?

MENDY: It wasn't my fault.

STEPHEN: Mendy, I was doing fine with that one guy until you came over and burst into the second act of *Tosca*.

MENDY: No one has a sense of humor in those places.

STEPHEN: Including me.

MENDY: I thought he looked like Richard Tucker in *Pagliacci* anyway. I'll be good. Take me. Please.

STEPHEN: I do better on my own. So would you.

MENDY: Then where are you going? Not home with some stranger? Even you're not that self-destructive.

STEPHEN: There's a couch in my office.

MENDY: That's crazy.

STEPHEN: I can always go to a hotel.

MENDY: That's even crazier. Why don't you stay here? I'll make a bed up, I'll fix us some Sleepytime tea, we'll put on our pajamas, we'll listen to the documentary, we'll giggle, we'll dish, it'll be wonderful.

STEPHEN: I don't think so.

MENDY: Don't worry. I'm not going to make a pass at you. Now take your coat off. Sit.

STEPHEN: I'd like to, but I've just got to get out of here and go someplace.

(MENDY *exits.*)

Where are you going? Mendy! What are you doing?

(MENDY *quickly returns with bedding, pajamas, and a robe for* STEPHEN.)

You don't have to do that.

MENDY: It's no trouble.

STEPHEN: I haven't decided yet.

MENDY: Take your time. I can't wait for you to hear this.

STEPHEN: It's too late for the documentary.

MENDY: I'll just play the last side.

STEPHEN: I have a deadline tomorrow.

MENDY: Just the last side, I promise.

STEPHEN: All right, but as soon as it's finished—

MENDY: I know. Just sit down.

STEPHEN: *(Sitting)* I mean it, too.

MENDY: Okay, okay.

(STEPHEN *sits and starts idly flipping through the issue of* Blueboy.)

You're not listening.

STEPHEN: I will, I will!

(HE *will continue to flip through the pages as the documentary begins to play. It is the PBS television documentary on the life of Maria Callas. Franco Zeffirelli is telling us about the life and legend of Maria Callas.*)

ZEFFIRELLI: On the morning of September 16, 1977, shortly after awakening, Maria Callas died of a heart attack in her Paris apartment. She was 54 years old.

MENDY: You're not listening.

STEPHEN: Yes, I am.

(HE *turns another page. He kicks off his shoes.*)

ZEFFIRELLI: There has been perhaps only one faithful companion to Maria throughout her life: her loneliness. The price sometimes one has to pay for the glory and the success. It's also the price for being God's instrument. It really seems to me that God used Maria's talent to communicate to us his planet of beauty. To enrich our souls, to make us better men. Maria Callas, the glory of opera. *(Callas beings to sing "Ah, non credea mirarti" from La Sonnambula.)*

MENDY: Stephen!

STEPHEN: I'm listening, I'm listening.

(The voice of Maria Callas on the soundtrack is beginning to fade. STEPHEN continues to turn more pages. MENDY is silent.)

END OF ACT I

ACT II
(Stephen & Mike)

Stephen and Mike's apartment. Early morning. Pale, gray light from the windows. The room is in much disarray. We notice a box of pizza. There is a pair of pants on the floor. The needle on the phonograph is endlessly tracking the runoff groove at the end of a record side. The red light on the telephone answering machine is blinking, indicating that a message has been received. The door to the bedroom is closed.

A key is heard in the door. STEPHEN *enters.* HE *is in the same clothes as the evening before, only now he is wearing his coat over them. He carries a small duffel bag, a copy of the* New York Times *and a brown paper bag that contains coffee and Danishes.*

STEPHEN: Good morning! It's me!
  *(*HE *is no sooner through the door than he is aware of the phonograph needle tracking the end of the record. He puts down his things and goes to the phonograph. He takes the arm off the record, stops the turntable, and removes the record, being careful to hold it by the edges and perhaps blowing off any dust that might have collected.)*
Where did they leave the goddamn jacket?
  *(*HE *is clearly looking for the record's protective inner-sleeve and outer album cover.)*
Goddamnit!
  *(*HE *has seen them on the coffee table under the box of pizza. Some of the pizza has gotten onto them. He returns the record to its sleeve and jacket, then looks at the album cover a moment.)*

50

George Michael. Who the hell is George Michael?

(HE *returns the album to the collection, filing it away alphabetically. Then he goes back to the stereo unit and switches it to an FM station. Rock music is heard. It is unbearably loud. Clearly, whoever was playing the stereo was running it at full volume.* STEPHEN *quickly lowers the volume and carefully tunes in a classical musical station. Schubert's "Wanderer" Fantasie is being played.* STEPHEN *satisfies himself with the volume and the reception. Next, he kicks off his shoes and takes off his coat. At the same time, he moves to the answering machine and rewinds the messages. As the following messages are played back, he will hang his coat up in the hall closet.*)

STEPHEN'S VOICE: Mike? He just called. We're on. Have fun. I plan to. Bye.

MENDY'S VOICE: Mike? It's Mendy. You want to pick up? Hello? Don't tell me you're not back yet? What did you two go see? *Berlin Alexanderplatz?* All right, I guess you're not there. You brought the wrong one. It's the Lisbon *Traviata* I'm after. Call me just as soon as you come in. I'll be up all night. Really. 4, 5 A.M. How could I sleep knowing there's a new Maria?

(HE *sings.*)

Nessun dorma, nessun dorma!

(HE *stops.*)

Hello? Mike? I thought I heard someone pick up. Hello? I guess not. Please, Mike, just as soon as you come in. I really would appreciate it. How are you anyway? No one ever sees you anymore. It was lovely seeing you tonight and I appreciated the gesture, as futile as it was. Call sometime. I mean, call as soon as you get this message but call some other time, too. You know what I mean!

(*To* STEPHEN)

Do you want to talk to him?

(*To* MIKE)

Okay. Ciao, Babe.

WOMAN'S VOICE: *(Somewhat slurred)* Hello, Stephen. It's your mother. Nothing important. Just calling to say hi. You don't have to call back, if you don't want to. I love you. *(Short pause)*. It's your mother. Say hello to Mike. Hello, Mike. I hate these things.

MAN'S VOICE: This is a message for Stephen Riddick. Hi, it's Larry Newman. I'd really like to get together with you to go over the revisions on my manuscript. It's been weeks. I hate to bother you at home but I'm getting kind of edgy. I don't even know if you've gotten my other messages. Thank you.

MAN'S VOICE: Mike? Uh, Michael Deller? It's Allan Weeks from Baltimore. I was in your neighborhood for the evening. Sorry I missed you. I'll try you next trip.

(There are no more messages. STEPHEN *goes to machine and turns it off. The bedroom door opens.* PAUL *starts into the living room. He is naked.)*

PAUL: Oh!

STEPHEN: Good morning.

PAUL: Good morning. Excuse me.

*(*HE *goes back into the bedroom and closes the door.* STEPHEN *sits with the coffee and a Danish and opens the* Times. *He reads for a few moments, then lowers the paper and looks toward the bedroom. Then he raises the paper and reads again. The bedroom door opens and* MIKE *comes out. He holds the bedclothes around his middle. He will begin to pick up the clothes scattered around the room.)*

MIKE: We didn't hear you come in. Sorry.

STEPHEN: It's all right.

MIKE: Have you been here long?

STEPHEN: I just got here.

MIKE: What time is it?

STEPHEN: I'm a little early. Sorry.

MIKE: We'll be out of your way.

STEPHEN: I haven't said you're in it. There's no rush.

*(*STEPHEN *continues to read.* MIKE *continues to look for and pick up clothing.)*

MIKE: How was your evening?

STEPHEN: Great.

MIKE: I got your message.

STEPHEN: Obviously.

MIKE: Obviously! Thanks. How was your friend?

STEPHEN: Great. How was yours?

MIKE: Terrific.

STEPHEN: You left the phonograph on all night.

MIKE: Not again!

STEPHEN: That clunk, clunk would drive me crazy.

MIKE: We must have gone into the other room.

STEPHEN: You sure did a job on this one.

MIKE: I was better off with my old record player. Maybe it wasn't high fidelity but at least it turned itself off. I'm sorry. From now on I'll stick to the radio.

STEPHEN: That's not what I said. *(HE lowers paper.)* What are you looking for?

MIKE: It's all right.

STEPHEN: I think there's something over there.

(HE motions with his head.)

MIKE: Where?

(STEPHEN repeats the motion, MIKE crosses and picks up a jockstrap.)

Thank you.

STEPHEN: Is that what they're wearing nowadays?

MIKE: So what did you two do?

STEPHEN: We had a couple of drinks in one of the bars and then went to his place and discussed Joyce Carol Oates to the wee hours. He's very intense.

MIKE: I hope that's not all you did.

STEPHEN: Wouldn't you like to know?

MIKE: I haven't been to a bar in years. Was anybody there?

STEPHEN: Are you speaking society or numbers?

MIKE: I'm asking a question.

STEPHEN: On the slow side, on both fronts.

MIKE: What a fucked-up time we picked to live in.

(HE's *finished gathering the clothes and starts going to the bedroom.*)

STEPHEN: I brought coffee.

MIKE: He's got to get to work.

STEPHEN: Where's that?

MIKE: Somewhere uptown. East '70s, I think.

STEPHEN: It's getting cold.

(MIKE *goes to paper bag with the coffee in it and sees that there are two more cardboard containers in it.*)

MIKE: They gave you three.

STEPHEN: I asked for three. I was trying to be nice. The Danish are just from Smilers. Jon Vie wasn't open yet.

MIKE: That's okay. Thanks.

(HE *goes into the bedroom. The door closes.* STEPHEN *resumes reading the* Times, *but a moment later he lets the paper fall and stares in front of him.*)

STEPHEN: They liked the new Stoppard.

(PAUL *enters from bedroom, smiles at* STEPHEN, *and exits into bathroom.* STEPHEN *resumes reading the* Times. *Now* MIKE *comes out of the bedroom. He has put a bathrobe on.*)

MIKE: What's it like out?

STEPHEN: Sort of raw.

MIKE: They said more rain.

(HE *has gone to the closet and taken out a clean towel.*)

STEPHEN: What are you doing?

MIKE: He asked to take a shower.

STEPHEN: I thought he was . . . !

MIKE: What?

STEPHEN: Nothing.

MIKE: What?

STEPHEN: Nothing. Do you have to use that towel? Use one of the old ones. I thought he was so late for work!

MIKE: *(Evenly)* He has time for a shower.

STEPHEN: Those are our best towels. They're a set. I'm sorry, but I see no reason to take one of them when you have a whole closetful of old, perfectly good, unmatched ones to choose from.

MIKE: Yes, Mother.

(HE *exchanges the towel he took for another one.*)

STEPHEN: I'm just being practical. Only you would take a brand new towel from a brand new set instead of a single one.

MIKE: Only you would care if I did.

STEPHEN: It's common sense for Christ's sake!

(MIKE *goes back into the bedroom and closes the door.* STEPHEN *is clearly upset with himself.*)

Shit, shit, shit!

(*Almost to himself*)

I'm sorry.

(HE *goes to bedroom door, starts to knock, then thinks better of it.*)

I'll make more coffee! Okay?

(*No response from the bedroom.* STEPHEN *starts for the kitchen but stops. The recording of the Schubert* Fantasie *being played by the FM station has gotten stuck. The same phrase is repeated over and over and over.* STEPHEN *shakes his head.* MIKE *comes out of the bedroom again. This time we can hear the sound of the shower running in the bathroom adjacent to the bedroom.*)

MIKE: Did you say something?

STEPHEN: NCN is fucking up. Listen to that. You'd think they'd care enough to listen to what they're broadcasting. Hello?

(*Someone at the station bumps the needle, and the record resumes playing properly.*)

If I ran a station, heads would roll if that ever happened. I said I'd make more coffee.

MIKE: Not for us.

(HE *sits and begins to eat his Danish.*)

STEPHEN: (*Moving to kitchen area and beginning to prepare coffee*) You know, with compact discs, stuck records, scratches, that sort of thing are going to be a thing of the past. The

Brahms fourth will be safe from people like you and Mendy.

MIKE: I said not for us, thank you.

STEPHEN: I heard you. Though actually I was in Tower Records the other day and there was this man returning a CD he was complaining was defective. The Beethoven Third. The new Bernstein performance on Deutsche Grammophone. "What's the matter with it?" the salesman sort of sniffed. "I can't get access to the third movement," the man said. Do you believe it? "I can't get access to the third movement." Welcome to the future. We who have lived so long and borne so much, salute you. You sure you don't have time for coffee?

MIKE: He doesn't drink it.

STEPHEN: Another health nut! I can understand not smoking but all this other shit! Will he take decaf?

MIKE: We're fine.

STEPHEN: What time does he have to be at work anyway? What is he, a milkman?

MIKE: We're going by his place first.

STEPHEN: The two of you? With his sister there? That's saucy of you.

MIKE: I said I'd drive him.

STEPHEN: Where does he live?

MIKE: 106th St. and Amsterdam Avenue.

STEPHEN: In our car? Lots of luck. So long hubcaps. So long tape deck. So long motor.

MIKE: It's Columbia.

STEPHEN: Fuck you, it's Columbia. It's fucking Harlem. I ought to know. I went there.

MIKE: The neighborhood has changed.

STEPHEN: They were saying that when Lou Gehrig went there and look what happened to him.

MIKE: The car will be fine.

STEPHEN: What does he have to go home for anyway?

MIKE: To change.

STEPHEN: Into what? Another jockstrap?

MIKE: I should have guessed!

STEPHEN: What's the matter? What did I say?

MIKE: I'm sorry you're home earlier than I thought we'd agreed.

STEPHEN: I'm sorry but I got tired of playing Orphan Annie in the fucking rain but have you heard me complaining? We're both going to need a sense of humor if we're going to get through this and so far I've been working mine for all it's worth. I just want to know what you have against the 7th Ave.-Broadway IRT all of a sudden? It was good enough for us.

MIKE: I said I'd drive him.

STEPHEN: The subway is faster.

MIKE: I want to drive him. I like him.

STEPHEN: Why didn't you say so? That's all you had to say. Like I understand. I can relate to like. Like is lovely. Like is nice. Like is human. Like is likable. I respect like.
(MIKE *goes to the stereo and changes radio stations. He finds a mellow-rock-type music and lowers the volume.*)

MIKE: Do you mind? That stuff is making me nuts.

STEPHEN: Schubert never made anyone nuts. Bruckner, maybe.

MIKE: His name is Paul.

STEPHEN: I know.

MIKE: He's a graduate student at Columbia.

STEPHEN: Social work.

MIKE: You know all this.

STEPHEN: So why are you telling me?

MIKE: I really like him.

STEPHEN: He looks like a . . .

MIKE: I'm not interested.

STEPHEN: . . . something in the rodent family.

MIKE: That's your opinion.

STEPHEN: Listen, I'm glad you see something in him. It must be his charm or his brain. God knows, it's not his meat.

MIKE: This is hopeless.

STEPHEN: So move.

MIKE: Maybe I should.

(Calls off)

Paul! Hurry up!

STEPHEN: Did you get your messages?

MIKE: I'm not on call for twenty-four hours. I'd like to enjoy them.

STEPHEN: It looks like you're off and running. So who's Allan Weeks?

(HE changes his voice.)

He was in the neighborhood last night and he's sorry he missed you but he'll try you next trip.

(It's a deadly accurate imitation.)

MIKE: He's a pathologist at Johns Hopkins. We met at a CMV seminar for Christ's sake.

STEPHEN: What's keeping you? Dr. Al sounds like a real firecracker.

MIKE: He's married.

STEPHEN: Maybe his wife is disposable, too.

MIKE: 106th St. and Amsterdam will be just fine.

STEPHEN: I'm sorry. I'm sorry, I'm sorry, I'm sorry! I'm sorry about the towels, I'm sorry about what I just said, I'm sorry about this whole mess.

PAUL *(off)*: Mike!

MIKE: This has got to stop, Stephen.

STEPHEN: I know.

PAUL *(off)*: I'm out.

MIKE: I mean it.

PAUL *(off)*: She's all yours.

STEPHEN: Go on, take your shower, I'll be nice.

MIKE: I'd settle for civil.

STEPHEN: It's hard sometimes, okay?

MIKE: For me, too!

(PAUL opens bathroom door.)

PAUL: Did you hear me? I'm out.

MIKE: Thanks.

(PAUL *exits into the bedroom. Then* MIKE *turns and exits into the bathroom. The door closes.* STEPHEN *looks at the door a beat. We hear the shower being turned on again. This time* STEPHEN *crosses quickly to the bedroom door, knocks and opens it at the same time.*)

STEPHEN: Excuse me. Can I get in here a second? Thank you.

(HE *goes into the bedroom, leaving the door open. We can hear voices but nothing distinct. The room is empty for maybe fifteen seconds. Then* PAUL *comes into the room, where he will finish dressing.*)

PAUL: That's all right. I'm just in your way. I think I've got everything.

(HE *moves across the room to the window and looks out, checking the weather. He is putting on his shirt when* STEPHEN *comes back into the room, closing the door behind him.*)

STEPHEN: It's all yours again. I was looking for a fresh shirt but I guess I forgot to pick them up at the cleaners.

PAUL: Oh. I'm sorry.

STEPHEN: It's not your fault. Don't let me keep you.

PAUL: This is fine. I'm sorry about . . . !

STEPHEN: In the movies, I think it's called "meeting cute." We're destined to be more than very good friends.

PAUL: We just didn't hear you.

STEPHEN: I'm not your sister from Boston. I think I can handle it. Don't tell anybody, but it's not exactly the first time.

PAUL: It's nice to finally meet you.

STEPHEN: Please! It's Jim, right?

PAUL: No, it's Paul.

STEPHEN: Paul, of course! Jim's fairer. Coffee?

PAUL: I don't drink it.

STEPHEN: Good thinking. Decaf?

PUAL: (*Shaking his head*) That's all right.

STEPHEN: I'm Stephen.

PAUL: I know. We spoke on the phone last night.

STEPHEN: You broke my friend Mendy's heart. Cleft it in twain. And that's without even seeing you.

PAUL: I didn't even know what he was talking about.

STEPHEN: The Lisbon *Traviata*.

PAUL: It sounds like a murder story. "The Lisbon Traviata."

STEPHEN: You think so?

PAUL: Well, a mystery anyway. Something with criminals. "The Lisbon Traviata." "The Maltese Falcon." "The . . ."

STEPHEN: You have a vivid imagination.

PAUL: I'm afraid it just ran out!

STEPHEN: Those are nice pants.

PAUL: Thank you. They're from Barney's

STEPHEN: I wish you'd put something on.

PAUL: I'm sorry. I am.

STEPHEN: The stereo. I get nervous when something's not playing. Go ahead, I'll get your coffee.

PAUL: I told you, I don't drink it.

STEPHEN: It's decaf, cross my heart. If you have a caffeine attack, you can ring me at Knopf and call me a liar. Go ahead, put something on.

PAUL: I wouldn't know where to begin.

STEPHEN: They're all in alphabetical order by composer, title, or performer. If they're not, we know who to blame.

PAUL: I didn't know they made this many records.

STEPHEN: One of my many obsessions. It keeps me off the streets. My father always wondered why I wanted yet another *Aida*. "Because it's different from the other ones, Dad. You go to the Army-Navy game every year. Same game, different players. Same opera, different singers." He didn't see my logic. I thought it was brilliant for a toddler. How are you doing?

PAUL: It's hopeless.

STEPHEN: What would you say to a little Lisbon *Traviata?*

PAUL: I'd say, "Hello, little Lisbon *Traviata*." (*He laughs.*) I don't think so. Opera's kind of not my thing.

STEPHEN: I like the fit.

PAUL: I guess if I understood what they were singing about . . . !

STEPHEN: Love and death. That's all they're ever singing about. There's an occasional Anvil Chorus, but its basically boy meets girl, boy gets girl, boy and girl croak. That's all you need to know, from *Aida* to *Zaide*. I'll take you some time.

PAUL: I'd be over my head.

STEPHEN: Nonsense. That's what you all think. Michael was the same way. Opera is about us, our life-and-death passions—we all love, we're all going to die. Maria understood that. That's where the voice came from, the heart, the soul, I'm tempted to say from some even more intimate place.

PAUL: Maria?

STEPHEN: Maria Callas, Greek-American soprano, 1923–1977, famous for the musical and dramatic intensity she brought to her characterization. When did you two meet?

PAUL: Me and Mike?

STEPHEN: Mike and I. Mendy introduced us. He insisted he was madly in love with me and then he introduced me to Michael. I believe that's called self-destructive.

PAUL: I met Mike where I used to work.

STEPHEN: Let me guess. His gym.

PAUL: No, I never worked in a gym. I never even joined one.

STEPHEN: You have a beautiful body.

PAUL: Thank you. We met in a restaurant. Claudia's. In the Village.

STEPHEN: I know Claudia's. It used to be wonderful. Still, it's very pricey. I'm impressed.

PAUL: No, I was a waiter there, part-time. I couldn't afford to eat at Claudia's. I doubt I ever will.

STEPHEN: It's lucky for you Michael could.

PAUL: No, it's lucky for me he got my table.

STEPHEN: Let me guess, he slipped you his number on a matchbook.

PAUL: No. I said, "I get off at eleven. I could meet you at the bar across the street."

STEPHEN: Pretty cheeky!

PAUL: He was alone. He wasn't wearing a wedding ring. They're always telling us to go for it, so I went for it.

STEPHEN: Tell me about your intentions. Are they honorable?

PAUL: I think so.

STEPHEN: Dr. Deller is a good man.

PAUL: I know.

STEPHEN: And you know what they say about good men!

PAUL: Hard to find. Easy to lose. Smart to keep. Now I'm working part-time in a light gallery on the Upper East Side. I'm a graduate student at Columbia working for an M.S.W.

STEPHEN: Master of Social Work.

PAUL: Right.

STEPHEN: What's a light gallery?

PAUL: A showroom for lights. Lighting fixtures. One of these.

STEPHEN: Are they twill?

PAUL: I don't know.

STEPHEN: What kind of social work?

PAUL: Medical. Eventually I'd like to end up in a hospital.

STEPHEN: Most of us usually do. I thought about being a priest—

PAUL: Me, too.

STEPHEN: —for about exactly five minutes. Then I thought about joining the Peace Corps for exactly one.

PAUL: I spent two years in Zaire with the Peace Corps.

STEPHEN: Good for you!

PAUL: It was no picnic.

STEPHEN: I bet. I admire people who devote themselves to public service.

PAUL: That's probably why we do it.

STEPHEN: Twill wouldn't fit like that.

PAUL: I'm sorry?

STEPHEN: You're very sweet when you smile like that. I can see what Michael sees in you. Now I'm sorry. We're even.

PAUL: I can see what you saw in Mike.

STEPHEN: What's that?

PAUL: I beg your pardon?

STEPHEN: What did I see in him?

PAUL: I shouldn't have to tell you. He's a wonderful man. He's warm. He's generous. He's funny.

STEPHEN: He's not that funny.

PAUL: You're right!

STEPHEN: I was hoping you could see what Michael sees in me.

PAUL: I can see what he saw in you but I don't think we ought to pursue this.

STEPHEN: Has Michael told you we're going skiing next month?

PAUL: No.

STEPHEN: We try to get to Aspen every year. Do you ski?

PAUL: Not really.

STEPHEN: What does that mean?

PAUL: No.

STEPHEN: We're both good skiers. Michael's terrific, in fact. I love calling him Michael when everyone else calls him Mike. I don't know why. Michael's been under a lot of strain. We need to get away a couple of times each year to get back in synch with each other. Every August we try to sail off Maine for two weeks. Do you sail?

PAUL: No. I'm strictly handball.

STEPHEN: You should try it sometime. It's very liberating. Couples need time alone together. I think especially two men. I can't wait for Aspen.

PAUL: I hope you have a good time.

STEPHEN: Thank you. I'm sure we will. I went to Columbia.

PAUL: I know. Mike told me. He says you're an editor. A very good one.

STEPHEN: He's right. I make talented writers almost very good ones.

PAUL: You're famous.

STEPHEN: Poo!

PAUL: That's what Mike says.

STEPHEN: I can get seats for *Phantom of the Opera*.

PAUL: I'm not much of a theatergoer, either. I'd like to go more but on my budget . . . ! I just saw *Cats*.

STEPHEN: You can die a happy man.

PAUL: Am I nuts, but I hated it? I'd rather see *Bambi*.

STEPHEN: I like your taste in theater, men, and extremely sexy pants. We're going to get along famously.

(The sound of the shower has stopped.)

MIKE *(off)*: Paul!

STEPHEN: We're in here!

MIKE *(off)*: Paul!

PAUL: Here I am.

STEPHEN: Am I anything like you expected?

PAUL: From Mike's description of you? Not in the least.

(The teakettle has started to whistle.)

STEPHEN: Your water's boiling.

(MIKE opens bathroom door.)

MIKE: Stephen!

STEPHEN: *(On his way to the bedroom)* Well, it's about time.

(HE opens the door and goes in. The teakettle continues to whistle. MIKE crosses quickly, a towel around him, still wet from the shower.)

MIKE: I'm sorry about all this. It's his fault. He's early.

PAUL: Early on purpose.

MIKE: Are you alright?

PAUL: I'm fine. I'd just like to get out of here.

MIKE: He didn't say anything to . . . ?

PAUL: I can handle him. Hurry up.

MIKE: Shit! He did! I knew it.

PAUL: I thought he knew.

MIKE: He does know.

PAUL: He sure hasn't accepted it.

MIKE: He's going to have to.

PAUL: That was practically the first thing I asked you. No strings, you said.

MIKE: I didn't want him to meet you like this.

PAUL: You think I did?

MIKE: He's really a very nice man.

PAUL: He spoke highly of you, too.

MIKE: I'm sorry.

PAUL: It's not anybody's fault. But you've got to tell him, Michael. Now go on, get dressed.

MIKE: You called me Michael.

PAUL: Do you mind?

MIKE: No . . . I liked it. I've got the whole day off. I can meet you for lunch.

(HE *hugs* PAUL. STEPHEN *comes out of the bedroom in time to see them.*)

STEPHEN: What are you trying to do? Burn the place down?

(HE *goes to the whistling kettle and turns the flame down.*)

How big a spoonful? I'm afraid it's instant.

PAUL: Really, nothing for me.

MIKE: Why don't you come in while I dress?

PAUL: I'm fine right here.

MIKE: I wish you would.

PAUL: Really! Hurry up.

(MIKE *goes into the bedroom, leaving door ajar.* STEPHEN *is preparing a cup of decaffeinated coffee for* PAUL.)

STEPHEN: Come and get it!

(PAUL *goes to* STEPHEN *and takes a cup from him.*)

Milk? Sugar?

PAUL: No, thanks.

STEPHEN: I found something I think you might get a kick out of.

(HE *crosses to bedroom door and sticks his head in.*)

Excuse us. We're going to put on a little music, loud.
(HE *closes the door.*)
Mike basically hates opera. That should've clued me in
years ago we weren't fated to last. After eight years, it
gets pretty hard coming home night after night to a man
who doesn't like *Idomeneo*.
(HE *hands* PAUL *an envelope, which* PAUL *will open while*
STEPHEN *goes to stereo unit and puts on a CD. Inside the
envelope is a collection of Polaroid photos.*)
Those were taken our first year together. We were insa-
tiable. Having each other for real wasn't enough. We
wanted tangible proof of our priapic good fortune. They
got me through a lot of nights when he was working
late. He went crazy when he couldn't find them. I told
him I'd destroyed them. I think he's forgotten all about
them.

PAUL: Why did you give me these?

STEPHEN: Because I'm a shit.

(HE *presses the Play button. The music is quite loud. It is
Alban Berg's* Wozzeck. MIKE *comes out of the bedroom.* HE *is
in his socks and underwear.*)

MIKE: Stephen!

STEPHEN: He requested it. I swear to God.

MIKE: Turn it off.

STEPHEN: Just a second. The big hit tune's coming up.

(MIKE *presses the Stop button.*)
Why no one's made a rap version of that!

MIKE: Stop it, Stephen!

STEPHEN: Now what would you say to a little Mad Scene
with Maria herself? The high E alone is guaranteed to
clear your sinuses.

MIKE: I said, cut it out.

STEPHEN: Okay, we'll stick with *Wozzeck*.

(HE *presses the Play button again. The music seems even
louder.* MIKE *hits him.* STEPHEN *goes down.*)

MIKE: Do it again and I'll break your fucking head open.

PAUL: Hey, come on you two, don't. I'm going.

(STEPHEN *is getting to his feet.*)

STEPHEN: Your friend is talking to you.

MIKE: I mean it, Stephen.

(HE *presses the Stop button.*)

STEPHEN: Maybe you want him to see this side of you.

MIKE: Don't you dare turn that on. Don't make me do this, Stephen.

STEPHEN: The only thing that makes you do anything is your dick and your sick deluded idea that if you stick it enough places maybe you'll forget what a miserable, fucked-up faggot you've become.

(HE *pushes the Play button.* MIKE *hits him again. Again* STEPHEN *goes down. This time there is blood.*)

PAUL: Jesus, Mike!

MIKE: I haven't hit anyone since the fifth grade! What are you doing to me?

(*To* PAUL)

I told you to come in there with me!

PAUL: That's it. I'm going.

MIKE: I'm sorry! I—!

(*To* STEPHEN)

Get up!

STEPHEN: If this is your idea of safe sex, I don't like it.

PAUL: I'll call you.

MIKE: Wait, I'm taking you.

PAUL: I'm late. Here, I don't want these.

MIKE: What are they?

PAUL: I don't care.

MIKE: Where did you get these?

PAUL: I said I don't care.

MIKE: This was years ago.

PAUL: It's okay. Call me. I'm late.

MIKE: What about lunch?

PAUL: I don't know. Make sure he's okay.

MIKE: I can be ready in a minute.

PAUL: I can't!

(MIKE *kisses* PAUL, *who pulls away after a few moments.*)

I'll call you.

(MIKE *kisses him again, this time more forcefully.* PAUL *never really responds or relaxes into it. Finally,* HE *pulls away.*)

I gotta go.

(HE *goes to the door, where he has some trouble with the different locks.*)

Making a graceful exit from a New York City apartment is just about impossible unless you're some sort of fucking Houdini.

MIKE: Now the lower one! There you go.

PAUL: Thanks.

(PAUL *goes.* MIKE *crosses to apartment door, opens it, and sticks his head out into the hallway.*)

MIKE: Can you hear the elevator? Is it coming? Push the "Up" button, too. Your hair is still wet. Don't you want to use the dryer?

(*Sound of raucous music from the hall*)

Good morning, Mrs. De Leon. I'll call you, Paul. What I said last night . . . I meant it. I really do . . . Could you ask your grandson to turn that down, Mrs. De Leon? Thank you. So long, Paul.

(*Sounds of elevator door opening and closing in the apartment corridor off.* MIKE *closes the door and turns back into the room. He looks at* STEPHEN, *who is still on the floor.*)

Look at you.

STEPHEN: You want to fuck me?

MIKE: You're pathetic.

STEPHEN: You want me to fuck you?

MIKE: You just did.

STEPHEN: I hope you know what you're doing.

MIKE: I wouldn't be surprised if he never wanted to see me again. I wouldn't walk into this mess.

STEPHEN: I worry about you. Has he been tested?

MIKE: Yes. We both have. Have you? (HE *is trying to rip up the Polaroids.*) I asked you to destroy these.

STEPHEN: You'll need scissors to do that.

MIKE: You said you had.

STEPHEN: I lied.

MIKE: Where were they?

STEPHEN: In the bookshelf behind *The Story of Civilization* by Will and Ariel Durant.

(MIKE *gives up trying to destroy the Polaroids.*)

I told you. I'd forgotten how funny blood tastes.

MIKE: Get up, will you?

STEPHEN: Sort of like metal.

MIKE: At least . . . Here!

(HE *tosses* STEPHEN *a kitchen towel.*)

Wipe your mouth.

STEPHEN: It's us. We're tasting ourselves.

MIKE: You're still bleed—!

(HE *goes to* STEPHEN, takes towel, and wipes the blood off his chin.)

STEPHEN: Why don't you want to fuck me? Ow! You used to love my ass. Ow, I said!

MIKE: Shut up. Hold it there until it stops.

(HE *holds towel to* STEPHEN*'s chin.*)

Put your head back. Here. Against me. Jesus, Stephen, what are you doing to me? What are we doing to each other?

STEPHEN: You know you're the only person I ever let fuck me. A lot of guys wanted to but I wouldn't let them. I guess I was saving myself for you.

MIKE: Let go. Let me look.

(HE *takes towel from* STEPHEN*'s chin, then looks and dabs at it.*)

STEPHEN: I never really liked fucking you. You said "ouch" too much. Well, not "ouch" exactly. It was more like a whining moan of general discomfort. "Are you okay, Mike?" "Unh-hunh." That "unh-hunh" was a real turn-off.

(MIKE *stops dabbing* STEPHEN's *chin, gets up, and goes to the bathroom.*)

Where are you going? That was nice. You want to hit me again?

(*No response from the other room. We hear* MIKE *going through the medicine chest in the bathroom.*)

What are you doing in there? Don't get carried away, doctor. I'm fine.

(MIKE *returns.* HE *has a small bottle of medicine in his hand.*)

What's that?

MIKE: Never mind.

STEPHEN: I said I'm fine.

MIKE: Hold still.

STEPHEN: Hasn't he ever asked you about your ring?

MIKE: No.

STEPHEN: I would have.

MIKE: It's not a wedding ring.

STEPHEN: It's hardly costume jewelry either.

MIKE: Do you want it back?

STEPHEN: That's not what I'm saying.

MIKE: Hold still.

STEPHEN: What is it? Do I get a lollipop?

(MIKE *puts medicine on* STEPHEN's *lip.*)

Is that it? Thank you.

(*A delayed reaction*)

Ow!

MIKE: Get up. It makes me sick to think I did that to you.

STEPHEN: I like it down here.

MIKE: Suit yourself.

STEPHEN: Mendy says I usually do.

MIKE: I told you I liked him, Stephen.

STEPHEN: I saw what you two are all about. K-Y and a joint.

MIKE: It's the best sex I've had in three years.

STEPHEN: That's not just my fault.

MIKE: Of course it's not.

STEPHEN: People go through phases.

MIKE: The pity is they stay there. I didn't deserve that. Neither did he.

(MIKE *moves away from him and retrieves the Polaroids.*)

Anybody who would show these to someone else . . . !

STEPHEN: Is what? Is sick? Is crazy?

MIKE: I trusted you. These weren't for other people.

STEPHEN: The real tragedy is neither one of us is ever going to look that good again.

(MIKE *sits and looks at the Polaroids.*)

Do you remember where we took those?

MIKE: No.

STEPHEN: Take a look.

MIKE: That weekend on the Cape?

STEPHEN: We thought those woods were so green and lush. Two days later we found out it was mostly poison ivy. You had to stand most of the way on the bus coming back. I had it all over my balls. It's probably the only time in my life I would have gladly exchanged a pair of pants for a simple skirt. I'm getting up. Last chance.

(STEPHEN *will get up and go to stereo and put on a CD during the following.*)

I'm going to put something on. Don't worry, something nice. I can't stand it without music. I'll put on something you'll like. Trust me. I'm not going to tell you what it is. You should be able to guess. We saw it together in Paris. It was Oscar Wilde's birthday and we were staying in that hotel he died in on the Seine.

(*The music begins. It is the prelude to Wagner's* Lohengrin. STEPHEN *sets it at a low, easy-listening level.*)

I'll give you three guesses and one hint: it's not *La Bohème*. Isn't that cold? I'll make some fresh.

(HE *takes* MIKE's *coffee cup, moves to kitchen area, empties it, and begins making coffee.*)

I wasn't planning on going in today. Maybe we can catch that Diebenkorn show at the Modern I was telling you about. And we could pick up your watch. It's ready. They sent you a card. I don't know why they don't just call. (MIKE *gets up, takes a scissors from the desk, and begins to methodically cut the Polaroids into little pieces.* STEPHEN *has come out of kitchen area.*)

Before you do that, did you see Sammy in one of them?

MIKE: No. Where?

STEPHEN: The one where we're . . . I can't describe it. Here. (HE *quickly dries his hands, comes to* MIKE, *takes Polaroids, finds the one he is looking for, and shows it to him.*) It's just the top of his head but still! Whatever we were doing that dog wanted to be doing it, too. Remember, there was that whole period whenever we were making love, he'd jump on the bed and bark. That wonderful stillness after coming. Arf arf arf!

MIKE: He thought you were attacking me.

STEPHEN: He was right.

MIKE: God, I miss him.

STEPHEN: Me, too. I still think we should get another one. Not the same breed maybe but . . .

(MIKE *resumes cutting the Polaroids.*)

You sure you want to do that? There's no more where those came from.

MIKE: I know what we looked like eight years ago, and this isn't the way I care to remember either one of us.

STEPHEN: You could always send one to Knopf with an anonymous letter—"Stephen R. sucks cock"—and sign it William F. Buckley.

MIKE: I think they know.

STEPHEN: The sadness? They couldn't possibly.

MIKE: Stephen, we better talk.

STEPHEN: We are talking. I've done nothing but. You're the silent one.

(HE *gestures towards the stereo.*)

You give up? The Prelude to *Lohengrin*. Remember? That's too bad. (HE *is taking the record off as he speaks.*)

First prize was a trip to Positano to hear Leontyne Price in *Gypsy*. Why not? Birgit Nilsson's doing it in Stockholm, Joan Sutherland in Sydney, Kiri at Guadalcanal. Jessye Norman turned it down. I think she was right. You used to love these games.

MIKE: I used to love a lot of things.

STEPHEN: Including me.

(HE *has turned on the radio to a rock-and-roll station. He dances to it.*)

You wanna dance? I'll let you lead.

(HE *abruptly stops.*)

You're not in the mood for this. Neither am I.

(HE *turns off the radio and start something for another CD.*)

MIKE: Could we have no music for a change?

STEPHEN: I'll keep it low.

MIKE: What's wrong with quiet?

STEPHEN: I dare you not to like this.

(*Villa-Lobos's* Bachianas Brasileiras #5 *is heard.*)

MIKE: Stephen, we have to talk.

STEPHEN: I am talking. You're not listening. (HE *means the music.*) I can't say it any better than that.

(HE *crosses to* MIKE *and stands behind him looking down at one last Polaroid he is about to destroy.*)

Is that the last one? Wait.

(MIKE *stops.*)

I still find the man in that picture very attractive.

MIKE: I don't recognize him.

STEPHEN: Look at those proportions. They're perfect.

MIKE: They're not perfect.

STEPHEN: To me they're perfect. My kind of perfect. The only kind I care about.

(THEY *are both looking at this last Polaroid,* STEPHEN *leaning over* MIKE's *shoulder, perhaps his hand on his shoulder.*)

Wonderful full lips on a generous mouth. I like that enormously. Wonderful thick neck. I like that, too. Or did I already tell you that? I told someone I did. Deep, burning, really nail-you eyes. Right at the camera, right through it and into mine. There's strength in that look but such a gentleness, too.

MIKE: Stephen.

STEPHEN: Where am I going to find that again?

MIKE: He wants to live with me, Stephen.

STEPHEN: Of course he wants to live with you. You're a catch, doctor. You have lousy hours but you're a catch. And see that line there? Defining the pelvis. I could trace it for hours. There's some wonderful name for it, somebody's girdle. Achilles' or Hercules' or Atlas' or . . . you took anatomy, help me out here.

MIKE: I don't remember.

STEPHEN: His is perfection. The thighs. Everything. He's everything I ever wanted. I can look at that picture and get hard. I used to look at them and masturbate when you were doing your residency and it seemed like you were never around. Even when you were sometimes. Once, I remember this so clearly, you were out here reading a new Updike, one of the Rabbits, and I was looking at those and jacking off. The last time you spent the night with him I did. The next time you spend the night with him I will.

MIKE: Jesus.

STEPHEn: Don't give me Jesus. Give me the picture.

MIKE: No.

STEPHEN: This isn't easy for me to say. I want the picture, Mike. Let me have that much of you. Something.

(MIKE *starts to cut up the final Polaroid.*)

Eight hundred years of analysis and I still say exactly what's on my mind. Do you want to live with him?

MIKE: I don't know. Maybe I should live alone.

STEPHEN: I have and believe me, it's not all it's cracked up to be.

(MIKE *gets up and disposes of the pieces of Polaroid.* STEPHEN *stays where he was.* MIKE *turns off stereo. There is a long silence.*)

MIKE: Why aren't you going in today?

STEPHEN: I don't feel like it.

MIKE: This will be the third time this month.

STEPHEN: What are you, spying on me?

MIKE: It's killing me. Watching you let it all slip away.

STEPHEN: Do you love him?

MIKE: I don't know.

STEPHEN: Ask a straight question, expect an evasive answer.

MIKE: I said I don't know!

STEPHEN: Let me rephrase that. Love is what we're supposed to have. Are you in love with him?

MIKE: Sometimes I think I am. That's about as straight an answer as I can give you.

STEPHEN: Was it like us?

MIKE: No.

STEPHEN: No whirlwind courtship?

MIKE: We didn't have a courtship.

STEPHEN: We didn't need one.

STEPHEN: What you said to him last night, what you just reminded him that you said, what was that?

MIKE: How fond I am of him.

STEPHEN: How "fond"? Did you say "fond," madam? Nay, you love. I know not "fond."

MIKE: Stephen, it's easy for you to play with words. Too easy. You can either hear what I want to say—it's pretty simple—or not. I don't have the time for anything else. This arrangement isn't working for either one of us.

STEPHEN: The arrangement is fine. It's me. I saw those records, the mess, and just went crazy. I'm sorry.

MIKE: That's how I am, Stephen. I always was. You just didn't notice. I scratch records, I eat pizza, I use the wrong towel.

STEPHEN: I said I was sorry.

MIKE: You can't have it both ways.

STEPHEN: I don't want it both ways. I want it this way. Just try to be careful next time.

MIKE: There will be a next time.

STEPHEN: I know.

MIKE: I like him.

STEPHEN: Fine.

MIKE: I really like him.

STEPHEN: Don't touch the phonograph and you can bring George Bush up here.

MIKE: This is about me. I'm trying to tell you how I feel. I know how you feel. I don't think you hear me anymore. You hear the words, but you don't hear what I'm saying.

STEPHEN: Try me.

MIKE: I have been.

STEPHEN: Try me!

MIKE: I'm tired, Stephen. I'm tired of saying I'm sorry all the time. I'm tired of tiptoeing through my life because it might interfere with yours. I'm tired of being told what opera to like, what book to read, what movies to go to. I'm tired of being your father, mother, big brother, best friend, your analyst, your cheerleader.

STEPHEN: You left out lover.

MIKE: I haven't been your lover since the first night I said to myself, "Who is this person lying at my side, this stranger, who hasn't heard or held me since the last time it pleased him?" That's the night I should have grabbed you by the shoulders and screamed, "I don't want this, Stephen. I don't need just another warm body next to mine. I'm much too needy to settle for so little. Look at me. Love me. Be with me." Now I've waited too long. You weren't even sleeping. You were reading. Your friend was on your cassette player on your side of the bed. Maria Callas. You had your back to me. I had my arm around you. I was stroking one of your tits. I asked you how you thought I should handle Sarah—she was coming up to New York and wanted to see me. It was the first time since the divorce and I was scared. I'd hurt her in a way I was ashamed of. I really needed you and you just shrugged and said, "You'll do the right thing" and turned the page. I didn't stop stroking your tit, but you weren't the same person anymore. Neither was I. I kept my arm around you only because I was suddenly so scared I was as alone as I must have made Sarah feel. I was holding on for dear life.

STEPHEN: Why didn't you tell me?

MIKE: You wouldn't have heard me. After you stopped reading I let you make love to me. I love you, Stephen, I'll always love you, but I haven't been your lover for a long time. I think you're a good man, a decent and caring man, a deserving one. You don't deserve this. You'll find someone else.

STEPHEN: I don't want someone else.

(There has been another blast of raucous music from the hallway outside the apartment. STEPHEN *explodes.)*

How can anyone goddamn expect themselves to think with that going on!

(HE goes to the door, opens it.)

What's the matter with you? Where do you think you are? I don't care if he's your *great*-grandson, Mrs. De Leon!

(HE slams the door.)

That's not a super. That's a spy from the Spanish Inquisition moonlighting as a fucking baby-sitter! *(HE sees* MIKE *at the phone.)* Hey! We're talking here. Who are you calling?

MIKE: I can't help the pain you're in.

STEPHEN: You can stop causing it.

MIKE: How, for Christ's sake?

STEPHEN: By loving me.

(HE breaks the phone connection.)

MIKE: I did love you.

STEPHEN: Not enough.

MIKE: There is no "enough" for you.

STEPHEN: I can't help that.

MIKE: You'd better. You're never going to find anyone who can.

STEPHEN: I'm sorry but I thought I had. I'll kill you first.

MIKE: I said I still love you.

STEPHEN: Good! Then you can tell what's-his-face that it's all off.

MIKE: I just don't want to be in this kind of relationship with you or anyone else.

STEPHEN: If I hear that asshole word one more time! I don't want a relationship. I want a lover.

MIKE: So do I!

(HE begins to dial again.)

STEPHEN: All right, I'm sorry I behaved that way. I'll apologize to him.

MIKE: Shit!

(HE hangs up and dials another number.)

STEPHEN: I doubt if he's there yet.

MIKE: I wasn't calling him.

STEPHEN: You want the truth, Michael? I had a lousy night. My date stood me up. I spent the night at Mendy's listening to Maria Callas.

MIKE: I'm sorry.

STEPHEN: *(HE goes to stereo and starts looking for a CD.)* Why? She was in great voice. Don't cry for me, Argentina. I'm sorry but I need something. I tried being good, I didn't like it. Wear earplugs. Get lost. Drop dead.

(HE begins to play another CD. The music is Beverly Sills singing the soprano aria from Mozart's Zaide.*)*

MIKE: *(Into the phone)* May I speak to Mr. Deller, please? . . . His brother . . . Thank you. I'll hold.

STEPHEN: You want to take a guess at the composer? Anyone would know this is Mozart. But you'll never guess the music. It's an aria from *Zaide*. He wrote it when he was two weeks old or something. It's hardly ever done. *Ruhe sanft, mein holdes Leben,* which I would translate roughly as, "Rest softly, my dearest life."

MIKE: *(To* STEPHEN*)* Why didn't you tell me about last night? We could've gone somewhere else. A hotel, something.

STEPHEN: Then why the hell didn't you?

MIKE *(Into the phone)* Bob! Hi. Listen, can I stay with you two for a while. It's really gotten impossible here.

STEPHEN: He knows?

MIKE: I hope Ginny won't mind. I tried to call her first but there was no answer. Thanks. I don't know how he is. I haven't talked to mom since Sunday. I'm sure she'd call if there were any change. Okay. Thanks. Who? He's fine. Yeah. Bye. (HE *hangs up.)*

STEPHEN: You told them?

MIKE: It was pretty obvious.

STEPHEN: I wish you'd made things more obvious to me. How is your father? I've been meaning to ask.

MIKE: The same, I guess. One of us would have heard.

STEPHEN: Who's fine?

MIKE: Paul. Do you know where that overnight bag is?

STEPHEN: We left it in St. Bart's. It was falling apart.

MIKE: The blue one?

STEPHEN: Oh, you mean the tote! If it's not here, it's out in Sag.

(MIKE *goes into the bedroom, leaving the door open.)*

How does he know Paul?

MIKE: We all had dinner and went to the theater.

STEPHEN: On his budget? What did you see? *Cats?*

MIKE: How did you know?

STEPHEN: Just a wild guess.

(MIKE *gets a dark suit on a hanger out of the closet.)*

I know it's none of my business as of thirty seconds ago, but why are you taking your black wool suit to sleep on your brother's sofa?

MIKE: It's for Billy Todd's funeral tomorrow.

STEPHEN: From your description of him, you'll be the only one there not in full drag.

MIKE: I'm speaking. I didn't think it would be quite appropriate.

STEPHEN: A church full of queens lusting for the humpy doctor delivering his standard eulogy. Who asked you to speak? His lover?

MIKE: His family. He didn't have a lover.

STEPHEN: Of course not, he was madly in love with you. If I were you, I'd shake everybody up. People are sick and tired of hearing the same old dreary things at these affairs. He was wonderful. He had so much life to give. He was brave. Sky, instead, "Aren't you sick and tired of these people depressing us just because they were unable to maintain a stable relationship? How many tears are we supposed to shed? Don't you wish they'd just get it over with? Wouldn't you rather be at a nice restaurant than sitting here moping over someone who probably, if the truth could be faced up to, even just a little bit, got what was coming to him?"

MIKE: Jesus, Stephen.

STEPHEN: *(HE busts into tears.)* I'm sorry, but ever since you started telling me about him, I've been so jealous of him. That you were caring for him. Isn't that crazy?

MIKE: Stephen, he was dying.

STEPHEN: So was I. And then when you said he'd died last night, my first thought was, he's free. No one can hurt him anymore. No one can leave him.

MIKE: Oh, I didn't want this either.

STEPHEN: I was a good lover, Michael.

MIKE: It's not just about sex.

STEPHEN: Yes it is. Right now it is. Most of the time it is. We were wonderful that way. What happened?

MIKE: I don't know.

STEPHEN: So why are we doing this?

MIKE: I don't know.

(MIKE exits to bedroom.)

STEPHEN: Nice try, Bubbles. The good doctor's got a heart of stone this morning.

(Calling off to MIKE*)*

What do you want to hear? What about Tebaldi? You always liked her more than Maria. That should have been a tip-off! Do you think people like us read too many books about people like us?

(The phone begins to ring.)

Aren't you going to get that?

*(*MIKE *appears at the door of the bedroom. The phone machine is set to answer on the fourth ring.)*

That could be him. He could be home now. I'm not going near it all day. The House of Knopf can think I'm dead. This is like waiting for water to boil.

Don't give up on me, Michael.

(The machine picks up, interrupting the fourth ring. MIKE *looks at phone, anxious to hear who's calling.)*

MENDY'S VOICE: Stephen, it's Mendy. I know you're there. Do you want to pick up?

*(*MIKE *goes back into the bedroom.)*

Stephen, this isn't funny. You promised you'd call the minute you got in. I'm dressed and ready to come over there and get it. I'm counting to three, Stephen. One. Two. Look what you've reduced me to! Three. Three! All right for you, Stephen. One day they will find Maria's Venice *Walküre* and her Genoa *Tristan* and her Chicago *Trovatore* with Jussi Björling, to refresh your feeble fart of a memory, and I will make it my life's work to see that no one on this entire planet allows you to hear those tapes. I hope I've made myself clear. You can take your Lisbon *Traviata* and shove it!

*(*HE *hangs up.)*

STEPHEN: The Lisbon *Traviata!* It's funny, but after all these years I still don't know why I even like Mendy. Sometimes I don't know who I like.

(Calls off to MIKE *in the bedroom)*

It's on the top shelf in my closet. The blue tote. Behind the tennis balls.

(HE *walks to the door and talks to* MIKE *without going into the bedroom.* MIKE *will continue to cross in and out of the bedroom and the bathroom, packing certain items to take with him.* STEPHEN *will seem superfluous to his activities.*)

What about the house anyway? What about Aspen? What do we tell George and Kenneth? That we're not coming? Just like that?

MIKE: This is difficult enough. Let's not make it worse.

STEPHEN: What am I supposed to tell my lawyer? I left everything to you. I'm not changing my will again.

MIKE: Tell him you want to leave everything to build a memorial statue to Maria Callas.

STEPHEN: You know, that's not a bad idea.

MIKE: Why not? She's dead. It's the living you have trouble with.

(HE *goes again.* STEPHEN *begins to play* La Traviata *and stands listening to the Prelude, which begins to fill the room.*)

STEPHEN: I'll never forget the night she did this at the old Met. The excitement in the air. Everybody was there. Jackie Kennedy was in a box with Leonard Bernstein. No, that was for the return as Tosca seven years later and she was Jackie Onassis and she was with Adlai Stevenson. I'd been in love with the sound of her voice since the first records. That strange, sad siren song I knew she was singing just for me. I could play those records for hours. I had them memorized. Every nuance, the slightest intake of breath, the fiercest tones, the hushed, still pianissimo. Hers was the only voice who heard what I heard, said what I wanted to hear. This would be the first time I'd seen her. I'd waited on line for days for standing room. The curtain rose. I didn't see her at first. She was to one side. I thought she'd be center. But then she sang those first phrases—"*Flora, amici*"—and I saw her. She took my breath away. She wasn't just a voice on a record. She was there, she was real. I was on the same planet at the same moment in time as Maria Callas. The rest of the evening passed like a dream, a dream I remember more clearly than the color of my lover's eyes. I miss you, Mme. Callas.

(HE *goes to the window and looks out. He stands with his back to us.* MIKE *comes out of the bedroom with a small tote bag and some final articles he will pack in the suitcase.*)

MIKE: You have my brother's number?

STEPHEN: Don't go. Please, don't go.

MIKE: Will you be going out to the house this weekend?

STEPHEN: What do you care?

MIKE: I think it will be easier to get my things out if you aren't here.

STEPHEN: So soon? I don't see the hurry.

MIKE: Yes or no?

STEPHEN: If Caballè cancels her recital, yes. If she deigns to put in an appearance, no.

MIKE: When will you know?

STEPHEN: With Caballè it's right down to the wire. Why don't you call her? She's staying at Burger King.

(*The phone begins to ring. This time the machine will answer after the first ring.*)

PAUL'S VOICE: Mike? It's Paul. Are you there? Do you want to pick up?

(MIKE *picks up the phone.*)

MIKE: Paul, where are you? What happened? I think we should, too. How soon? What did you tell them at work? The whole day? Great. I'll be there.

(HE *hangs up.*)

STEPHEN: Let me guess. He said, "I think we should talk" and you said, "I think we should too." Now he's calling in sick. You see the effect you have on people?

(MIKE *is dialing another number.*)

MIKE: Go to hell.

STEPHEN: Now who are you calling?

MIKE: (*Into phone*) This is Dr. Deller. Number 52. The blue BMW. Thank you. How soon?

STEPHEN: What did they tell you? Ten minutes? That should be the name of that garage. It's probably the only English they speak. "Ten minutes." Please don't go. I don't want him in our car.

MIKE: Fine. I'll take a cab.

STEPHEN: I didn't mean that. You know what I mean. What if we get a bigger apartment? Two bedrooms.

MIKE: Ten bedrooms wouldn't be big enough.

STEPHEN: Does it have to be this morning?

MIKE: It should have been three years ago. You can't love what we've become.

STEPHEN: I don't know how to deal with it!

MIKE: Neither do I.

STEPHEN: I was hoping it would go away or one of us would get used to it or both of us would or a new soprano would come along, another Callas, but I suppose that was too much to ask for, or I could see one of your tricks and not be ripped by jealousy.

MIKE: Stephen. I think you're a good man. A decent and caring man.

STEPHEN: Shut up. Please, shut up. Just hold me. Or I could not mind so desperately being stood up by a cute waiter who's too young for me anyway. But at his age and given half a choice in this city of a million of them, I wouldn't want to sleep with me either. You can't leave. No one else will want me.

MIKE: That's not true.

STEPHEN: I look in the mirror and see a young, attractive man, but no one else does.

MIKE: You are attractive.

STEPHEN: I said young, attractive.

MIKE: Oh my Stephen. My dear, sweet, wonderful Stephen, why can't I stay here with you?

STEPHEN: Or I could castrate myself or I could castrate you or we could just get heavily into saltpeter and just pretend that none of this mattered—none of it, none of it—get another dog and gracefully grow old together.

MIKE: I don't know what to say, Stephen.

STEPHEN: Sure you do.

MIKE: I can't anymore.

STEPHEN: Sometimes I think this is the most beautiful music ever written.

(HE *puts the phonograph needle to the beginning of "Ah, forse lui."*)

MIKE: I do love you, you know.

STEPHEN: Other times it's the Good Friday Music from *Parsifal*. Or *The Magic Flute,* Pamina's aria, or *Fidelio,* the entire second act.

MIKE: Stephen.

STEPHEN: I heard you. You just don't want to hold my hand when I'm afraid of the dark.

MIKE: I just want to be away from you.

STEPHEN: So you can hold someone else's hand when he's afraid of the dark.

MIKE: You'll be fine without me.

STEPHEN: I won't make it without you.

MIKE: You just think you won't.

STEPHEN: Don't tell me what I think. I'll tell you what I think and what I think is this: you're leaving me at a wonderful moment in our long, happy history of queerness to seek a new mate to snuggle up with right at the height of our very own Bubonic Plague.

MIKE: You'll find someone.

STEPHEN: I don't want someone. No, thank you. I'll stay right here. Those are dark, mean, and extremely dangerous streets, right now. You can say all you want against Maria, no one's ever accused her of causing AIDS. Renata Scotto, yes; Maria, no.

MIKE: Why can't you be serious?

STEPHEN: It hurts too much, okay? Asshole. Self-centered, smug, shit-kicking, all-his-eggs-in-one-basket, stupid asshole.

(HE *goes to the stereo and moves the needle to Callas singing the* *recitative leading to* "Sempre Libera," *beginning with* "Follie, follie!")

MIKE: That's not going to make it hurt any less.

STEPHEN: Shut up! Shut up and listen to this. The least you can do is sit there and listen to one last *"Sempre libera"* with me. "Always free!," that's you, Michael.

MIKE: I don't want to.

STEPHEN: It's from the by-now-almost-legendary Lisbon *Traviata.*

MIKE: I don't care if it's the Hoboken one.

STEPHEN: Mendy would kill to hear Maria sing this.

MIKE: I'm not Mendy! I've spent the past half-hour trying to get through to you; I've spent the past eight years. You live in *Tosca.* You live in *Turnadot.* You live in some opera no one's ever heard of. It's hard loving someone like that.

STEPHEN: Maria does this phrase better than anyone.

MIKE: Listen to me! Turn that down and listen to me.

STEPHEN: It's hard loving someone like me!

(HE *turns up the volume to a painfully loud level. Callas is all we can hear.* MIKE *tries to move past* STEPHEN, *who pushes him back.*)

Where are you going?

MIKE: Let me go.

(STEPHEN *pushes* MIKE *again and picks up the pair of scissors* MIKE *had previously used to destroy the Polaroids. He will brandish them to keep* MIKE *from moving.*)

STEPHEN: You love him, don't you?

MIKE: I said, let me go.

STEPHEN: You're not getting past me.

MIKE: Come on, Stephen, put those down. I'm not staying here with you.

(HE *takes a step forward.* STEPHEN *forces him back with the scissors.*)

STEPHEN: You're going to him. You do love him.

MIKE: Yes. I love him.

STEPHEN: Then you don't love me anymore? Then you don't love me anymore?

MIKE: No, I don't love you anymore.

STEPHEN: But I still love you. I adore you.

MIKE: What's the point of this? I have to go.

(*Again he tries to move past* STEPHEN, *who again forces him back with a violent lunge with the scissors.*)

STEPHEN: I am to lose my life's salvation so that you can run to someone else and laugh at me? You're not going. You're staying here with me.

MIKE: Give way, Stephen.

STEPHEN: I'm not going to warn you again.

MIKE: (*Stepping forward, opening his arms wide*) All right, do it! Do it or let me by.

STEPHEN: (*Raising the scissors above his head*) For the last time, will you stay here?

(MIKE *holds his hand with the ring in front of* STEPHEN's *face.*)

MIKE: You gave me this ring. (HE *pulls it off.*) I don't want it anymore. (HE *throws it down.*) Now will you let me by?

(MIKE *walks directly past* STEPHEN, *who still stands with the scissors raised. Just as* MIKE *passes him,* STEPHEN *grabs him from behind with a cry and pulls* MIKE *towards him. His hand with the scissors is poised to strike. Their eyes lock.* MIKE *does not flinch. The scissors do not move. There is a terrible, tremendous moment between them. The only sound is Maria Callas singing* La Traviata.

Finally, MIKE *disengages himself from* STEPHEN's *embrace and goes to gather his suitcase and things.* STEPHEN *is still holding the scissors.*

MIKE *exits the apartment without looking back.* STEPHEN *stands clutching the scissors, unable to watch what is happening. His back stiffens as* MIKE *closes the apartment door. Callas continues to sing* "Sempre Libera" *on the stereo. The telephone begins to ring. The answering machine picks up.* STEPHEN *still hasn't moved.*

MENDY'S VOICE: The only reason I called back, Stephen, is to tell you that Albert Benedetti has just come by with a copy of the Lisbon *Triaviata* and we have just put it on and so there!

(STEPHEN's *head turns slowly toward the answering machine. He still holds the scissors. He still hasn't moved.*)

He also brought over Sutherland's first *Adriana* from San Diego if you really want to laugh. He also said to tell you, since he's the only one still speaking to you, that Vickers has cancelled all his *Parsifals.* Such is life. You're still a cunt but I'll probably forgive you, though I can't for the life of me see how Mike puts up with you.

(STEPHEN *closes his eyes and listens to the music. He is no longer aware he is holding the scissors.*)

It's begun! She just sang *"Flora, amici"!* Divine woman! What would we do without her?

(STEPHEN *opens his eyes.* HE *looks straight ahead.*)

Remember, we have *Meistersingers* tonight!

(HE *hangs up.* STEPHEN *slowly sits on the edge of the coffee table. Callas is spinning an elaborate web of coloratura.* STEPHEN *is drawn into it. He throws his head back with her as she reaches for a climactic high note, but no sound comes out. The lights are fading.*

STEPHEN's *mouth is open, his head is back, his eyes are closed. Callas is all we can hear.*

Blackout.)

THE END

Frankie
and Johnny
in the
Clair de Lune

For Maurine McElroy

Frankie and Johnny in the Clair de Lune was first produced by Manhattan Theatre Club Stage II at City Center in New York City on June 2, 1987, with the following cast:

FRANKIE .... Kathy Bates
JOHNNY........................ F. Murray Abraham
VOICE OF RADIO ANNOUNCER...... Dominic Cuskern

It transferred to Manhattan Theater Club Stage I at City Center on October 14, 1987, with the following cast:

FRANKIE .... Kathy Bates
JOHNNY........................ Kenneth Welsh
VOICE OF RADIO ANNOUNCER...... Dominic Cuskern

Both productions were directed by Paul Benedict. Sets by James Noone. Costumes by David Woolard. Lighting by David Noling. Sound by John Gromada. The Production Stage Manager was Pamela Singer.

This production transferred to the Westside Arts Theatre in New York City on December 4, 1987. It was produced by Steven Baruch, Thomas Viertel, Richard Frankel, and Jujamcyn Theatres/Margo Lion.

THE CHARACTERS

FRANKIE—Striking, but not conventional, good looks. She has a sense of humor and a fairly tough exterior. She is also frightened and can be very hard to reach.

JOHNNY—Johnny's best feature is his personality. He works at it. He is in good physical condition.

TIME

The present.

PLACE

New York City.

SETTING

Frankie's one-room apartment in a walk-up tenement in the west '50s. The fourth wall looks onto the backyard and the apartments behind. When the sofa bed is down, as it is for much of the play, the room is quite cramped.

ACT I

AT RISE: Darkness. We hear the sounds of a man and woman making love. They are getting ready to climax. The sounds they are making are noisy, ecstatic, and familiar. Above all, they must be graphic. The intention is a portrait in sound of a passionate man and woman making love and reaching climax together.
The real thing.
They came.
Silence. Heavy breathing. We become aware that the radio has been playing Bach's Goldberg Variations *in the piano version.*
By this point, the curtain has been up for at least two minutes. No light, no dialogue, just the sounds of lovemaking and now the Bach.

FRANKIE: God, I wish I still smoked. Life used to be so much more fun. *(JOHNNY laughs softly.)* What?

JOHNNY: Nothing. *(HE laughs again, a little louder.)* Oh, God!

FRANKIE: Well it must be something!

JOHNNY: It's dumb, it's gross, it's stupid, it's . . . *(HE howls with laughter.)* I'm sorry. Jesus, this is terrible. I don't know what's gotten into me. I'll be all right.
(HE catches his breath. FRANKIE turns on a bedside lamp.)
Really, I'm sorry. It has nothing to do with you.

FRANKIE: Are you okay now?

JOHNNY: Yes. No!
(HE bursts into laughter again. And now FRANKIE bursts into laughter: a wild, uncontrollable, infectious sound.)

What are you laughing at?

FRANKIE: I don't know!

(Now THEY *are both laughing hilariously. It is the kind of laughter that gets out of control and people have trouble breathing.* FRANKIE *rolls off the bed and lands on the floor with a slight thud.)*

JOHNNY: Are you okay?

FRANKIE: No!

(Now it is FRANKIE *who is laughing solo. It is a wonderful joyful sound: a lot of stored-up feeling is being released.)*

JOHNNY: Should I get you something?

FRANKIE: Yes! My mother!

JOHNNY: A beer, a Coke, anything?

FRANKIE: A bag to put over my head!

JOHNNY: You really want your mother?

FRANKIE: Are you crazy?

JOHNNY: You have the most . . . the most wonderful breasts.

FRANKIE: Thank you.

*(*SHE *bursts into new laughter. This time* JOHNNY *doesn't join in at all. Eventually* THEY *are both still. They listen to the Bach in silence and without moving.)*

That's nice music. Very . . . I want to say "chaste."

JOHNNY: I'll tell you why I was laughing. All of a sudden— just like that!—I remembered this time back in high school when I was making out with this really beautiful girl and was feeling incredibly suave and sophisticated and wondering if anybody would believe my good fortune and worrying if she was going to let me go all the way—I think it would have been her first time too—when all of a sudden I let out this incredibly loud fart. Like that. Only louder. It was awful. *(*HE *laughs again.)* And there was no pretending it wasn't me. You couldn't say something like "Boy, did you hear that thunder?" or "Jesus, Peggy, was that you?" The best I could come up with was "May I use your bathroom?" which only made it worse. And there in the bathroom was her mother taking a bath at ten o'clock at night. She had one arm up, washing her armpit. I said something real cool like, "Hello, Mrs. Roberts." She screamed and I ran out of the house. I tripped over the garbage cans and tore my pants climbing over the back-yard fence. I must've run twenty blocks, most of them with dogs chasing me. I thought my life was over. We never mentioned what happened and I never dated her again and I lost my virginity with someone else. But why that fart banged back into my consciousness just then . . . !

FRANKIE: Could we change the subject?

JOHNNY: What's the matter?

FRANKIE: I'm not a prude . . .

JOHNNY: I know that! Any woman who . . .

FRANKIE: I just . . . we all draw the line somewhere.

JOHNNY: And with you it's farts?

FRANKIE: Is that going to be a problem?

JOHNNY: You don't think any kind of farting is funny?

FRANKIE: Not off the top of my head I don't.

JOHHNY: Hunh! I always have. I don't know why I find a lot of things funny. Like Corgies.

FRANKIE: Corgies?

JOHNNY: You know the dogs the Queen of England has?

FRANKIE: No.

JOHNNY: Sure you do. They're about this big, tan, and look like walking heads. Everytime I see one, I get hysterical. Show me a Corgie and I'm yours.

FRANKIE: I guess a farting Corgie would really lay you out!

JOHNNY: See? You do have a sense of humor about it!

(THEY *both laugh. Then silence. The Bach plays on.*)

FRANKIE: You know what I mean? About the music? It's pure.

JOHNNY: Did you come?

FRANKIE: No one's that good at faking it.

JOHNNY: I thought so. Good. I'm glad.

FRANKIE: There! Hear that? It makes me think of . . . grace.

JOHNNY: You mean, the thing it's good to be in the state of?

FRANKIE: The movement kind. You know . . .

(SHE *moves her arm in a flowing gesture and sways her shoulders to the music.*)

Flowing.

JOHNNY: So why were you laughing?

FRANKIE: I don't know. Because you were, I guess. You sounded so happy. Little did I know!

JOHNNY: I *was* happy. I'm still happy. Where are you going?

FRANKIE: Nowhere.

JOHNNY: You're going somewhere.

FRANKIE: The closet.

JOHNNY: Why?

FRANKIE: A robe.

JOHNNY: You don't need a—

JOHNNY: I'm cold.

JOHNNY: I want to bask in your nakedness.

FRANKIE: Sure you do.

(FRANKIE *turns on the overhead room light.*)

JOHNNY: Ow!

FRANKIE: I'm sorry, I'm sorry!

(SHE *turns off the overhead light. The first quick impression we have of the room is that it is modest and not especially tidy.*)

JOHNNY: Warn somebody when you're going to do that! I hate bright lights but especially right after making love. Talk about a mood changer! Besides, I think you see the other person better in the light of the afterglow. *(Pause)* Did you hear what I just said?

FRANKIE: Yes.

JOHNNY: Just checking.

(*While* FRANKIE *gets robe out of the closet,* JOHNNY *goes through her purse on the bed table until he finds a pair of sunglasses.*)

FRANKIE: Remember when everybody used to light up the second it seemed they were through making love? "I'm coming, I'm coming, I came. You got a match?"

JOHNNY: I didn't smoke.

FRANKIE: Never?

JOHNNY: Ever.

FRANKIE: You've got a smoker's personality.

JOHNNY: That's what they tell me.

FRANKIE: I just made that up.

JOHNNY: So did I. And I didn't like women who did.

FRANKIE: Did what? Smoked? Then you would have hated me. Marla the Human Furnace.

JOHNNY: Marla? I thought your name was Francis.

FRANKIE: It is, it is! Don't panic. I just made that up, too. I don't know where it came from. From what Freudian depth it sprung.

JOHNNY: Marla! Ecch!

FRANKIE: You put too much stock in this name business, John.

(SHE *comes back to bed wearing a bathrobe.* JOHNNY *looks fairly ridiculous in her sunglasses.*)

JOHNNY: It's Johnny, please.

FRANKIE: Are those mine? I wish you'd stay out of my—

JOHNNY: I hate John.

FRANKIE: Did you hear me?

JOHNNY: I heard you.

FRANKIE: I wish you'd act like you heard me.

JOHNNY: May I wear your sunglasses?

FRANKIE: Yes.

JOHNNY: Thank you. God, you're beautiful. Are you coming back to bed?

FRANKIE: I don't know.

JOHNNY: John sounds like a toilet or a profession. And Jack only works if you're a Kennedy or a Nicholson.

FRANKIE: I read somewhere there are millions of young people, a whole generation, who don't have a clue who John Kennedy was. Do you believe it? To me, he was only yesterday. I love Jack Nicholson. Did you see *Prizzi's Honor?*

JOHNNY: Six times.

FRANKIE: Six times?

JOHNNY: The first time I popped for it, six bucks, the good old days, remember them? Seven bucks gets my goat, don't get me started! Then five on VCR, you know a rental, when I was getting over my hernia and I couldn't get out of bed so hot.

FRANKIE: You've got a VCR?

JOHNNY: Oh sure. Stereo TV, VCR. I'm working on a dish.

FRANKIE: And you've got a hernia?

JOHNNY: Had, had. Here, I'll show you.

FRANKIE: Wow. That's big. Did it hurt?

JOHNNY: Comme çi, comme ça. You got any scars?

FRANKIE: Everybody has scars.

JOHNNY: Where? I'll just look.

FRANKIE: No.

JOHNNY: Okay, okay. You know, they filmed it right near where I live.

FRANKIE: *Prizzi's Honor?*

JOHNNY: Oh sure.

FRANKIE: In Brooklyn?

JOHNNY: Brooklyn Heights. Please, don't get us confused with the rest of the borough. Would you like it if I referred to your neighborhood as Chinatown?

FRANKIE: Fifty-third and Tenth?

JOHNNY: Anyway! You know the house that guy lived in, the one with the funny voice? Hinley or something? He got nominated for an Oscar or something but I don't think he won. Or maybe he did.

FRANKIE: The one who played the Don?

JOHNNY: That's the one. Headley, Henkley, Hinley.

FRANKIE: You live in that house?

JOHNNY: No, but I can see their roof from my bathroom window.

FRANKIE: Oh.

JOHNNY: You know what those movie stars get when they're on location like that? Their own trailers with their name

on the door. Big long trailers. Not like the kind you see
in Montauk, those ugly little Airstream jobbies. At least I
think they're ugly. No, these are the big long kind like
you see sitting up on blocks in a trailer park that people
live in full time, people who aren't going anywhere in
'em they're so big! I'm talking trailers with bedrooms and
bathtubs. I'm talking major mobile homes.

FRANKIE: I hate trailers.

JOHNNY: So do I. That's not the point.

FRANKIE: I'd rather die than live in a trailer. The very words
"mobile home" strike me with such terror.

JOHNNY: I believe I had the floor.

FRANKIE: Who the hell wants a living room that moves for
Christ's sake? Ecch! Sorry.

JOHNNY: Anyway, they each have their own trailer, I mean,
Jack Nicholson is on one side of the street in his block-
long trailer and Kathleen Turner is on the other in hers.

FRANKIE: I'm sorry but I don't get her message.

JOHNNY: Will you let me finish?

FRANKIE: Do you?

JOHNNY: Yes, but that's not the point either. They also give
these trailers to people you never even heard of, like this
Hinley, Headley, Hinckley, what's-his-face character.

FRANKIE: Is that the point?

JOHNNY: I'm not saying he's not a good actor but his own
trailer? I'm in the wrong business.

FRANKIE: We both are.

JOHNNY: Do you think I talk too much?

FRANKIE: I don't think you always give the other person a
chance to—

JOHNNY: That's what my best friend says. "I talk because I
got a lot to say, Ernie," I tell him, but he doesn't seem to
understand that. Talking to you comes real easy. I appreciate that. And I won't pretend I wasn't looking forward
to this evening.

FRANKIE: Well, it's been very . . .

JOHNNY: What do you mean, "been"? It still is. "The night is young, the stars are clear, and if you care to go walking, dear." I admit I love the sound of my own voice. So shoot me, give me the electric chair, it ain't over till the fat lady sings. Can I have a beer?

FRANKIE: I'm sorry.

JOHNNY: You say that too much.

(HE *goes to refrigerator as* FRANKIE *crosses to floor lamp by easy chair and turns it on.*)

FRANKIE: Is this okay? I hate gloom.

JOHNNY: Light like this is fine. It's the harsh blinding kind I can't stand. Now where are you going?

FRANKIE: Just in here.

(SHE *goes to bathroom door, opens it, turns on light, goes in, leaving door open so that more light spills into the room.*)
Keep talking. I can hear you.

JOHNNY: You mean about the light? There are some delicatessens I just won't go into, they're so bright. There's one over on Madison Avenue and 28th Street that is so bright from the overhead fluorescents that you wouldn't believe it. I complained. I don't even shop there and I complained. "What are you trying to do? Get an airplane to land in here?" They just looked at me like I was an idiot. Of course, I doubt if they even spoke English. Most Koreans don't. It's getting to the point where you can count on one hand the number of people who speak English in this city.

(HE *goes to bathroom door and stands watching* FRANKIE *within.*)
Look, I know I talk too much. It's just that certain things get my goat. Things like ninety-foot trailers for people I never heard of . . .

(FRANKIE *comes out of the bathroom.* SHE *has changed into a brightly colored kimono. She has a hairbrush in her hand and will brush her hair during the following.*)
Hi there.

FRANKIE: Hello.

JOHNNY: . . . waste, especially water—you got a leaky faucet around here? Lady, I'm your plumber—and the fact this is supposed to be an English-speaking nation only nobody speaks English anymore. Other than that, I'm cool and I'll shut up now and won't say another word. I'm locking my mouth and throwing away the key.

(HE *watches* FRANKIE *brush her hair.*)

FRANKIE: Did you get Easter off? *(*JOHNNY *shakes his head.)* Neither did I. And watch us twiddle our thumbs. Last Easter you could've shot moose in there. Forget tips. I've already decided, I'm gonna call in sick. Life's too short, you know? You want some juice? It's homemade. I mean, I squeezed it myself. That's right, you're working on a beer. I'd offer you a joint but I don't do that anymore. Not that I think other people shouldn't. It's just that I can't personally handle it anymore. I mean, I didn't like what it was doing to me. I mean, the bottom line is: it isn't good for you. For me, I mean. It isn't good for me. Hey, come on, don't!

JOHNNY: Can I say one more thing?

FRANKIE: I wish you would.

JOHNNY: I could watch you do that for maybe the rest of my life.

FRANKIE: Get real.

JOHNNY: I think a woman brushing and fixing her hair is one of the supremely great sights of life. I'd put it up there with the Grand Canyon and a mother nursing her child. Triumphant facts of nature. That's all. Now I'm locking my eyes shut and throwing away the key.

(HE *closes his eyes.*)

FRANKIE: What am I supposed to do?

JOHNNY: Sshh, pretend you can't hear. Next thing she'll want is your ears.

FRANKIE: Oh my God, it's three o'clock! Look, I'd ask you to stay over but . . . I don't know about you but I'm kind of drained, you know? I mean, that was pretty intense

back there. Harrowing. No, not harrowing, that doesn't
sound right. I'm too pooped to pop, all right? Oh come
on, you know what I mean!

(JOHNNY inhales very slowly and very deeply.)

JOHNNY: She's wearing something new. This part is called
Scent Torture. I love it, I love it!

FRANKIE: You know, you're a very intense person. One
minute you're making love like somebody just let you out
of jail and the next you're telling me watching me brush my
hair is like the Grand Canyon. Very intense or very crazy.
Look, I'm glad what happened happened. If we both play
our cards right, maybe it will happen again. . . . Hello?

JOHNNY: I hear you.

FRANKIE: I wish you'd open your eyes.

*(JOHNNY very slowly opens his eyes and turns to face FRANKIE.
HE reacts as if blinded.)*

JOHNNY: Aaaagggg! It's worse than the delicatessen! Such
blinding beauty!

FRANKIE: I'm serious.

(JOHNNY stops screaming and looks at her again.)

JOHNNY: *(Quietly)* So am I.

FRANKIE: That's exactly what I mean. One minute you're
kidding and the next you're looking at me like that.

JOHNNY: Like what?

FRANKIE: Like that! People don't go around looking at one
another like that. It's too intense. You don't look, you
stare. It gives me the creeps. I suppose it's very flattering
but it's not something I feel real comfortable with. It's
like if you would send me a million roses, I'd be impressed but I wouldn't know where to put them. I don't
need a million roses. One would be just fine. So if you
just looked at me *occasionally* in the future like that. Look,
obviously I like you. I like you a lot. What's the matter?

JOHNNY: I'm just drinking all this in.

FRANKIE: You're not the easiest person to talk to anybody
ever met.

JOHNNY: I certainly hope not. How old are you?

FRANKIE: None of your business. How old are you?

JOHNNY: What do you think?

FRANKIE: Mid-forties.

JOHNNY: Ouch!

FRANKIE: Maybe late thirties.

JOHNNY: I can live with that.

FRANKIE: Come on, how old are you?

JOHNNY: I don't know.

FRANKIE: Everybody knows how old they are.

JOHNNY: I used to, then I forgot.

FRANKIE: That's a great answer. Can I borrow it?

JOHNNY: I did.

FRANKIE: Who from?

JOHNNY: Some old lady on the Carson show? I don't re-member. Half the things I got up here, I don't remember where they came from. It doesn't seem fair. People ought to get credit for all the things they give and teach us. You're fabulous.

FRANKIE: I feel like I'm supposed to say "thank you."

JOHNNY: It's not necessary.

FRANKIE: Instead, I want to ask you to quit sneaking up on me like that. We're talking about one thing, people who teach, and wham! you slip in there with some kind of intimate, personal remark. I like being told I'm fabulous. Who wouldn't? I'd like some warning first, that's all. This is not a spontaneous person you have before you.

JOHNNY: You're telling me that wasn't spontaneous?

FRANKIE: That was different. I'm talking about the larger framework of things. What people are doing in your life. What they're doing in your bed is easy or at least it used to be back before we had to start checking each other out. I don't know about you but I get so sick and tired of living this way, that we're gonna die from one another, that every so often I just want to act like Saturday night really is a Saturday night, the way they used to be.

JOHNNY: I'm very glad we had this Saturday night.

FRANKIE: I never would have said that if I knew you better.

JOHNNY: How well do you want to know me?

FRANKIE: I'll let you know Monday between orders. "I got a BLT down working!" "Tell me about your childhood." "Take the moo out of two!" "Were you toilet trained?"

JOHNNY: Come here.

FRANKIE: Are you sure you don't want something before you go?

JOHNNY: Come here.

FRANKIE: I've got some meatloaf in the fridge.

JOHNNY: Come here.

(FRANKIE *moves a few steps towards* JOHNNY, *who is sitting on the edge of the bed.*)

FRANKIE: What?

JOHNNY: Closer.

(FRANKIE *moves closer to* JOHNNY, *who pulls her all the way towards him and buries his face in her middle.*)

FRANKIE: I can toast some bread. Butter and catsup. A cold meatloaf sandwich. All the way back to Brooklyn . . .

JOHNNY: Heights.

FRANKIE: Heights! This time of night. Aren't you hungry?

JOHNNY: I'm starving.

FRANKIE: No!

JOHNNY: Why not?

FRANKIE: We just did.

JOHNNY: So?

FRANKIE: I can't.

JOHNNY: What do you mean, you can't?

FRANKIE: I don't want to.

(JOHNNY *immediately stops nuzzling* FRANKIE. *Both hands fly up with palms outwards.*)

You don't have to take it like that. I'm sorry. Just not right now. You know, you're right: I do say "I'm sorry" a lot around you. There's something about you that makes me feel like I'm letting you down all the time. Like you have all these expectations of me that I can't fulfill. I'm sorry—there I go again!—but what you see here is what you get. I am someone who likes to eat after making love and right now I feel like a cold meatloaf sandwich on white toast with butter and catsup with a large glass of very cold milk and I wish you would stop looking at me like that.

JOHNNY: Open your robe.

FRANKIE: No. Why?

JOHNNY: I want to look at your pussy.

FRANKIE: No. Why?

JOHNNY: It's beautiful.

FRANKIE: It is not. You're just saying that.

JOHNNY: I think it is. I'm telling you, you have a beautiful pussy—!

FRANKIE: I hate that word, Johnny!

JOHNNY: —alright, thing! And I'm asking you to open your robe so I can look at it. Just look. Fifteen seconds. You can time me. Then you can make *two* cold meatloaf sandwiches and *two* big glasses of milk. Just hold the catsup on one.

FRANKIE: I don't know if you're playing games or being serious.

JOHNNY: Both. Serious games. Do you have to name everything? If I had said "You have a beautiful parakeet" you'd have let me see it and we'd be eating those sandwiches already.

FRANKIE: I had a parakeet. I hated it. I was glad when it died. (SHE *opens her robe.*) Okay?

JOHNNY: Oh! Yes!

FRANKIE: (*Continuing to hold her robe open as* JOHNNY *sits on edge of bed and looks*) I'm timing this! I told my cousin I didn't want a bird. I hate birds. She swore I'd love a parakeet. What's to love? (SHE *almost drops the robe.*) They don't do anything except not sing when you want them to, sing when you don't, and make those awful scratching

noises on that awful sandpaper on the floor of their cell. I mean cage! If I ever have another pet it'll be a dog. A Golden Lab. Something that shows a little enthusiasm when you walk through the door. Something you can hold. The only time I got my hands on that goddamn parakeet was the day it dropped dead and I had to pick it up to throw in the garbage can. Hey, come on! This has gotta be fifteen seconds. (FRANKIE *closes her robe.* JOHNNY *takes her hand, kisses it, rubs his cheek against it.* FRANKIE *stands awkwardly.*)
You really would like a sandwich?

JOHNNY: But no catsup.

FRANKIE: Catsup's what makes a cold meatloaf sandwich good.

JOHNNY: I'm allergic. Catsup and peaches.

FRANKIE: Ugh!

JOHNNY: Well not in the same dish!
(HE *is still nuzzling her fingers.*)

FRANKIE: Can I have my hand back?

JOHNNY: Do you want it back?

FRANKIE: Well you want a sandwich, don't you?

JOHNNY: I want you to notice how we're connecting. My hand is flowing into yours. My eyes are trying to see inside yours.

FRANKIE: That's not connecting. That's holding and staring. Connecting is when the other person isn't even around and you could die from just thinking of them.

JOHNNY: That's missing. This is connecting.

FRANKIE: Yeah, well it ain't how a sandwich gets made.
(SHE *takes her hand from* JOHNNY *and goes to kitchen area of the apartment, where she takes out all the makings of her meatloaf sandwich and begins to prepare them.* JOHNNY *will just watch her from his place on the bed.*)
My father used to say a good meatloaf and gravy with mashed potatoes was food fit for the gods.

JOHNNY: You're kidding! That's exactly what my old man used to say.

FRANKIE: Of course, considering our family budget we didn't have too many other options. Guess what, pop? I still don't.

(SHE *laughs*. JOHNNY *laughs with her*.)

You want to turn on the television?

JOHNNY: Why?

FRANKIE: We don't have to watch it. You know, just sound. I do it all the time. Company. It beats a parakeet.

JOHNNY: I'd rather watch you.

FRANKIE: Do you ever watch the Channel 5 Movie Club on Saturday night? That's right, you got a VCR. They have this thing called the Movie Club. Talk about dumb gimmicks. You put your name and address on a postcard. If they draw it, you go on the air and tell everybody what your favorite movie is and they show it, along with intermission breaks where they tell you certain little-known facts about the movie I just as soon wouldn't have known, such as "Susan Hayward was already stricken with a fatal cancer when she made this sparkling comedy." Kind of puts a pall on things, you know?

JOHNNY: I was on that program.

FRANKIE: You were not.

JOHNNY: Sure I was.

FRANKIE: What was your favorite movie?

JOHNNY: I forget.

FRANKIE: You probably don't even have one.

(JOHNNY *has gotten up off the bed and come over to where* FRANKIE *is working*. HE *finds a place to sit very close to where* SHE *stands making the sandwiches*.)

JOHNNY: You know what I was thinking while I was looking at you over there?

FRANKIE: I should have guessed this was coming!

JOHNNY: I was thinking "There's got to be more to life than this" but at times like this I'll be goddamned if I know what it is.

FRANKIE: You don't give up, do you?

JOHNNY: I want to drown in this woman. I want to die here. So why is she talking about parakeets and meatloaf? The inequity of human relationships! I actually thought that word: "inequity." I didn't even know it was in my vocabulary. And what's the other one? Disparity! Yeah, that's it. The disparity between us at that moment. I mean, there I was, celebrating you, feasting on your loveliness, and you were talking about a fucking, pardon my French, parakeet!

FRANKIE: Maybe it's because I was ill at ease.

JOHNNY: Because of me?

FRANKIE: Maybe I don't like being looked at down there that way, how the hell should I know?

JOHNNY: Bullshit! You don't like being looked at, period.

FRANKIE: Ow!

JOHNNY: What happened?

FRANKIE: I cut myself.

JOHNNY: Let me see.

FRANKIE: It's all right.

JOHNNY: Let me see.

(HE sucks the blood from her finger.)

FRANKIE: Look, I don't think this is going to work out. It was very nice while it lasted but like I said . . .

JOHNNY: You'll live.

(HE releases her hand.)

FRANKIE: . . . I'm a BLT down sort of person and I think you're looking for someone a little more pheasant under glass. Where are you going?

JOHNNY: I'll get a bandage.

FRANKIE: That's okay.

JOHNNY: No problem.

FRANKIE: Really. What are you doing?

(JOHNNY has gone into the bathroom. We hear him going through the medicine cabinet looking for a bandage as HE continues to speak through the open door.)

JOHNNY: I don't remember you saying you were a BLT down sort of person.

FRANKIE: I thought I implied it when I was talking about that meatloaf.

(JOHNNY comes out of the bathroom with a box of Band-Aids and a bottle of iodine.)

JOHNNY: It's because I said you had a beautiful pussy, isn't it? Give me your finger.

(FRANKIE holds out her finger while JOHNNY disinfects and dresses it.)

FRANKIE: It's because you said a lot of things. Ow!

JOHNNY: A man compliments a woman. All right, maybe he uses street talk but it's nice street talk, affectionate. It's not one of them ugly words, like the one I'm sure we're both familiar with, the one that begins with "c." I didn't say you had a beautiful "c." I was saying something loving and you took offense.

FRANKIE: I told you I wasn't very spontaneous!

JOHNNY: Boy, if you had said to me, "Johnny, you have the most terrific dick on you" I would be so happy.

(HE finishes with the Band-Aids.)

There you go.

FRANKIE: Thank you.

JOHNNY: You want to see scarred fingers!

(HE holds up his hands to FRANKIE.)

FRANKIE: *(Wincing at the sight)* Please!

JOHNNY: They don't hurt.

FRANKIE: I don't want to look.

JOHNNY: *(Looking at them)* It's hard to connect to them. I mean, I'm not the type who should have scarry hands.

FRANKIE: You're so good with knives. I've watched you.

JOHNNY: She admits it. The haughty waitress has cast a lustful gaze on the Knight of the Grill.

FRANKIE: "Can that new guy chop and dice," Dena tells me. "Look at him go."

JOHNNY: Now, sure! It's a breeze. I can dice an onion blindfolded. These scars were then. On my way up the culinary ladder. I knew you were looking at me.

FRANKIE: It's human curiosity. A new face in the kitchen. Male. Look, I never said I was a nun.

JOHNNY: Hey, it's okay. It was mutual. I was looking at you.

FRANKIE: Besides, there aren't that many short-order cooks who have a dictionary and a copy of Shakespeare in their locker.

JOHNNY: You'd be surprised. We're an inquiring breed. We have our own quiz shows: *Cooks Want to Know*.

FRANKIE: The one before you, Pluto, I'm not kidding, he said his name was Pluto, I swear to God! You know what he would have done with your books? Cooked 'em!

JOHNNY: So you noticed what I was reading, too?

FRANKIE: Call me the Bionic Eye. I don't miss a trick.

JOHNNY: You know what I liked about you? The way you take the time to talk to that old guy who comes in every day about 3:30.

FRANKIE: Mr. Leon.

JOHNNY: With the cane and a copy of the *Post* and always has a flower in his lapel. You really are nice with him.

FRANKIE: He's really nice with me.

JOHNNY: You really talk to him. I also like the way you fluff up that thing you wear on your uniform. It looks like a big napkin.

FRANKIE: It's supposed to be a handkerchief.

JOHNNY: I like the way you're always fluffing at it.

FRANKIE: What are you? Spying on me from the kitchen?

JOHNNY: Not spying. Watching.

FRANKIE: I'm going to be very self-conscious from now on.

JOHNNY: Watching and liking what I see.

FRANKIE: You in night school or something?

JOHNNY: This is my kind of night school.

FRANKIE: I meant the Shakespeare and the big words.

JOHNNY: I'm doing that on my own.

FRANKIE: Why?

JOHNNY: You don't want to be going out with a semi-illiterate, subcretinous, protomoronic asshole do you?

FRANKIE: Listen, it's easy to use words I don't know.

JOHNNY: What? Asshole? God, I like you.

FRANKIE: You still want a sandwich before you go?

JOHNNY: I still want a sandwich.

FRANKIE: Then you're going. You're not staying over.

JOHNNY: We'll cross that bridge when we get to it.

FRANKIE: There's no bridge to cross.

JOHNNY: What are you scared of?

FRANKIE: I'm not scared.

(SHE *has resumed making sandwiches.* JOHNNY *watches her intently.*) I'm not scared. I'm . . .

JOHNNY: Yes, you are.

FRANKIE: Well not like a horror movie. I don't think you're going to pull out a knife and stab me, if that's what you mean. Could we change the subject?

JOHNNY: What do you mean?

FRANKIE: Oh come on! You're gonna stand there and tell me you're not weird?

JOHNNY: Of course I'm weird.

FRANKIE: There's a whole other side of you I never saw at work.

JOHNNY: You thought all I did was cook?

FRANKIE: There's a whole other side of you I never saw when we were doing it either.

JOHNNY: It was probably your first experience with a passionate, imaginative lover.

FRANKIE: My first experience with an animal is more like it.

JOHNNY: Did you ever see an animal do to another animal's toes what I did to yours?

FRANKIE: Will you keep your voice down?

JOHNNY: You got this place bugged?

FRANKIE: I'm sure the whole building heard you. Ooooo! Ooooo! Ooooo!

JOHNNY: What do you expect, the way you kept twirling your fingers around inside my ears?

FRANKIE: Nobody ever put their fingers in your ears before?

JOHNNY: Maybe for a second but not the way you did, like you were drilling for something. I thought to myself, "Maybe she gets off on putting her fingers in guys' ears." But did I say anything? Did I call you weird?

FRANKIE: You should have said something.

JOHNNY: Why?

FRANKIE: I would have stopped.

JOHNNY: Are you crazy? I loved it. I'll try anything once, especially in that department. You got any new ideas? Keep 'em coming, keep 'em coming. I'll tell you when to stop.

FRANKIE: I can just hear you now at work: "Hey, guys, that Frankie puts her fingers in your ears!"

JOHNNY: That is probably just about the last thing in the entire world I would ever do about tonight: talk about it to anyone, especially those animals at work. You really don't know me.

FRANKIE: It wouldn't be the first time one of the guys had yak-yak-yakked about it.

JOHNNY: Women yak, too. Hey, no catsup!

FRANKIE: Yeah, but about dumb things.

JOHNNY: All yakking is dumb. "I slept with Frankie." "Oh yeah, well I slept with Nancy Reagan." "Big effing pardon-my-French deal, the two of yous. I slept with Mother Teresa." So it goes. This wall of disparity between us, Frankie, we gotta break it down. So the only space left between us is just us.

FRANKIE: Here's your sandwich.

JOHNNY: Here's my guts.

FRANKIE: I'm sorry. I'm not good at small talk.

JOHNNY: This isn't small talk. This is enormous talk.

FRANKIE: Whatever you call it, I'm not good at it.

JOHNNY: Sure you are. You just have to want to be.

FRANKIE: Maybe that's it. I forgot the milk.

JOHNNY: Something's going on in this room, something important. You don't feel it?

FRANKIE: I told you what I felt.

JOHNNY: You don't want to feel it. Two people coming together: sure, it's a little scarey but it's pardon-my-French-again fucking wonderful, too. My heart is so full right now. Put your hand here. I swear to God, you can feel the lump. Go on, touch it.

FRANKIE: You're too needy. You want too much. I can't.

JOHNNY: That's where you're wrong.

FRANKIE: You had the whole thing. There's no more where it came from. I'm empty.

JOHNNY: I know that feeling. It's terrible. The wonderful thing is, it doesn't have to last.

FRANKIE: Turn the light off! I want to show you something.

(JOHNNY turns off the light.)

Down one floor, over two buildings, the window with the kind of gauzey curtains. You see?

(JOHNNY has joined her at the window.)

JOHNNY: Where?

FRANKIE: There!

JOHNNY: The old couple in the bathrobes? What about 'em?

FRANKIE: I've been watching them ever since I moved in. Almost eight years now. I have never seen them speak to one another, not once. He'll sit there reading the paper and she'll cook an entire meal without him looking up. They'll eat it in total silence. He'll help her wash up sometimes but they still won't say a word. After a while the lights go out and I guess they've gone to bed.

(JOHNNY has seen something else out the window.)

JOHNNY: Jesus!

FRANKIE: Those two! The Raging Bull I call him. She's Mary the Masochist. They moved in about eighteen months ago.

JOHNNY: Hey!

FRANKIE: It's their thing.

JOHNNY: He's beating the shit out of her.

FRANKIE: She loves it.

JOHNNY: Nobody could love getting hit like that. We ought to do something.

FRANKIE: I saw her in the A&P. She was wearing a nurse's uniform. Living with him, that was a smart career choice. She had on sunglasses, you know, to hide the bruises. I went up to her, I figured it was now or never, and I said, "I live in the building behind you. I've seen how he hits you. Is there anything I can do?" and she just looked at me and said, "I don't know what you're talking about."

JOHNNY: Jesus, Jesus, Jesus.

FRANKIE: Some nights when there's nothing on television I sit there in the dark and watch them. Once I ate a whole bunch of grapes watching them. One night she ended up on the floor and didn't move till the next morning. I hate being used to them.

JOHNNY: I would never hit you. I would never hit a woman.

FRANKIE: I think you had better finish that and go.

JOHNNY: You are missing one hell of an opportunity to feel with your own hand the human heart. It's right here.

FRANKIE: Maybe next time.

(JOHNNY *looks at her and then downs the glass of milk in one long, mighty, gulp.*)

Thank you.

JOHNNY: Your meatloaf is directly from Mount Olympus. Your father was a very lucky guy.

FRANKIE: It's his recipe. He taught me.

JOHNNY: Yeah? My old man was a great cook, too.

FRANKIE: Mine didn't have much choice.

JOHNNY: How do you mean?

FRANKIE: My mother left us when I was seven.

JOHNNY: I don't believe it! My mother left us when I was seven.

FRANKIE: Oh come on!

JOHNNY: Boy, you really, really, really and truly don't know me. Just about the last thing in the entire world I would joke about is a mother who wasn't there. I don't think mothers are sacred. I just don't think they're especially funny.

FRANKIE: Me and my big mouth! I don't think you realize how serious I am about wanting you to leave now.

JOHNNY: I don't think you realize how serious I am about us.

FRANKIE: What us? There is no us.

JOHNNY: I'm working on it. Frankie and Johnny! We're already a couple.

FRANKIE: Going out with someone just because his name is Johnny and yours is Frankie is not enough of a reason.

JOHNNY: I think it's an extraordinary one. It's fate. You also said you thought I had sexy wrists.

FRANKIE: One of the biggest mistakes in my entire life!

JOHNNY: It's gotta begin somewhere. A name, a wrist, a toe.

FRANKIE: Didn't they end up killing each other?

JOHNNY: She killed him. The odds are in your favor. Besides, we're not talking about ending up. I'm just trying to continue what's been begun.

FRANKIE: If he was anything like you, no wonder she shot him.

JOHNNY: It was a crime of passion. They were the last of the red-hot lovers. We're the next.

FRANKIE: You're not from Brooklyn.

JOHNNY: Brooklyn Heights.

FRANKIE: I knew you were gonna say that! You're from outer space.

JOHNNY: Allentown, Pennsylvania, actually.

FRANKIE: Very funny, very funny.

JOHNNY: You've never been to Allentown.

FRANKIE: Who told you? Viv? Martin? I know, Molly the Mouth!

JOHNNY: Now who's from outer space? What the pardon-my-French fuck are you talking about?

FRANKIE: One of them told you I was from Allentown so now you're pretending you are so you can continue with this coincidence theory.

JOHNNY: You're from Allentown? I was born in Allentown.

FRANKIE: Very funny. Very funny.

JOHNNY: St. Stephen's Hospital. We lived on Martell St.

FRANKIE: I suppose you went to Moody High School, too.

JOHNNY: No, we moved when I was eight. I started out at Park Lane Elementary though. Did you go to Park Lane? This is incredible! This is better than anything in Shirley MacLaine.

FRANKIE: It's a small world and Allentown's a big city.

JOHNNY: Not that small and not that big.

FRANKIE: I still don't believe you.

JOHNNY: Of course you don't. It's one big pardon-my-French again fucking miracle and you don't believe in them.

FRANKIE: I'll tell you one thing: I could never, not in a million years, be seriously involved with a man who said "Pardon my French" all the time.

JOHNNY: Done. Finished. You got it.

FRANKIE: I mean, where do you pick up an expression like that?

JOHNNY: Out of respect for a person. A woman in this case.

FRANKIE: The first time you said it tonight I practically told you I had a headache and had to go home.

JOHNNY: That's so scary to me! That three little words, "Pardon my French," could separate two people from saying the three little words that make them connect!

FRANKIE: What three little words?

JOHNNY: I love you.

FRANKIE: Oh. Them. I should've guessed.

JOHNNY: Did you ever say them to anyone?

FRANKIE: Say them or mean them? My father, my first true love, and a couple of thousand men since. That's about it.

JOHNNY: I'm not counting.

FRANKIE: You're really from Allentown?

(JOHNNY *nods, takes a bite out of his sandwich, and makes a "Cross My Heart" sign over his chest. Then he pushes his empty milk glass toward* FRANKIE, *meaning* HE *would like a refill, which* SHE *will get.)*

How did you get so lucky to get out of there at eight?

JOHNNY: *(Talking and eating)* My mother. She ran off with somebody she'd met at an A.A. meeting. My father took us to Baltimore. He had a sister. She couldn't cope with us. We ended up in foster homes. Could I have a little salt? I bounced all over the place. Washington, D.C. was the best. You go through that Smithsonian Institute they got there and there ain't nothing they're gonna teach you in college! That place is a gold mine. Portland, Maine, is nice, too. Cold though.

FRANKIE: You didn't miss much not staying in Allentown . . . My big highlight was . . .

JOHNNY: What?

FRANKIE: Nothing. It's stupid.

JOHNNY: I've told you stupid things.

FRANKIE: Not this stupid.

JOHNNY: No fair.

FRANKIE: All right! I played Fiona in our high school production of *Brigadoon.*

JOHNNY: What's stupid about that? I bet you were wonderful.

FRANKIE: It's hardly like winning a scholarship to Harvard or being the class valedictorian. It's an event; it shouldn't be a highlight.

JOHNNY: So you're an actress!

FRANKIE: You mean at this very moment in time?

JOHNNY: I said to myself, "She's not just a waitress."

FRANKIE: Yeah, she's an unsuccessful actress! What are you really?

JOHNNY: I'm really a cook.

FRANKIE: Oh. When you put it like that, I'm really a waitress. I haven't tried to get an acting job since the day I decided I never was gonna get one. Somebody told me you gotta have balls to be a great actress. I got balls, I told 'em. No, Frankie, you got a big mouth!

JOHNNY: Would you . . . ? You know . . . ?

FRANKIE: What?

JOHNNY: Act something for me.

FRANKIE: What are you? Nuts? You think actors go around acting for people just like that? Like we do requests?

JOHNNY: I'm sorry. I didn't know.

FRANKIE: Acting is an art. It's a responsibility. It's a privilege.

JOHNNY: And I bet you're good at it.

FRANKIE: And it looks like I'll die with my secret. Anyway, what happened to your mother?

JOHNNY: I tracked her down when I was eighteen. They were still together, living in Philadelphia and both drinking again. They say Philadelphia will do that to you.

FRANKIE: So you saw her again? You see, I never did.

JOHNNY: But how this potbellied, balding, gin-breathed stranger could have been the object of anyone's desire but especially my mother's! She was still so beautiful, even through the booze, but he was one hundred percent turkey.

FRANKIE: Mine was killed in a car wreck about three, no, four years ago. She was with her turkey. He go it, too. I didn't hear about it for almost a month.

JOHNNY: What people see in one another! It's a total mystery. Shakespeare said it best: "There are more things in heaven and on earth than are dreamt of in your philosophy, Horatio." Something like that. I'm pretty close. Did you ever read *Hamlet?*

FRANKIE: Probably.

JOHNNY: I like him. I've only read a couple of his things. They're not easy. Lots of old words. Archaic, you know? Then all of a sudden he puts it all together and comes up with something clear and simple and it's real nice and you feel you've learned something. This Horatio was Hamlet's best friend. He thought he had it all figured out, so Hamlet set him straight. Do you have a best friend?

FRANKIE: Not really.

JOHNNY: That's okay. I'll be your best friend.

FRANKIE: You think a lot of yourself, don't you?

JOHNNY: Look, I'm going all over the place with you. I might as well come right out with it: I love you. I'm in love with you. I personally think we should get married and I definitely want us to have kids, three or four. There! That wasn't so difficult. You don't have to say anything. I just wanted to get it out on the table. Talk about a load off!

FRANKIE: Talk about a load off? Talk about a crock of shit.

JOHNNY: Hey, come on, don't. One of the things I like about you, Frankie, is that you talk nice. Don't start that stuff now.

FRANKIE: Well fuck you how I talk! I'll talk any fucking way I fucking feel like it! It's my fucking apartment in the fucking first place and who the fuck are you to come in here and start telling me I talk nice. (SHE *has started to cry.*)

JOHNNY: I'm sorry.

FRANKIE: Out of the blue, just like that, you've decided we're going to get involved?

JOHNNY: If you want to understate it like that.

FRANKIE: Whatever happened to a second date?

JOHNNY: We were beyond that two hours ago.

FRANKIE: Maybe you were.

JOHNNY: I like your apartment. That's a nice robe. You're a very pretty woman but I guess all the guys tell you that. Is that what you want?

FRANKIE: I don't want this.

JOHNNY: That has occurred to me. Dumb, I am not. Nervy and persistent, those I plead guilty to. I'm also something else people aren't too accustomed to these days: courageous. I want you and I'm coming after you.

FRANKIE: Has it occurred to you that maybe I don't want you?

JOHNNY: Only a couple of hundred times. I got my work cut out for me.

FRANKIE: Just because you take me out to dinner—!

JOHNNY: That wasn't my fault!

FRANKIE: Then the movies—!

JOHNNY: It got four stars!

FRANKIE: And end up making love—!

JOHNNY: Great love.

FRANKIE: Okay love.

JOHNNY: Great love. The dinner and the movie were lousy. We were dynamite.

FRANKIE: Okay, good love. So why do you have to go spoil everything?

JOHNNY: I told you I loved you. That makes me unlovable?

FRANKIE: It makes you a creep!

JOHNNY: Oh.

FRANKIE: No, I take that back. You're not a creep. You're sincere. That's what's so awful. Well, I'm sincere, too. I sincerely do not want to continue this.

JOHNNY: Pretend that we're the only two people in the entire world, that's what I'm doing, and it all falls into place.

FRANKIE: And I was looking forward to seeing you again.

JOHNNY: I'm right here.

FRANKIE: "God," I was thinking, "make him want to see me again without him knowing that's what I want."

JOHNNY: I already did know. God had nothing to do with it.

FRANKIE: I said "see you again," not the stuff you're talking about. Kids for Christ's sake!

JOHNNY: What's wrong with kids?

FRANKIE: I hate kids.

JOHNNY: I don't believe that.

FRANKIE: I'm too old to have kids.

JOHNNY: No, you're not.

FRANKIE: I can't have any. Now are you happy?

JOHNNY: We'll adopt.

FRANKIE: You just don't decide to fall in love with people out of the blue.

JOHNNY: Why not?

FRANKIE: They don't like it. How would you like it if Helen came up to you and said, "I'm in love with you. I want to have your baby."

JOHNNY: Who's Helen?

FRANKIE: At work.

JOHNNY: That Helen?

FRANKIE: You'd run like hell.

JOHNNY: She's close to seventy.

FRANKIE: I thought love was blind.

JOHNNY: It's the exact opposite. Besides, I'd tell her I was in love with you.

FRANKIE: You don't know me.

JOHNNY: Is that what all this is about? Of course I don't know you. You don't know me either. We got off to a great start. Why do you want to stop?

FRANKIE: Does it have to be tonight?

JOHNNY: Yes!

FRANKIE: Who says?

JOHNNY: We may not make it to tomorrow. I might get knifed if you make me go home. You might choke on a chicken bone. Unknown poison gases could kill us both in our sleep. When it comes to love, life's cheap and it's short. So don't fuck with it and don't pardon my French.

FRANKIE: This is worse than *Looking for Mr. Goodbar*.

JOHNNY: Look, Frankie, I might see someone on the BMT tonight, get lucky and get laid, and think I was in love with her. This is the only chance we have to really come together, I'm convinced of it. People are given one moment to connect. Not two, not three, one! They don't take it, it's gone forever and they end up not only pardon-my-French-for-the-very-last-time screwing that person on the BMT but marrying her.

FRANKIE: Boy, are you barking up the wrong tree.

JOHNNY: I never thought I could be in love with a woman who said "barking up the wrong tree."

FRANKIE: You've driven me to it. I never used that expression in my entire life.

JOHNNY: You sure you don't want to feel this lump?

FRANKIE: Why won't you go?

JOHNNY: The only difference between us right now is I know how this is going to end—happily—and you don't. I need a best friend, too. Could I trouble you for another glass of milk?

FRANKIE: Okay, milk, but then I really want you to go. Promise?

JOHNNY: You drive a hard bargain. Milk for exile from the Magic Kingdom.

FRANKIE: Promise?

JOHNNY: Promise.

FRANKIE: Say it like you mean it.

JOHNNY: I promise.

FRANKIE: It's a good thing you're not an actor.

JOHNNY: All right, I don't promise.

FRANKIE: Now I believe you.

(SHE goes to refrigerator and pours a glass of milk.)

JOHNNY: It's just words. It's all words. Words, words, words. He said that, too, I think. I read somewhere Shakespeare said just about everything. I'll tell you one thing he didn't say: I love you, Frankie.

(FRANKIE brings him a glass of milk.)

FRANKIE: Drink your milk.

JOHNNY: I bet that's something else he never said: "Drink your milk," *The Merry Wives of Windsor*, Act III, scene ii. I don't think so. The Swan of Avon ain't got nothing on us.

FRANKIE: Did anybody ever tell you you talk too much?

JOHNNY: Yeah, I told you about half an hour ago. There's no virtue in being a mute.

FRANKIE: I'm not a mute.

JOHNNY: Did I say you were?

FRANKIE: I talk when I have something to say.

JOHNNY: Did I say she was a mute?

FRANKIE: You know, not everybody thinks life is a picnic. Some of us have problems. Some of us have sorrows. But people like you are so busy telling us what you want, how you feel you don't even notice the rest of us who aren't exactly jumping up and down for joy.

JOHNNY: I haven't done anything but notice you.

FRANKIE: Shut up!

JOHNNY: Who's jumping up and down!

FRANKIE: I said, shut up! Just drink your milk and go. I don't want to hear your voice again tonight.

JOHNNY: What do you want?

FRANKIE: I want to be alone. I want to watch television. I want to eat ice cream. I want to sleep. I want to stop worrying I'm trapped in my own apartment with a fucking maniac.

JOHNNY: We all have problems, you know.

FRANKIE: Right now, mine begin and end with you. You said you'd go.

JOHNNY: I lied.

FRANKIE: All I have to do is open that window and start screaming.

JOHNNY: In this city? Lots of luck.

FRANKIE: I have neighbors upstairs, friends . . .

JOHNNY: No one's gonna want to get involved in us. They'll just tell you to call the police.

FRANKIE: Don't think it hasn't crossed my mind.

JOHNNY: They'll come, give or take an hour or two. They'll make me leave but I'll be right back. That's a very handy fire escape. If not tonight, then tomorrow or the day after that. Sooner or later, you're gonna have to deal with me. Why don't we just get it over with? Besides, tomorrow's Sunday. We can sleep in.

(At some point before this, the music on the radio has changed to Scriabin's Second Symphony. Neither FRANKIE *nor* JOHNNY *heard the announcement. Ideally, the audience didn't either.)*

FRANKIE: I *am* trapped in my own apartment with a fucking maniac!

JOHNNY: You don't mean that. I'm trying to improve my life and I'm running out of time. I'm still going around in circles with you. There's gotta be that one thing I say that makes you listen. That makes us connect. What station are you on?

FRANKIE: What?

JOHNNY: It looks like it's around about ninety. You got a paper?

(HE *starts rummaging about for a newspaper.*)

FRANKIE: What do you think you're doing?

JOHNNY: I want to get the name of that piece of music you liked for you.

FRANKIE: I don't care anymore.

JOHNNY: Well, I do. When you come across something beautiful, you gotta go for it. It doesn't grow on trees, beautiful things.

(JOHNNY *has found the radio station call letters in the newspaper.*)

WKCC. (*As* HE *dials information*)

I owe you a quarter.

FRANKIE: He's nuts. Out and out loco!

JOHNNY: (*Into phone*) Give me the number for WKCC. Thank you. (*To* FRANKIE) Without the name, we'll lose that music and I'll never find it on my own. You let something like that slip through your fingers and you deserve rock and roll!

(HE *hangs up and immediately redials.*)

I hate these recordings that give you the number now. One less human contact. (*To* FRANKIE) Where are you going?

FRANKIE: Out, and you better not be here when I get back.

JOHNNY: You want to pick up some Haagen-Dazs Vanilla Swiss Almond while you're out?

FRANKIE: I said get out! (SHE *starts throwing things.*) You're a maniac! You're a creep! You're a . . . Oh!

JOHNNY: *(Into phone)* May I speak to your disc jockey? . . . Well excuse me! *(HE covers phone; to FRANKIE)* They don't have a disc jockey. They have someone called Midnight With Marlon. *(Into phone)* Hello, Marlon? My name is Johnny. My friend and I were making love and in the afterglow, which I sometimes think is the most beautiful part of making love, she noticed that you were playing some really beautiful music, piano. She was right. I don't know much about quality music, which I could gather that was, so I would like to know the name of that particular piece and the artist performing it so I can buy the record and present it to my lady love, whose name is Frankie and is that a beautiful coincidence or is it not? *(Short pause)* Bach. Johann Sebastian, right? I heard of him. The Goldberg Variations. Glenn Gould. Columbia Records. *(To FRANKIE)* You gonna remember this?
(FRANKIE smacks him hard across the cheek. JOHNNY takes the phone from his ear and holds it against his chest. HE just looks at her. SHE smacks him again. This time he catches her hand while it is still against his cheek, holds it a beat, then brings it to his lips and kisses it. Then, into phone, he continues, but what he says is really for FRANKIE, his eyes never leaving her.)
Do you take requests, Marlon? Then make an exception! There's a man and a woman. Not young, not old. No great beauties, either one. They meet where they work: a restaurant and it's not the Ritz. She's a waitress. He's a cook. They meet but they don't connect. "I got two medium burgers working" and "Pick up, side of fries" is pretty much the extent of it. But she's noticed him, he can feel it. And he's noticed her. Right off. They both knew tonight was going to happen. So why did it take him six weeks for him to ask her if she wanted to see a movie that neither one of them could tell you the name of right now? Why did they eat ice cream sundaes before she asked him if he wanted to come up since they were in the neighborhood? And then they were making love and for

maybe an hour they forgot the ten million things that
made them think "I don't love this person. I don't even
like them" and instead all they knew was they were
together and it was perfect and they were perfect and
that's all there was to know about it and as they lay there,
they both began the million reasons not to love one
another like a familiar rosary. Only this time he stopped
himself. Maybe it was the music you were playing. They
both heard it. Only now they're both beginning to forget
they did. So would you play something for Frankie and
Johnny on the eve of something that ought to last, not
self-destruct? I guess I want you to play the most beautiful music ever written and dedicate it to us.

(HE *hangs up.*)

Don't go.

FRANKIE: Why are you doing this?

JOHNNY: I'm tired of looking. Everything I want is in this
room.

(HE *kisses her.* FRANKIE *responds. It quickly gets passionate.*
FRANKIE *starts to undress.*)

JOHNNY: Let me.

FRANKIE: Hunh?

JOHNNY: Let me do it.

(HE *helps her out of her raincoat. Then he takes it and hangs it
up.* FRANKIE *stands a little awkwardly in the center of the
room, waiting for him to come back to her.*)

Make yourself at home. That was a little joke. No, that
was a little bad joke.

(HE *turns off a lamp.*)

FRANKIE: What's the matter?

JOHNNY: Nothing.

FRANKIE: Leave the lights on.

JOHNNY: It's better off.

FRANKIE: I want to see you this time.

(JOHNNY *has started unbuttoning her blouse.*)

JOHNNY: I don't like to make love with the lights on.

FRANKIE: Why not?

JOHNNY: I can't.

FRANKIE: That's a good reason.

(JOHNNY *is having a little difficulty undressing her.*)

JOHNNY: It's because of Archie.

FRANKIE: Okay, I'll bite. Who's Archie?

JOHNNY: A huge Great Dane at one of my foster families. I mean, massive. Whenever I'd jack off, he'd just stare at me. At it. Talk about serious castration anxiety! So I got in the habit of doing it with the lights off.

FRANKIE: Sometimes I am so glad I'm a girl.

JOHNNY: I'm also a romantic. I think everything looks better in half-light and shadows.

FRANKIE: That's not romance, that's hiding something. Romance is seeing somebody for what they really are and still wanting them warts and all.

JOHNNY: I got plenty of them.

(HE *stops undressing her.*)

I'm forty-five.

FRANKIE: You look younger. I'm thirty-seven.

JOHNNY: So do you. I'm forty-six.

FRANKIE: Honest?

JOHNNY: I'll be forty-eight the tenth of next month.

FRANKIE: What do you want for your birthday?

JOHNNY: To be able to stop bullshitting about things like my age.

FRANKIE: I'll be thirty-nine on the eleventh.

JOHNNY: We're both what-do-you-ma-call-its!

FRANKIE: Figures! Gimme a hand with the bed. I hate it when the sheets get like that.

(FRANKIE *starts straightening up the bed.* JOHNNY *turns off another light in the room before helping her to smooth the sheets and blankets.*)

I'm the one who ought to be hiding from the light. Me and my goddamn inverted nipples. I hate the way they look.

JOHNNY: Don't be silly.

FRANKIE: Yeah? You be a woman and have someone invert your nipples and see how you like it.

JOHNNY: I love your nipples.

FRANKIE: Well I hate 'em.

JOHNNY: What do you know?

(THEY *stand on opposite sides of the bed shaking out the sheets.*)

Listen, I wish I was circumcised.

FRANKIE: Sounds like you had your chance and blew it.

JOHNNY: Hunh?

FRANKIE: The dog. Skip it, skip it! I'll be forty-one on the eleventh.

JOHNNY: Big deal. So what do you want?

FRANKIE: The same thing you do and a new pair of tits.

JOHNNY: Hey, it means a lot to me you talk nice.

(JOHNNY *crosses to window to close the shade.* FRANKIE *goes to bed and lies down on it.*)

Jesus.

(HE *points to something outside the window and above it.*)

FRANKIE: Come away from there. It's not good for you.

JOHNNY: Come here. Quick.

(HE *stands at the window. Moonlight covers his body.*)

FRANKIE: I mean it. I've looked too long.

JOHNNY: There's a full moon! You can just see it between the buildings. Will you look at that! Now that's what I call beautiful!

FRANKIE: I ordered it just for you. Macy's. Twenty-five bucks an hour.

JOHNNY: Look at it!

FRANKIE: Later.

JOHNNY: It won't be there later.

(FRANKIE *joins him at the window.*)

You can almost see it move.

FRANKIE: (*Lowering her gaze*) All quiet on the Western front. For now. Come on.

(SHE *moves to bed.*)

Come on. I want you to make love to me.

(JOHNNY turns from the window.)

JOHNNY: I want to make love to you.

FRANKIE: Woof! Woof! *(Nothing)* It was a joke, I'm sorry.

RADIO ANNOUNCER: This young man was very persuasive . . .

JOHNNY: Sshh! Listen!

(HE moves quickly to the bedside radio and turns up the volume.)

RADIO ANNOUNCER: So although it's against my policy to play requests, there's an exception to every rule. I don't know if this is the most beautiful music ever written, Frankie and Johnny—and how I wish that really were your names but I know when my leg is being pulled—but whoever you are, wherever you are, whatever you're doing, I hope this is something like what you had in mind.

(Debussy's "Clair de Lune" is heard. JOHNNY switches off the bedside lamp and kisses FRANKIE. Then HE gets up quickly and goes to the window and reaches for the shade. He sees the two couples in the apartment across the courtyard. He looks up at the moon. There is moonlight spilling onto his face and body. He decides not to pull the shade, allowing the moonlight to spill into the room. He moves away from the window and disappears in the shadows of the bed. We hear a distant siren. We hear the Debussy. We hear the sounds of FRANKIE and JOHNNY starting to make love. Fifteen seconds of this. Abrupt silence. Total blackout.)

END OF ACT I

ACT II

AT RISE: *The only illumination in the room comes from the television set. In its gray light, we can see* FRANKIE *and* JOHNNY *in the bed, under the covers. They both stare at it. The only sound is coming from the radio: now it is playing "The Ride of the Valkyries." Thirty seconds of the Wagner.*

JOHNNY: Is that Charles Bronson?
  *(*JOHNNY *turns down radio.)*
  Is that Charles Bronson?
FRANKIE: Or the other one. I always get people in those kinds of movies confused.
JOHNNY: James Coburn?
FRANKIE: I think that's his name.
JOHNNY: Whoever he is, I hate him. It's not Clint Eastwood?
FRANKIE: No. I know what Clint Eastwood looks like. Look, you don't have to make such a big deal about it.
JOHNNY: I'm not making a big deal about it.
FRANKIE: Then how come we stopped?
JOHNNY: I haven't stopped. We're taking a little break. Will you look at that! I am appalled at the violence in the world today.
FRANKIE: It's okay if we don't.
JOHNNY: I know.
FRANKIE: Really.
JOHNNY: I said I know. Jesus, he drove a fucking nail through his head!

FRANKIE: I had my eyes shut.

JOHNNY: And when did that asshole go from playing our song to those screaming meemies? I thought he liked us. That kind of music is bad enough during normal hours. But when you're trying to make love to someone . . . ! Talk about not knowing how to segue from one mood to the next! I ought to call that station and complain.

(We hear him trip over something.)

Goddamnit!

*(*FRANKIE *turns on the bedside lamp.)*

FRANKIE: Are you all right?

JOHNNY: I wish you wouldn't leave—. Yeah. Since I'm up, you want something?

FRANKIE: Johnny.

JOHNNY: You're the one who's making a big deal about it. I'm fine. I'm not upset. Look, I'm dancing. Now yes or no? What do you want?

FRANKIE: A Western on white down and a glass of milk.

JOHNNY: Very funny. What do want? A beer?

(We can see him in the light of the open refrigerator as HE *searches it for food and drink.)*

FRANKIE: I want a Western and a glass of milk.

JOHNNY: We're in the middle of something. This is a little rest, not a major food break. Besides, you just ate.

FRANKIE: I'm still hungry.

JOHNNY: I'm opening a beer.

FRANKIE: I want a Western and a glass of milk.

JOHNNY: I never know when you're kidding me or not. I think that's one of the things I like about you but I'm not sure.

FRANKIE: I'm not kidding you. I'm starving and what I would like is one of your Westerns and a glass of milk. Everyone says you make a great Western.

JOHNNY: They do?

FRANKIE: So come on, Johnny, Johnny . . . ravish me with your cooking.

JOHNNY: You mean, since I couldn't ravish you with my body?

FRANKIE: No, that's not what I mean.

JOHNNY: Look, this is a temporary hiatus. I would like to keep it that way.

FRANKIE: So would I. I'll eat fast.

JOHNNY: All I'm saying is that if we get into real food now and I start cooking you a Western and chopping onions and peppers, it's going to be very hard to get back into the mood for what we were doing and which, contrary to your impression perhaps, I was enjoying enormously. All I asked for was a little breather for Christ's sake!

FRANKIE: I only asked for a sandwich.

JOHNNY: You asked for a Western. Westerns mean chopping and dicing and sautéing and . . . you know what goes into a Western! Come on, Frankie, it's not like you asked for a peanut butter and jelly on a Ritz cracker. You want food food.

FRANKIE: I suppose I could call out.

JOHNNY: All right, all right!

(HE *starts getting ingredients out of the refrigerator and slamming them onto the work counter.*)

I just wish somebody would tell me how we got from a mini-sex problem to a major pigout.

FRANKIE: I don't think there's a connection.

JOHNNY: I wasn't going to tell you this but since you're not sparing my feelings, I'm not going to go on sparing yours: this is the first time anything like this ever happened to me.

FRANKIE: So?

JOHNNY: Well if you can't make the connection . . . !

FRANKIE: Between what and what?

JOHNNY: It takes two to tango.

FRANKIE: You mean it's my fault you conked out?

JOHNNY: I didn't say it was anybody's fault. And I didn't conk out, I'm resting.

FRANKIE: Oh, the old And-On-The-Seventh-Day Syndrome!

JOHNNY: There's no need to be sarcastic.

FRANKIE: Then don't blame me your dancing dog didn't dance when you told it to. That sounds terrible. Don't blame me for your limp dick. Now what about my Western?

JOHNNY: You expect me to make you a sandwich after that?

FRANKIE: After what?

JOHNNY: Insulting my manhood.

FRANKIE: I didn't insult your manhood. I merely described a phase it was going through. Everything has phases. To talk about the new moon doesn't insult the old one. You have a lovely manhood. It's just in eclipse right now so you can make one of your terrific Westerns.

JOHNNY: This is the first time this has ever happened to me. I swear to God.

FRANKIE: I believe you.

JOHNNY: I hate it. I hate it a lot.

FRANKIE: Just be glad you have someone as sympathetic as me to share it with.

JOHNNY: Don't make fun.

FRANKIE: I'm not.

(SHE *goes to him and comforts him.*)

It's okay.

JOHNNY: You're lucky women don't have problems like this.

FRANKIE: We've got enough of our own in that department.

JOHNNY: It's male menopause. I've been dreading this.

FRANKIE: You know what I think it was? The moonlight. You were standing in it. It was bathing your body. I've always been very suspicious of what moonlight does to people.

JOHNNY: It's supposed to make them romantic.

FRANKIE: Or turn you into a werewolf. That's what I was raised on. My grandmother was always coming into my bedroom to make sure the blinds were down. She was convinced sleeping in the moonlight would turn you into the wolfman. I thought if I slept in the moonlight I'd wake up a beautiful fairy princess, so I kept falling asleep with the blinds open and she kept coming in and closing them. She always denied it was her. "Wasn't me, precious. Must have been your Guardian Angel." Remember them?

JOHNNY: What do you mean, "remember"?

FRANKIE: One night I decided to stay awake and catch her in the act. It seemed like forever. When you're that age, you don't have anything to stay awake *about*. So you're failing geography, so what? Finally my grandmother came into the room. She had to lean across my bed to close the blinds. Her bosom was so close to my face. She smelled so nice. I pretended I was still sleeping and took the deepest breath of her I could. In that one moment, I think I knew what it was like to be loved. Really loved. I was so safe, so protected! That's better than being pretty. I'll never forget it. The next thing I knew it was morning and I still didn't look like Audrey Hepburn. Now when I lie in bed with the blinds up and the moonlight spilling in, I'm not thinking I want to be somebody else. I just want my Nana back.

JOHNNY: Nana? You called your grandmother Nana? That's what I called mine.

FRANKIE: It's not that unusual.

JOHNNY: It's incredible! I don't know anybody else who called their grandmother Nana. I always thought it was very unusual of me and more than anything else I wanted to be like everyone else.

FRANKIE: You, like everybody else?

JOHNNY: It was a disaster. "Why do we call her Nana?" I used to ask my mother—this was before Philadelphia—"Everyone else says grandma." "We just do," she told me. My mother was not one for great answers. Sort of a Sphinx in that department. Anyway, I for one am very glad you didn't wake up Audrey Hepburn. She's too thin. People should have meat on their bones. "Beware yon Cassius. He hath a lean and hungry look."

FRANKIE: Who's Cassius?

JOHNNY: I don't know. But obviously he was thin and Shakespeare thinks we should be wary of skinny people.

FRANKIE: Why?

JOHNNY: Well you know how they are. Grim. Kind of waiting and watching you all the time.

FRANKIE: Like Connie?

JOHNNY: Who?

FRANKIE: Connie Cantwell. She works weekends. Red hair, wears a hairnet?

JOHNNY: Exactly! Wouldn't you beware her?

FRANKIE: I've actually seen her steal tips.

JOHNNY: There you go! He's filled with little tips like that. "Neither a borrower nor a lender be."

FRANKIE: That's just common sense. You don't have to be a genius to figure that one out.

JOHNNY: Of course not. But he put it in poetry so that people would know up here what they already knew in here and so they would remember it. "To be or not to be."

FRANKIE: Everyone knows that. Do I want to kill myself?

JOHNNY: Well?

FRANKIE: Well what?

JOHNNY: Do you want to kill yourself?

FRANKIE: Of course not. Well not right now. Everybody wants to kill themself some of the time.

JOHNNY: They shouldn't.

FRANKIE: Well they do! That doesn't mean they're gonna do it. Could we get off this?

JOHNNY: The list just gets longer and longer.

FRANKIE: What list?

JOHNNY: The us list, things we got in common.

FRANKIE: What do you want to kill yourself about sometimes?

JOHNNY: Right now? My limp dick. I'm kidding. I'm kidding. I'm going to start warning you before I say something funny.

FRANKIE: You don't have to warn me. Just say something funny.

JOHNNY: I want to kill myself sometimes when I think I'm the only person in the world and the part of me that feels that way is trapped inside this body that only bumps into other bodies without ever connecting with the only person in the world trapped inside of them. We gotta connect. We just have to. Or we die.

FRANKIE: We're connecting.

JOHNNY: Are we?

FRANKIE: I am. I feel very . . .

JOHNNY: Say it.

FRANKIE: I don't know what it is.

JOHNNY: Say it anyway.

FRANKIE: Protective, but that's crazy!

JOHNNY: It's nice.

FRANKIE: I'm looking for somebody to take care of me this time.

JOHNNY: We all are.

FRANKIE: Why do we keep going from one subject I don't like to another?

JOHNNY: We're like an FM station when you're out driving in a car. We keep drifting and we gotta tune ourselves back in.

FRANKIE: Who says?

JOHNNY: Hey, I'm being nice.

FRANKIE: May I say something without you biting my head off?

JOHNNY: Aw, c'mon!

FRANKIE: I mean it!

JOHNNY: You are the woman I've been looking for all my adult life. You can say anything you want. Speak, Queen of my heart, speak!

FRANKIE: That's just what I was talking about.

JOHNNY: What? Queen of my heart?

FRANKIE: I'm not the queen of anybody's heart.

JOHNNY: Fine. So what is it?

FRANKIE: This is going to sound awfully small potatoes now.

JOHNNY: You couldn't speak in small potatoes if you wanted to.

FRANKIE: I still want a Western.

JOHNNY: You don't give up. You're like a rat terrier with a bone.

FRANKIE: I'm sorry.

JOHNNY: I didn't hear that.

FRANKIE: All right, I'm *not* sorry. I'm a very simple person. I get hungry and I want to eat.

JOHNNY: I'm also a very simple person.

FRANKIE: Sure you are!

JOHNNY: I see something I want, I don't take no. I used to but not anymore.

FRANKIE: What is that supposed to mean?

JOHNNY: My life was happening to me. Now I'm making it happen. Same as with you and this sandwich. You wanted it, went for it, and won.

(HE *turns and opens the refrigerator.*)

You can tell a lot about someone from what they keep in their icebox. That and their medicine chest. I would've made a terrific detective.

FRANKIE: Just stay out of my medicine chest. And I didn't appreciate you going through my purse either.

JOHNNY: Someone is clearly not prepared for the eruption into her what-she-thinks-is-humdrum life of an extraordinary man, chef, and fellow worker. Why don't you try our friend on the radio again.?

(FRANKIE *will go to radio and turn it on.*)

Personally, I think it was all his fault. When it comes to music, I'm a mellow sort of guy. That last thing he played was for people playing with themselves, not one another. "If music be the food of love, play on." You-Know-Who.

FRANKIE: *(At the radio)* I would love a cigarette.

JOHNNY: Over my dead body.

FRANKIE: That doesn't mean I'm going to smoke one.

(SHE turns up volume. We hear the Cesar Franck Sonata for Piano and Violin.)

How's that?

JOHNNY: Comme çi, comme ça.

FRANKIE: It's pretty.

JOHNNY: Let's put it this way: he's no Bach. The first thing in the morning I'm going to buy you those Goldberg Variations.

FRANKIE: It's Sunday. Everything'll be closed.

JOHNNY: Monday then.

FRANKIE: I guess Bach was Jewish. The Goldberg Variations.

JOHNNY: I read somewhere a lot of great composers were.

FRANKIE: I thought you were Jewish.

JOHNNY: In New York, that's a good assumption.

FRANKIE: I just realized I don't know your last name.

JOHNNY: I don't know yours.

FRANKIE: Mine's right on the bell. It's all over this place.

JOHNNY: We don't need last names. We're Frankie and Johnny. *(Closing refrigerator door)* Boy, you just shot my icebox theory all to hell. You should be an Irish long-shoreman from what you've got in there.

FRANKIE: I am. Had you fooled for a while there, didn't I?

(JOHNNY is getting ready to make the Western.)

JOHNNY: Now watch how I do this. After this, you're on your own!

(JOHNNY begins to work with the food and the utensils. HE works swiftly, precisely, and with a great élan. He is a virtuoso in the kitchen. FRANKIE will pull up a stool and watch him work.)

FRANKIE: I know I'm going to regret saying this, but I thought I was the only person I knew who referred to one of those things as an "icebox."

JOHNNY: Now who's pulling whose leg?

FRANKIE: And I don't say things like "phonograph" or "record player." Just "icebox" and I only dimly remember us having one when I was about that big.

JOHNNY: Do you know what the population of New York City is?

FRANKIE: Eight million?

JOHNNY: Nine million, six hundred eighty-four thousand, four hundred eleven. Exactly two of them refer to those things as iceboxes. Those two, after you-know-what-ing their brains out, are now engaged in making a Western sandwich somewhere in Hell's Kitchen.

FRANKIE: It's Clinton actually.

JOHNNY: You still gonna call that a coincidence? Boy, I bet the Swan of Avon would have had something to say about that!

FRANKIE: I believe there's a reason for everything and I like to know what it is. One and one are two.

JOHNNY: That's mathematics. We're talking people.

FRANKIE: One and one should be two with them, too. Too many people throw you a curve nowadays and you end up with a three.

JOHNNY: Do I hear the voice of bitter experience?

FRANKIE: I wasn't born yesterday, if that's what you're talking about.

(SHE *has watched* JOHNNY *intently during this as he has continued to prepare the Western.*)

That's something I've never see anyone do.

JOHNNY: What?

FRANKIE: Chop the pepper that fine.

JOHNNY: 'Cause they're looking for shortcuts.

FRANKIE: You're incredible with that knife.

JOHNNY: Thank you.

FRANKIE: And don't say it's all in the wrists.

JOHNNY: It is.

FRANKIE: I hate that expression. It's such a "fuck you." What people really mean is "I know how to do it and you don't. Ha ha ha!"

JOHNNY: What brought that on? We're talking nice and Bingo! the armor goes up.

FRANKIE: What about your armor?

JOHNNY: I don't have any.

FRANKIE: Everybody has armor. They'd be dead if they didn't.

JOHNNY: Bloody but unbowed.

FRANKIE: Besides, I wasn't talking about you.

JOHNNY: Where's your cayenne?

FRANKIE: I don't have any. I don't even know what it is. What's that you just put in?

JOHNNY: Wouldn't you like to know? (HE *does a good imitation of* FRANKIE.) "Ha ha ha!"

FRANKIE: C'm'on!

JOHNNY: Salt, just salt!

FRANKIE: Is that all?

JOHNNY: Cooking's no big deal.

FRANKIE: It is if you can't.

JOHNNY: You just never had anyone to cook for. The way I feel about you I feel a Duck à l'Orange Flambé with a puree of water chestnuts coming on!

FRANKIE: I like food. I just never saw the joy in cooking it. My mother hated cooking. Her primary utensil was a can opener. I even think she resented serving us on plates. She used to eat right out of the pots and pans. "One less thing to clean. Who's to know? We ain't got company."

JOHNNY: This isn't the right kind of bread.

FRANKIE: Gee, I'll run right out!

JOHNNY: There you go again! You want a good Western down, you need the right bread.

FRANKIE: Did you always want to be a cook?

JOHNNY: About as much as you wanted to be a waitress.

FRANKIE: That bad, hunh?

JOHNNY: When I look at some of the choices I made with my life, it seems almost inevitable I would end up slinging hash.

FRANKIE: Same with me and waitressing. I was supposed to graduate high school and work for a second cousin who had a dental laboratory.

JOHNNY: That place down by the old train station?

FRANKIE: Yeah, that's the one.

JOHNNY: His son was in my class. Arnold, right?

FRANKIE: You knew my cousin Arnold?

JOHNNY: Enough to say hello. Finish your story.

FRANKIE: Anyway, they made bridges, plates, retainers, stuff like that there. A dentist would take a paraffin impression of the patient's mouth and make plaster of paris molds for the technicians to work from.

JOHNNY: No wonder the acting bug bit.

FRANKIE: I never had what it takes. I hope I have what it takes to be something but I know it's not an actress. You know what I'm thinking about?

JOHNNY: What?

FRANKIE: You won't laugh?

JOHNNY: Of course not.

FRANKIE: I can't. It's too . . . I'll tell you later. I can't now.

JOHNNY: Okay. I'll tell you one thing. You didn't miss much not graduating high school. I had almost two years of college. We both ended up working for a couple of crazed Greeks. (HE *imitates their boss.*) "Cheeseburger, cheeseburger" is right.

FRANKIE: That was very good.

JOHNNY: Thank you.

FRANKIE: A teacher.

JOHNNY: Hunh?

FRANKIE: What I'm thinking of becoming.

JOHNNY: Why would I laugh at that?

FRANKIE: I don't know. It just seems funny. Someone who can't spell "cat" teaching little kids to. I'll have to go back to school and learn before I can teach them but . . . I don't know, it sounds nice.

(SHE *hasn't stopped watching* JOHNNY *work with the eggs.*)
Aren't you going to scramble them?

JOHNNY: It's better if you just let them set.

FRANKIE: In the restaurant, I've seen you beat 'em. That's when I noticed you had sexy wrists.

JOHNNY: That's in the restaurant. I'm in a hurry. These are my special eggs for you.

(HE *starts cleaning up while the eggs set in a skillet on the stovetop.*)

FRANKIE: You don't have to do that.

JOHNNY: I know.

FRANKIE: Suit yourself.

JOHNNY: I bet I know what you're thinking: "He's too good to be true."

FRANKIE: Is that what you want me to think?

JOHNNY: Face it, Frankie, men like me do not grow on trees. Hell, *people* like me don't.

(HE *holds his wet hands out to her.*) Towel? (FRANKIE *picks up a dish towel on the counter and begins to dry his hands for him.*)

So you think I have sexy wrists?

FRANKIE: I don't think you're gonna break into movies on 'em.

JOHNNY: What do you think is sexy about them?

FRANKIE: I don't know. The shape. The hairs. That vein there. What's that?

JOHNNY: A mole.

FRANKIE: I could live without that.

JOHNNY: First thing Monday morning, it comes off.

(HE *is kissing her hands.* FRANKIE *lets him but keeps a certain distance, too.*)

FRANKIE: Are you keeping some big secret from me?

JOHNNY: It's more like I'm keeping several thousand little ones.

FRANKIE: I'd appreciate a straight answer.

JOHNNY: No, I'm not married.

FRANKIE: Men always think that's the only question women want to ask.

JOHNNY: So fire away.

FRANKIE: Well were you?

JOHNNY: I was.

FRANKIE: How many times?

JOHNNY: Once. Is that it?

FRANKIE: Men have other secrets than being married. You could be a mass murderer or an ex-convict.

JOHNNY: I am. I spent two years in the slammer. Forgery.

FRANKIE: That's okay.

JOHNNY: The state of New Jersey didn't seem to think so.

FRANKIE: It's no skin off my nose.

JOHNNY: Anything else?

FRANKIE: You could be gay.

JOHNNY: Get real, Frankie.

FRANKIE: Well you could!

JOHNNY: Does this look like a gay face?

FRANKIE: You could have a drug problem or a drinking one.

JOHNNY: All right, I did.

FRANKIE: Which one?

JOHNNY: Booze.

FRANKIE: There, you see?

JOHNNY: It's under control now.

FRANKIE: You could still be a real shit underneath all that.

JOHNNY: But I'm not.

FRANKIE: That's your opinion.

JOHNNY: You just want a guarantee we're going to live happily ever after.

FRANKIE: Jesus God knows, I want something. If I was put on this planet to haul hamburgers and french fries to pay the rent on an apartment I don't even like in the vague hope that some stranger will not find me wanting enough not to want to marry me then I think my being born is an experience that is going to be equaled in meaninglessness only by my being dead. I got a whole life ahead of me to feel like this? Excuse me, who do I thank for all this? I think the eggs are ready.

JOHNNY: Everything you said, anybody could say. I could give it back to you in spades. You didn't invent negativity.

FRANKIE: I didn't have to.

JOHNNY: And you didn't discover despair. I was there a long time before you ever heard of it.

FRANKIE: The eggs are burning.

JOHNNY: Fuck the eggs! This is more important!

FRANKIE: I'm hungry.

(FRANKIE has gone to the stove to take the eggs off. JOHNNY grabs her from behind and pulls her toward him.)

JOHNNY: What's the matter with you?

FRANKIE: Let go of me!

JOHNNY: Look at me!

(THEY struggle briefly. FRANKIE shoves JOHNNY who backs into the hot skillet and burns his back.)

Aaaaaaaaaaaaaaaa!

FRANKIE: What's the matter—?

JOHNNY: Oooooooooooooo!

FRANKIE: What happened—?

JOHNNY: Ow! Ow! Ow! Ow! Ow! Ow! Ow!

FRANKIE: Oh my God!

JOHNNY: Oooo! Oooo! Oooo! Ooooo! Oooo! Oooooo!

FRANKIE: I'm sorry, I didn't mean to—!

JOHNNY: Jesus, Frankie, Jesus Christ!

FRANKIE: Tell me what to do!

JOHNNY: Get something!

FRANKIE: What?

JOHNNY: Ice.

FRANKIE: Ice for burns? Don't move.

(FRANKIE *puts the entire tray of ice cubes on* JOHNNY's *back. The scream that ensues is greater than the first one.*)

JOHNNY: AAAAAAAAAAAAAAAAAAAAAAAAA!!!!!!!!!!

FRANKIE: You said to—! (JOHNNY *nods vigorously.*) Should I keep it on? (JOHNNY *nods again, only this time he bites his fingers to keep from crying out.*) We'd be a terrific couple. One of us would be dead by the end of the first week. One date practically did it. All I asked you to do was turn off the eggs but no! everything has to be a big deal with you. I would have made the world's worst nurse.

JOHNNY: (*Between gasps of pain*) Butter.

FRANKIE: What?

JOHNNY: Put some butter on it.

FRANKIE: Butter's bad on burns.

JOHNNY: I don't care.

FRANKIE: I may have some . . . oh what-do-you-call-it-when-you-have-a-sunburn, it comes in a squat blue bottle?

JOHNNY: Noxzema!

FRANKIE: That's it!

JOHNNY: It breaks me out. Get the butter.

FRANKIE: It's margarine.

JOHNNY: I don't care.

(FRANKIE *gets the margarine out of the refrigerator.*)

FRANKIE: It sounds like you got a lot of allergies.

JOHNNY: Just those three.

FRANKIE: Catsup, Noxema, and . . . what was the other one?

JOHNNY: Fresh peaches. Canned are okay.

(FRANKIE *puts the margarine on* JOHNNY's *back*).

Ooooooooooooo!

FRANKIE: Does that feel good?

JOHNNY: You have no idea.

FRANKIE: More?

JOHNNY: Yes, more. Don't stop.

FRANKIE: You're gonna smell like a . . . whatever a person covered in margarine smells like.

JOHNNY: I don't care.

FRANKIE: To tell the truth, it doesn't look all that bad.

JOHNNY: You think I'm faking this?

FRANKIE: I didn't say that.

JOHNNY: What do you want? Permanent scars? *(Pause. FRANKIE puts more margarine on JOHNNY's back.)*

FRANKIE: Did your first wife do this for you?

JOHNNY: Only wife. I told you that.

FRANKIE: Okay, so I was fishing.

JOHNNY: No, checking. Were you married?

FRANKIE: No, never.

JOHNNY: Anyone serious?

FRANKIE: Try "terminal."

JOHNNY: What happened?

FRANKIE: He got more serious with who I thought was my best friend.

JOHNNY: The same thing happened to me.

FRANKIE: You know what the main thing I felt was? Dumb.

JOHNNY: I know, I know!

FRANKIE: I even introduced them. I lent them money. Money from my credit union. I gave her my old televison. A perfectly good Zenith. They're probably watching Charles Bronson together at this very moment. I hope it explodes and blows their faces off. No, I don't. I hope it blows up and the fumes kill them. Aren't there suppose to be poison gases in a television set?

JOHNNY: I wouldn't be surprised.

FRANKIE: That or he's telling her she looks like shit, who told her she could change her hair or where's his car keys or shut the fuck up, he's had a rough day. I didn't know how exhausting unemployment could be. God, why do we get involved with people it turns out hate us?

JOHNNY: Because . . .

FRANKIE: . . . we hate ourselves. I know. I read the same book.

JOHNNY: How long has it been?

FRANKIE: Seven years.

(JOHNNY *lets out a long stream of air.*)

What? You, too? (JOHNNY *nods.*) Any kids?

JOHNNY: Two.

FRANKIE: You see them?

JOHNNY: Not as much as I'd like. She's remarried. They live in Maine in a beautiful house overlooking the sea.

FRANKIE: I bet it's not so beautiful.

JOHNNY: It's beautiful. I could never have provided them with anything like that. The first time I saw it, I couldn't get out of the car. I felt so ashamed. So forgotten. The kids came running out of the house. They looked so happy to see me but I couldn't feel happy back. All of a sudden, they looked like somebody else's kids. I couldn't even roll down the window. "What's the matter, daddy?" I started crying. I couldn't stop. Sheila and her husband had to come out of the house to get me to come in. You know what I wanted to do? Run that crewcut asshole insurance salesman over and drive off with the three of them. I don't know where we would've gone. We'd probably still be driving.

FRANKIE: That would've been a dumb thing to do.

JOHNNY: I never said I was smart.

FRANKIE: I'll tell you a secret: you are.

JOHNNY: I said I was passionate. I don't let go of old things easy and I grab new things hard.

FRANKIE: Too hard.

JOHNNY: There's no such thing as too hard when you want something.

FRANKIE: Yes, there is, Johnny. The other person.

(*There is a pause.* FRANKIE *has stopped working on* JOHNNY's *back. Instead* SHE *just stares at it.* JOHNNY *looks straight ahead. The music has changed to the Shostakovich Second String Quartet.*)

JOHNNY: What are you doing back there?

FRANKIE: Nothing. You want more butter or ice or something? (JOHNNY *shakes his head.*)

JOHNNY: It's funny how you can talk to people better sometimes when you're not looking at them. You're right there. *(HE points straight ahead.)* Clear as day.

FRANKIE: I bet no one ever said that was the most beautiful music ever written.

JOHNNY: I don't mind.

FRANKIE: I don't know what the radio was doing on that station in the first place. That's not my kind of music. But I could tell you were enjoying it and I guess I wanted you to think I had higher taste than I really do.

JOHNNY: So did I.

FRANKIE: I liked what he played for us though, but he didn't say its name.

JOHNNY: Maybe it doesn't need one. You just walk into a fancy record shop and ask for the most beautiful music ever written and that's what they hand you.

FRANKIE: Not if I was the salesperson. You'd get "Michelle" or "Eleanor Rigby" or "Lucy in the Sky with Diamonds." Something by the Beatles. I sort of lost interest in pop music when they stopped singing.

JOHNNY: The last record I bought was the Simon and Garfunkel Reunion in Central Park. It wasn't the same. You could tell they'd been separated.

FRANKIE: Sometimes I feel like it's still the sixties. Or that they were ten or fifteen years ago, not twenty or twenty-five. I lost ten years of my life somewhere. I went to Bruce Springsteen last year and I was the oldest one there.

JOHNNY: Put your arms around me.

(FRANKIE puts her arms over JOHNNY's shoulders.)
Tighter.

(FRANKIE's hands begin to stroke JOHNNY's chest and stomach.)
Do you like doing that?

FRANKIE: I don't mind.

JOHNNY: We touch our own bodies there and nothing happens. Something to do with electrons. We short-circuit ourselves. Stroke my tits. There!

(HE *tilts his head back until he is looking up at her.*)
Give me your mouth.
(FRANKIE *bends over and kisses him. It is a long one.*)
That tongue. Those lips.
(HE *pulls her down towards him for another long kiss.*)
I want to die like this. Drown.

FRANKIE: What do you want from me?

JOHNNY: Everything. Your heart. Your soul. Your tits. Your mouth. Your fucking guts. I want it all. I want to be inside you. Don't hold back.

FRANKIE: I'm not holding back.

JOHNNY: Let go. I'll catch you.

FRANKIE: I'm right here.

JOHNNY: I want more. I need more.

FRANKIE: If I'd known what playing with your tit was gonna turn into . . . !

JOHNNY: Quit screwing with me, Frankie.

FRANKIE: You got a pretty weird notion of who's screwing with who. I said I liked you. I told you that. I'm perfectly ready to make love to you. Why do you have to start a big discussion about it. It's not like I am saying "no."

JOHNNY: I want you to do something.

FRANKIE: What?

JOHNNY: I want you to go down on me.

FRANKIE: No.

JOHNNY: I went down on you.

FRANKIE: That was different.

JOHNNY: How?

FRANKIE: That was then.

JOHNNY: Please.

FRANKIE: I'm not good at it.

JOHNNY: Hey, this isn't a contest. We're talking about making love.

FRANKIE: I don't want to right now.

JOHNNY: You want me to go down on you again?

FRANKIE: If I do it will you shut up about all this other stuff?

JOHNNY: You know I won't.

FRANKIE: Then go down on yourself.

JOHNNY: What happened? You were gonna do it.

FRANKIE: Anything to get you to quit picking at me. Go on, get out of here. Get somebody else to do down on you.

JOHNNY: I don't want somebody else to go down on me.

FRANKIE: Jesus! I just had a vision of what it's going to be like at work Monday after this! I'm not quitting my job. I was there first.

JOHNNY: What are you talking about?

FRANKIE: I don't think we're looking for the same thing.

JOHNNY: We are. Only I've found it and you've given up.

FRANKIE: Yes! Long before the sun ever rose on your ugly face.

JOHNNY: What scares you more? Marriage or kids?

FRANKIE: I'm not scared. And I told you: I can't have any.

JOHNNY: I told you: we can adopt.

FRANKIE: I don't love you.

JOHNNY: That wasn't the question.

FRANKIE: You hear what *you* want to hear.

JOHNNY: Do you know anybody who doesn't?

FRANKIE: Not all the time.

JOHNNY: You're only telling me you don't love me so you don't have to find out if you could. Just because you've given up on the possibility, I'm not going to let you drag me down with you. You're coming up to my level if I have to pull you by the hair.

FRANKIE: I'm not going anywhere with a man who for all his bullshit about marriage and kids and Shakespeare . . .

JOHNNY: It's not bullshit!

FRANKIE: . . . Just wants me to go down on him.

JOHNNY: Pretend it was a metaphor.

FRANKIE: Fuck you it was a metaphor! It was a blowjob. What's a metaphor?

JOHNNY: Something that stands for something else.

FRANKIE: I was right the first time. A blowjob.

JOHNNY: A sensual metaphor for mutual acceptance.

FRANKIE: Fuck you. Besides, what's mutual about a blowjob?

JOHNNY: I made that up. I'm sorry. It wasn't a metaphor. It was just something I wanted us to do.

FRANKIE: And I didn't.

JOHNNY: Let go, will you! One lousy little peccadillo and it's off with his head!

FRANKIE: Stop using words I don't know. What's a peccadillo?

JOHNNY: A blowjob! Notice I haven't died you didn't do it!

FRANKIE: I noticed.

JOHNNY: And let me notice something for you: you wouldn't have died if you had. Thanks for making me feel about this big.

(HE *gets up and starts gathering and putting on his clothes.*)

I'm sorry, I mistook you for a kindred spirit. Kindred: two of a kind, sharing a great affinity.

FRANKIE: I know what kindred means!

JOHNNY: Shall we go for affinity!

FRANKIE: That's the first really rotten thing you've said all night. Somebody who would make fun of somebody else's intelligence, no worse, their education or lack of— that is somebody I would be very glad not to know. I thought you were weird, Johnny. I thought you were sad. I didn't think you were cruel.

JOHNNY: I'm sorry.

FRANKIE: It's a cruelty just waiting to happen again and I don't want to be there when it does.

JOHNNY: Please!

(*There is an urgency in his voice that startles* FRANKIE.)

I'm not good with people. But I want to be. I can get away with it for long stretches but I always hang myself in the end.

FRANKIE: Hey, c'm'on, don't cry. Please, don't cry.

JOHNNY: It's not cruelty. It's a feeling I don't matter. That nobody hears me. I'm drowning. I'm trying to swim back to shore but there's this tremendous undertow and I'm not getting anywhere. My arms and legs are doing a mile a minute but they aren't taking me any closer to where I want to be.

FRANKIE: Where's that?

JOHNNY: With you.

FRANKIE: You don't know me.

JOHNNY: Yes, I do. It scares people how much we really know one another, so we pretend we don't. You know me. You've known me all your life. Only now I'm here. Take me. Use me. Try me. There's a reason we're called Frankie and Johnny.

FRANKIE: There's a million other Frankies out there and a billion other Johnnys. The world is filled with Frankies and Johnnys and Jacks and Jills.

JOHNNY: But only one this Johnny, one this Frankie.

FRANKIE: We're too different.

JOHNNY: You say po-tah-toes? All right, I'll say po-tah-toes! I don't care. I love you. I want to marry you.

FRANKIE: I don't say po-tah-toes. Who the hell says po-tah-toes?

JOHNNY: Are you listening to me?

FRANKIE: I'm trying very hard not to!

JOHNNY: That's your trouble. You don't want to hear anything you don't think you already know. Well I'll tell you something, Cinderella: your Prince Charming has come. Wake up before another thousand years go by! Don't throw me away like a gum wrapper because you think there's something about me you may not like. I have what it takes to give you anything and everything you want. Maybe not up here . . . (HE *taps his head.*) . . . or here . . . (HE *slaps his hip where he wears his wallet.*) . . . but here. (HE *touches his heart*). And that would please me enormously. All I ask back is that you use your capacity to be everyone and everything for me. It's within you. If we could do that for each other we'd give our kids the universe. They'd be Shakespeare and the most beautiful music ever written and a saint maybe or a champion athlete or a president all rolled into one. Terrific kids! How could they not be? We have a chance to make everything turn out all right again. Turn our back on everything that went wrong. We can begin right now and all over again but only if we begin right now, this minute, this room and us. I know this thing, Frankie.

FRANKIE: I want to show you something, Johnny. (SHE *pushes her hair back.*) He did that. The man I told you about. With a belt buckle.

(JOHNNY *kisses the scar.*)

JOHNNY: It's gone now.

FRANKIE: It'll never go.

JOHNNY: It's gone. I made it go.

FRANKIE: What are you? My guardian angel?

JOHNNY: It seems to me the right people are our guardian angels.

FRANKIE: I wanted things, too, you know.

JOHNNY: I know.

FRANKIE: A man, a family, kids . . . He's the reason I can't have any.

JOHNNY: He's gone. Choose me. Hurry up. It's getting light out. I turn into a pumpkin.

FRANKIE: (*Looking toward the window*) It is getting light out! (FRANKIE *goes to the window.*)

JOHNNY: You are so beautiful standing there.

FRANKIE: The only time I saw the sun come up with a guy was my senior prom.

(JOHNNY *has joined her at the window. As they stand there looking out, we will be aware of the rising sun.*)

His name was Johnny Di Corso but everyone called him Skunk.

(SHE *takes* JOHNNY's *hand and clasps it to her, but her eyes stay looking out the window at the dawn.*)

He was a head shorter than me and wasn't much to look

at but nobody else had asked me. It was him or else. I was dreading it. But guess what? That boy could dance! You should have seen us. We were the stars of the prom. We did Lindys, the Mambo, the Twist. The Monkey, the Frug. All the fast dances. Everybody's mouth was down to here. Afterwards we went out to the lake to watch the sun come up. He told me he was going to be on American Bandstand one day. I wonder if he ever made it.

(JOHNNY *puts his arm around her and begins to move her in a slow dance step.*)

JOHNNY: There must be something about you and sunrises and men called Johnny.

FRANKIE: You got a nickname?

JOHNNY: No. You got to be really popular or really unpopular to have a nickname.

FRANKIE: I'll give you a nickname.

(THEY *dance in silence a while. Silence, that is, except for the Shostakovich, which they pay no attention to.*)

You're not going to like me saying this but you're a terrible dancer.

JOHNNY: Show me.

FRANKIE: Like that.

JOHNNY: There?

FRANKIE: That's better.

JOHNNY: You're going to make a wonderful teacher.

(HE *starts to hum.*)

FRANKIE: What's that supposed to be?

JOHNNY: Something from *Brigadoon.*

FRANKIE: That isn't from *Brigadoon.* That isn't even remotely from *Brigadoon.* That isn't even remotely something from anything.

(THEY *dance.* FRANKIE *begins to hum.*)

That's something from *Brigadoon.* You can't have kids in a place this size.

JOHNNY: Who says?

FRANKIE: How big is your place?

JOHNNY: Even smaller. We'll be a nice snug family. It'll be wonderful.

FRANKIE: Does it always get light so fast this time of year?

JOHNNY: Unh-unh. The sun's in a hurry to shine on us.

FRANKIE: Pardon my French but that's bullshit.

JOHNNY: You can sleep all day today.

FRANKIE: What are you planning to do?

JOHNNY: Watch you.

FRANKIE: You're just weird enough to do it, too. Well forget it. I can't sleep with people watching me.

JOHNNY: How do you know?

FRANKIE: I was in the hospital for my gallbladder and I had a roommate who just stared at me all the time. I made them move me. I got a private room for the price of a semi. Is this the sort of stuff you look forward to finding out about me?

JOHNNY: Unh-hunh!

FRANKIE: You're nuts.

JOHNNY: I'm happy!

FRANKIE: Where are you taking me?

JOHNNY: The moon.

FRANKIE: That old place again?

JOHNNY: The other side this time.

(JOHNNY *has slow-danced* FRANKIE *to the bed. The room is being quickly flooded with sunlight.*)

FRANKIE: If you don't turn into a pumpkin, what do you turn into?

JOHNNY: You tell me. (HE *kisses her very gently.*)

FRANKIE: Just a minute.

(SHE *gets up and moves quickly to the bathroom.* JOHNNY *turns off all the room lights.* HE *starts to close the blinds but instead raises them even higher. Sunlight pours across him. The Shostakovich ends.* JOHNNY *moves quickly to the radio and turns up the volume as the announcer's voice is heard.*)

RADIO ANNOUNCER: . . . that just about winds up my stint in the control room. This has been Music Till Dawn with

Marlon. I'm still thinking about Frankie and Johnny. God, how I wish you two really existed. Maybe I'm crazy but I'd still like to believe in love. Why the hell do you think I work these hours? Anyway, you two moonbeams, whoever, wherever you are, here's an encore.

(Debussy's "Clair de Lune" is heard again. JOHNNY *sits, listening.* HE *starts to cry he is so happy. He turns as* FRANKIE *comes out of the bathroom.* SHE *is brushing her teeth.)*

JOHNNY: They're playing our song again.

FRANKIE: Did they say what it was this time?

JOHNNY: I told you! You just walk into a record shop and ask for the most beautiful music . . .

FRANKIE: Watch us end up with something from *The Sound of Music*, you'll see! You want to brush?

*(SHE *motions with her thumb to the bathroom. She steps aside as* JOHNNY *passes her to go in.)*

Don't worry. It's never been used.

(Still brushing her teeth, SHE *goes to the window and looks out.)*

Did you see the robins?

*(SHE *listens to the music.)*

This I can see why people call pretty.

*(SHE *sits on the bed, listens and continues to brush her teeth. A little gasp of pleasure escapes her.)*

Mmmmm!

*(JOHNNY *comes out of the bathroom.* HE *is brushing his teeth.)*

JOHNNY: I'm not going to ask whose robe that is.

FRANKIE: Sshh!

*(SHE *is really listening to the music.)*

JOHNNY: We should get something with fluoride.

FRANKIE: Sshh!

JOHNNY: Anti-tartar buildup, too.

FRANKIE: Johnny!

*(JOHNNY *sits next to her on the bed.* THEY *are both brushing their teeth and listening to the music. They continue to brush their teeth and listen to the Debussy. The lights are fading.)*

THE END

It's Only
a Play

For Edgar Bronfman Jr.

It's Only a Play was produced by Manhattan Theatre Club at The Space at City Center Theater. It opened on December 17, 1985, with the following cast:

GUS WASHINGTON	Jihmi Kennedy
JAMES WICKER	James Coco
VIRGINIA NOYES	Joanna Gleason
FRANK FINGER	David Garrison
JULIA BUDDER	Christine Baranski
IRA DREW	Paul Benedict
PETER AUSTIN	Mark Blum
EMMA	Florence Stanley

It was directed by John Tillinger. Sets designed by John Lee Beatty. Lighting designed by Pat Collins. Costumes designed by Rita Ryack. Sound designed by Stan Metelits. Hairstyles by Brad Scott. The Production Stage Manager was Tracy B. Cohen.

The time of the play is now.
The place of the play is Julia Budder's townhouse.
The people of the play are:

PETER AUSTIN—The playwright. Don't let his nice looks
fool you.

JULIA BUDDER—The producer. Attractive and genuinely
pleasant.

IRA DREW—The critic. Wears glasses. Very sure of himself.

FRANK FINGER—The director. Seething. Dark. Intense.

VIRGINIA NOYES—The star. High cheekbones. Throaty voice.
A firecracker.

GUS WASHINGTON—The temporary help. Black, cool and
street smart.

JAMES WICKER—The best friend. Pleasant, open features and
a personality of great charm.

EMMA—A taxi driver. A no-nonsense lady of indeterminate
years.

ACT I

The bedroom in Julia Budder's townhouse. It is a large room with a king-sized bed, a chaise, several armchairs, a television set with a remote control, a bookcase, a desk with several telephones and, most curiously, a spinet piano.

There are two doors: one leads to the bathroom and dressing area; the other to the hallway and stairs. Thus, we can see people on the stairs before they enter the room itself. There are two windows, drapes drawn, fronting the street.

AT RISE: *there is a party in progress downstairs. Although the bedroom is empty, we can hear voices, laughter, and piano music drifting up from the living room one floor below. It sounds like a lot of people. Also, the bed is heaped with mink coats and purses.*

GUS WASHINGTON *is seen coming up the stairs. He is dressed in a dinner jacket. He is carrying a load of mink coats. He comes into the bedroom and closes the door. The party sounds grow fainter.*

He tosses the mink coats onto the pile and crosses to the desk, picks up the phone and excitedly punch dials a number.

GUS: Hello, Homer? It's me again. Guess who just blew in down there this time? Lena Horne! Can you bear it? . . . The hell you say it isn't. I guess I know what Lena Horne looks like. It sure as shit ain't Leontyne Price. I'm telling you, Homer, this place is crawling with celebrities. The party of the year for the play of the season. There's one old dude down there talking to Shirley MacLaine I'm pretty sure is the Pope. If I'd've known it was gonna be

161

this kind of gig, I'd've brought my Instamatic. Homer, this could be my Golden Opportunity. I feel one mighty song coming on.

(JAMES WICKER *enters.*)

JAMES: Wasn't it wonderful? I'll be right down. Thank you.

GUS: I seen this one somewhere, too.

JAMES: Hello.

GUS: You looking for the bathroom? Across the hall.

JAMES: The telephone. I couldn't hear a thing down there.

GUS: I gotta go.

JAMES: That's perfectly all right.

GUS: It's all yours.

JAMES: Thank you. Hello? Hello?

GUS: Push the button.

JAMES: The button! Thank you. Hello, operator? This is Mr. Wicker again. Thank you. *(To* GUS*)* California. They're all dying to know how the play went tonight.

GUS: How did it go?

JAMES: Wonderful, just wonderful.

GUS: Mrs. Budder will be pleased. Too bad you're not a critic.

JAMES: We're all critics. You haven't seen the show?

GUS: I'm temporary help. This party is just a one-night stand for me.

JAMES: This party is a one-night stand for a lot of people.

GUS: I'm Gus, Gus Washington. See, I don't do this for a living. I'm a singer-slash-actor-slash-dancer-slash-comedian-slasha-black-belt karate expert-period.

JAMES: Oh. *(Into phone)* Hello? Hello?

GUS: I have studied acting in the Village with Norman Orland, of whom I guess you are familiar. If not, he studied with Evelyn Galyon, who was a man [did you ever hear of a man called Evelyn? Weird!]. He's a wonderful teacher and I'd recommend him to you and anybody you might know.

JAMES: Thank you. *(Back into phone)* Yes, I'm still here, operator. Thank God, you're back. Where else would I be? I didn't place this call. *(To* GUS) My agent calls me and I have to wait. She wouldn't do this to Don Johnson.

GUS: Ain't I seen you some place?

JAMES: It's very likely.

GUS: Where?

JAMES: It all depends. The Broadway stage?

GUS: No.

JAMES: Motion pictures maybe?

GUS: No.

JAMES: Then it must be television.

GUS: No.

JAMES: No? What do you mean, no?

GUS: Maybe I saw you walking your dog.

JAMES: I don't have a dog. Besides, I live in Beverly Hills. I have a series.

GUS: Yeah?

JAMES: *Out on a Limb.*

GUS: *Out on a Limb?* Is that you in that show?

JAMES: I'm afraid so.

GUS: I've watched that program.

JAMES: I'm glad you don't have a Nielson box. *(Into phone)* Hello? There you are! Finally! What? I can hardly hear you. Who's party are you at? Does he know his series has been cancelled? Give him my love. "How did it go tonight?" Wonderful, just wonderful.

(HE *covers the phone and holds his empty champagne glass towards* GUS.)

Gus? Would you mind terribly?

GUS: Some more of the bubbly, right?

JAMES: And close the door on your way out.

(TORCH *is heard in the bathroom, a terrible sound to behold.)*

What in God's name is that?

GUS: The dog.

JAMES: What dog?

GUS: The Budders' dog. They call him Torch. Ain't nobody supposed to let him out. He got out when the party first started and bit that woman who was on *What's My Line*.

JAMES: Not Arlene Francis?

GUS: That's the one.

JAMES: Torch bit Arlene Francis?

GUS: Went right for her face.

JAMES: How horrible. I'm supposed to do her show next week.

GUS: They took her to Mt. Sinai along with Mr. Budder.

JAMES: Hold on, darling, this is too good. What happened to Mr. Budder?

GUS: He got mugged right after the play tonight.

JAMES: Where was he? Eighth Avenue trying to get a cab?

GUS: The men's room in Sardi's taking a leak.

(GUS goes.)

JAMES: *(Into phone)* I'm sitting ten feet from a rabid dog who just bit Arlene Francis in the townhouse of a lady producer whose husband got mugged in the men's room at Sardi's. I will never knock California again. Where was I? Oh, the play!

(HE makes himself comfortable for a long haul on the telephone. His voice glows with relish.)

Darling, what is your traditional Thanksgiving dinner? . . . Well this one is a thirty-six pound Butterball. Bob Fosse asked me what I thought at intermission and all I said was "Gobble, gobble" and he wet himself. Of course I don't want you to give that to Liz Smith. Are you crazy? I may want to work with these people. How was Jack Nimble? He was terrible, just terrible. But tell me this and tell me no more: when was he every any good? All of my mannerisms and none of my warmth. Of course I would have been wonderful in it. It was written for me. And you want to hear the killer? I wasn't even mentioned in Peter's biography in the Playbill. I mean, let's face it. I did create the lead in his one and only hit but do you think I got so much as even a mention in his bio tonight? Well, that's a best friend for you. I fly in three thousand miles on the goddamn Red Eye for his opening and I'm not even mentioned in the goddamn Playbill. The egos in this business! What about Virginia Noyes? Terrible, just terrible. I haven't seen a performance like that since her last one. Well of course she wanted to come back to Broadway. After her last couple of pictures, she had to go somewhere. Terrible direction, just terrible. Boy wonder he may well be; the new Trevor Nunn he's not. He's not even the old Mike Nichols. Frank something. He's out of Chicago. Aren't they all? Sets? What sets? It took place on a goddamn tilted disk. Give me scenery or count me out. Hideous costumes. Darling, I would have made my first entrance in a leather codpiece and sort of antlers. I kid you not. There but for the grace of ABC went I! Darling, Arnold Schwarzenegger couldn't have held this one up. Oh, and guess who was sitting next to me at the theater? Rita Moreno in a Day-Glo turban. She was with Calvin Klein. I wish you could have seen her face when he introduced her to Jean Kennedy as Chita Rivera! Who? Rita or Chita? Terrible, just terrible. But listen, darling, what do I know? What do any of us old gypsies know? I liked *The Rink*.

(VIRGINIA NOYES *enters the bedroom.*)

VIRGINIA: Is there a can in here? That fucking Shirley MacLaine's had me in a corner telling me who she was in her previous lives until I thought I would burst.

JAMES: You were wonderful tonight, just wonderful. I'm just telling the Coast.

VIRGINIA: You got the Coast on there? Give me that mother.

(SHE *takes the receiver.*)

Hey, California. This is Virginia Noyes. I'm back on Broadway, feeling fabulous and you can all go fuck yourself!

(*Hands phone back to* JAMES)

Am I going to regret that?

JAMES: Only if you're going back to California.

VIRGINIA: After tonight? No way!

(SHE *exits into bathroom.*)

JAMES: Oh my God! Miss Noyes, Miss Noyes!

VIRGINIA: What do you want? I just got in here!

JAMES: Be careful of that dog in there.

VIRGINIA: What dog?

JAMES: There's a dog in there with you.

VIRGININA: Is that what that is? *(Laughs)*

JAMES: *(Into phone)* Virginia Noyes, looking like Pocohantas and feeling no pain. Washed up at thirty-seven, that's the tragedy . . . Thirty-seven, darling, I know these things. Listen, what were our ratings like this week? . . . . That's not good.

(GUS *returns with a bottle of champagne.*)

I don't like that, Sue, I don't like that at all. I told them not to put us in that time slot.

(*To* GUS, *who leaves*)

Thank you, Gus. *(Back into phone)* I can't compete with trained dolphins. *Cagney and Lacey* I can handle but I draw the line at fish. They can't cancel us. I'll kill myself. Tell ABC I'll kill myself. Besides, I'm having a tennis court moved. Don't they know what that costs? Please, Sue, I don't need stress. I'm here to celebrate the opening of my best friend's play. I'll be back late tomorrow. We'll schmooze. Yes, mother. Yes, yes, yes. Big kisses. Ciao.

(HE *hangs up.* GUS *enters, struggling with a fur coat of exaggerated length.*)

Don't tell me. Let me guess. Tommy Tune, right?

GUS: I just take coats. I don't ask names. Mrs. Budder just got back from the hospital.

JAMES: Where is she, the dear?

GUS: She'll be right up. She wants you to wait for her.

JAMES: Up here? What for? I'm missing everything.

GUS: She didn't say.

JAMES: I want to go to the party.

(VIRGINIA *comes out of the bathroom.*)

VIRGINIA: You know, there is a dog in there when you get right up close to it.

JAMES: What did you think it was?

VIRGINIA: My first husband.

GUS: You let somebody in there?

VIRGINIA: I hope you guys are cool.

(SHE *has already sat with her drug stash.*)

It's straight city down there. My agent said, "Ginny, don't let anyone see you doing that. You're not in Hollywood. That's Helen Hayes over there." I said, "Honey, I don't give a flying fuck if it's Gabby Hayes. I am going to get a little buzz on."

GUS: You got some stuff there, lady?

VIRGINIA: I got some of everything. Grass, Thai stick, hash, coke, ludes, uppers, downers, saccharine, this stuff'll kill you, vitamin E, Revlon Lip Gloss, Tiger Balm. (*To* JAMES) You want a hit?

JAMES: No, thank you. I had some at home.

VIRGINIA: (*To* GUS) You?

GUS: No, thank you, I gotta stay on the ball. Maybe I'll catch you later.

(HE *goes*)

VIRGINIA: He's kinda cute.

JAMES: He didn't have a clue who I was and he wants to be an actor!

VIRGINIA: Who are you?

JAMES: I'm James Wicker.

VIRGINIA: Right.

JAMES: We did a film together.

VIRGINIA: Which one?

JAMES: *Red Dawn.*

VIRGINIA: Was I in that? I'm sure it'll come back. Did you ever have more hair?

JAMES: No, that was Marlo Thomas. We're often mistaken.

VIRGINIA: I'm sorry. James Wicker! Of course! How could I forget? *Flashes*, Peter's first play. He really put you on the map with that one.

JAMES: Some people would say it's the other way around.

VIRGINIA: Hello again. I love your work. I love it, I love it.

JAMES: Thank you.

VIRGINIA: When I forget someone, I really forget someone. How the hell are you? You look marvelous.

JAMES: I came in on the Red Eye.

VIRGINIA: When they sent me Peter's play, they told me you were doing Jack's part.

JAMES: There was some talk about it, they wanted me desperately, as a matter of fact, but with my series . . .

VIRGINIA: You got a series?

JAMES: For five years now.

VIRGINIA: I'm sorry. I do a lot of self-destructive things but I draw the line at television. I don't watch it and I won't do it.

JAMES: I just take the money and run.

VIRGINIA: Yeah. But are you happy?

JAMES: Relatively. Are you?

VIRGINIA: Fan-fucking-tastic.

JAMES: Speaking of Peter.

VIRGINIA: Peter? I wrote the book. Oh, that Peter!

JAMES: Where is he?

VIRGINA: Beats me. Maybe he's just hiding until the reviews are out. Speaking of which, have you heard anything?

JAMES: You're home free with this one.

VIRGINIA: You really think so?

JAMES: Darling, I could phone these raves in.

VIRGINIA: I hope so. Living in L.A. so long, you forget what being on a real stage is like. My only mistake was going out there in the first place. I guess I just wanted to see myself forty feet tall.

JAMES: We all do.

VIRGINIA: I wanted to see what they'd do with my tits.

JAMES: Me, too.

VIRGINIA: I don't see the crime in that.

JAMES: It's the American Dream.

VIRGINIA: I see the asshole but I don't see the crime. Thank God for this play. Don't you miss all this?

JAMES: No way. Wild horses couldn't get me up there again.

VIRGINIA: I don't know about you but my loins are girded.

JAMES: I'd love to but I'm waiting for our hostess. If Mary Martin sings, I'll come down.

VIRGINIA: If Carol Channing sings, I'll come up!

(VIRGINIA goes; JAMES looks at his watch.)

JAMES: It must be getting time for the first reviews.

(HE turns on the television with remote-control module.)

Oh God, I dread this. They're gonna crucify him.

(FRANK FINGER comes into the bedroom.)

FRANK: I don't wanna hear. I don't wanna know. Hi.

JAMES: Hi! I'm James Wicker. Do you know who's reviewing for Channel 5 now?

FRANK: No. Do you have to have that thing on? Reviews are killing the theater.

JAMES: Good ones aren't.

FRANK: *(HE is holding up a small enamel box.)* How much do you think something like this is worth?

JAMES: I don't know. Several hundred dollars, I should think. It used to be . . . what was his name? He gave me that incredible rave.

FRANK: You an actor?

JAMES: Yes.

FRANK: New York?

JAMES: Ex—L.A.

FRANK: L.A. sucks. Several hundred dollars for a box?

JAMES: It's more than just a box. It's an antique box.

FRANK: Puh!

(HE pockets the box. JAMES's eyes widen in disbelief. FRANK looks right at him.)

What?

JAMES: I saw that.

FRANK: So?

JAMES: I . . .

(For once HE *is speechless.)*

FRANK: What's upstairs?

JAMES: I don't know. More rooms, I should think. Whoever you are, you're putting me in an extremely difficult position.

*(*FRANK *presses the remote-control module. The sound comes back up at once.)*

TV: Stewart Klein was at the Barrymore Theatre for the opening of a new play tonight.

JAMES: I would like to be able to enjoy this.

(But the lure of the first review is too much for him. HE *rushes for a seat in front of the television.)*

STEWART KLEIN'S VOICE: Well, it's like this. Peter Austin's eagerly awaited new play, *The Golden Egg*, love that title, is—

*(*FRANK *presses the remote again. The sound goes off.)*

JAMES: What happened?

FRANK: You don't want to watch that.

JAMES: The hell I don't.

*(*FRANK *turns the sound back up for a second.)*

STEWART KLEIN'S VOICE: . . . working in an idiom totally dissimilar from his previous plays, almost as if they were in preparation for this, his broadway debut, Mr. Austin has given us a play that is both—

*(*FRANK *turns the sound off. This time* JAMES *spins around.)*

FRANK: Watching only encourages them.

JAMES: What's the matter with you? Are you crazy? Now turn that set on.

FRANK: I'd rather know what you thought.

JAMES: I loved it. And now I'd like to know what he thought.

FRANK: What do you care?

JAMES: He's a critic.

FRANK: He's an asshole.

JAMES: That's not the point.

FRANK: What is the point?

JAMES: What the assholes think.

FRANK: I'd rather know what you thought.

JAMES: I told you. I loved it. Please.

(HE *has fallen to his knees. The reviews for* PETER'*s play are a matter of life and death to* JAMES.)

FRANK: Why?

JAMES: Because my best friend wrote it. What do you want from me?

FRANK: A better reason.

JAMES: All right. My best friend wrote it for me and I turned it down because I thought it was a piece of shit and I want to see if that asshole agrees with me.

FRANK: Your best friend?

JAMES: Peter. Peter Austin.

FRANK: Peter Austin wrote a piece of shit for you.

JAMES: Not on purpose. In this business, we're all capable of shit.

(FRANK *turns up the volume.*)

STEWART KLEIN'S VOICE: . . . superb, no, I take that back: perfect staging by Frank Finger, the brilliant young director who gave us last season's ravishing *Arden of Feversham* in Prospect Park. Thank you and goodnight.

(*There is a burst of applause from the party downstairs.*)

TV ANNOUNCER: That was Stewart Klein with the very first review of tonight's big opening at the Ethel Barrymore. I'll be right back with Ticho Parley and the sports.

(FRANK *turns off TV with remote control. There is an enormous cheer and another burst of applause from the party downstairs.*)

JAMES: He liked it? He must have liked it!

FRANK: Why not? Look who directed it.

JAMES: Please, don't give me Frank Finger. You're talking to someone who actually sat through his all-male *Wild Duck*.

FRANK: I'm Frank Finger.

JAMES: And it was wonderful, just wonderful. So you're Frank Finger.

(The bedroom door opens. JULIA BUDDER *is seen on the landing calling over her shoulder to some guests on the floor below.)*

JULIA: Thank you! Isn't it exciting? I won't be a moment.

FRANK: *(Tossing the purloined antique box to* JAMES*)* I'll tell Peter what you thought of his play.

JAMES: I'll deny every word of it.

*(*JULIA *comes into the bedroom just as* FRANK *is on his way out.)*

JULIA: Congratulations, Frank.

FRANK: I don't want to hear! I don't want to know! *(*FRANK *is gone.)*

JAMES: There she is!

JULIA: I'm sorry.

JAMES: Congratulations, darling. How does it feel to have the biggest hit on Broadway since *Virginia Woolf?*

JULIA: You really think so?

JAMES: Not only is Julia Budder the luckiest producer on Broadway, she's also the prettiest.

JULIA: I have never been so embarrassed in my entire life.

JAMES: What happened?

JULIA: This!

*(*SHE *raises her skirt to reveal a pair of men's galoshes under her evening gown.)*

I've had them on all evening. I was so excited, I completely forget.

JAMES: So what. Darling, this is your night. You can take the dress off and keep the boots on. It's opening night, anything goes. You can do, say or feel anything you want.

*(*HE *will quickly be worried he said this.* JULIA *lets out a scream. Actually, it is more of a happy squeal.* SHE *even twirls herself around a time or two.* JAMES *looks at her with some amazement and much impatience.)*

JULIA: I did it. I did it. I did it. I'm a real live Broadway producer. You really think we have a chance?

JAMES: *(Sticking out his hand)* Dinner at Lutece.

JULIA: *(Without a moment's hesitation)* You're on. (SHE *shakes his hand.)* You heard Stewart Kling?

JAMES: Stewart Kling?

JULIA: He reviews for Channel 11 or 9 or . . . he was just on.

JAMES: Stewart Klein, Channel 5.

JULIA: That's him. You didn't watch?

JAMES: Thanks to your director.

JULIA: *(Taking off her mink coat)* Frank just has a phobia about reviews. I don't know why. His are always good. *(Shaking her head at it all)* Irving Berlin said it best: "There's no business like the one we're in."

JAMES: What did he say?

JULIA: "There's no business like—"

JAMES: Stewart Klein.

JULIA: I'll never forget it. My first review. It's engraved right here in great big letters. "Good solid theater."

JAMES: "Good solid theater?"

JULIA: You have to imagine it blown up.

JAMES: "Good solid theater."

JULIA: To tell you the truth, I was hoping for something with a little more oomph in it myself, but coming from him our press agent says it's a rave.

JAMES: Who's your press agent?

JULIA: Buzz, Buzz Something. *(Heading for bathroom)*

JAMES: Buzz Something?

JULIA: He's tops in his field. Hello, Torch. Mummy's home, darling. We were a bad boy tonight. James, would you bring me Torch's Yummies? They're in the silver dish on the coffee table.

(SHE goes back into the bathroom. A strong reaction from JAMES, who had been unknowingly eating TORCH's Yummies throughout his telephone conversation with the Coast. JAMES

brings JULIA *the Yummies, then pours himself another glass of champagne as* JULIA *comes out of the bathroom.)*

JAMES: Gus said you wanted to speak to me?

JULIA: Just let me collect myself. The hospital was a nightmare.

JAMES: So he told me. What happened exactly?

JULIA: Well, first Elliott gets mugged in the men's room at Sardi's. No one gets mugged at the men's room at Sardi's. It's never happened in their entire history and they're not a new restaurant. Thank God, they caught him.

JAMES: Who was it?

JULIA: Just some radical busboy. And then Torch bites Arlene Francis and it's off to Mount Sinai with *her*. I said to her, "Relax, Arlene, he just wants to sniff you." People don't know how to behave around dogs, horses either for that matter. I'm not budging from this house again tonight. Have you seen that mob down there?

*(*SHE *has caught her breath by now.)*

JAMES: No, But I'd like to.

JULIA: I don't know half of them. I think I saw Candice Bergen in the library. I used to listen to her father. I'm sure she did too. I said to one woman, "Excuse me, you look just like Marilyn Horne." She said, "I am Marilyn Horne."

JAMES: Oh, Jackie's here? Come on, I'll introduce you.

JULIA: I hate to do this to you but I'm very worried about Peter.

JAMES: What's wrong?

JULIA: This. *(*SHE *produces a sealed envelope.)* Just before the play tonight, I was backstage with the actors, giving them their ashtrays, when the stage manager handed me this note.

JAMES: May I?

JULIA: I had to promise not to read it until after the reviews were in.

JAMES: And so you opened it at once?

JULIA: Of course not. But now that there's no sign of him, I'll never forgive myself if anything happens to him.

JAMES: *(His hand out for the note)* Julia.

JULIA: But James, I promised.

JAMES: I didn't. *(HE takes the note and tears it open.)*

JULIA: If it's bad news, I don't want to hear it.

JAMES: *(Reading rather quickly; the party still beckons.)* "Dear Julia, Thank you for producing my play. I know it cost you a lot of money, none of which you may ever see again."

JULIA: The money! As if I cared about that.

JAMES: "And thank you for your beautiful opening-night gift. I have always wanted a handmade ashtray with the name of one of my plays on it."

JULIA: I had Little Elliott make everyone in the cast an ashtray with the name of the play and opening date on it.

JAMES: Little Elliott?

JULIA: Our eight-year-old.

JAMES: I think Peter's being sarcastic.

JULIA: Oh, no, they're really quite lovely. Look.

(JAMES looks at it a beat, then resumes with the letter.)

JAMES: "I wish you the best. I even wish Frank break a leg."

JULIA: That's a theatrical expression. It means good luck.

JAMES: What does he mean "even"?

JULIA: You should've heard some of the names Frank called him during rehearsal. Failure. Has-been. Hack.

JAMES: No!

JULIA: Loser. Fake. Phony. Written out.

JAMES: I get the picture.

JULIA: He said I was just an amateur, dilettante, rich bitch.

JAMES: Why did you stand for it?

JULIA: I didn't. My husband said, "You can't speak to my wife like that," and he punched him right in the mouth.

JAMES: Good for Elliott.

JULIA: You don't understand. Frank punched Elliott. He knocked him out and then barred him from the theater.

JAMES: As the producer you should have done something.

JULIA: I'd already been barred from the theater.

JAMES: This play sounds like a total nightmare for you from the first day of rehearsal right up until tonight.

JULIA: It's been bliss. Sheer creative bliss.

JAMES: "As for me, my dearest Julia (and I love you like a mother)—"

JULIA: And I love him like a son.

JAMES: "I don't think I can face anyone, most of all you, if I let us down tonight. If anything happens to me, it will be an accident and you are in no major way to blame."

JULIA: *(A knife cutting through her)* Major!

JAMES: "Goodbye for now. Remember me a little bit. And good luck with the Lanford Wilson."

JULIA: A new play I've optioned.

JAMES: "P.S. I still wish you'd given me that turntable in the second act." *(HE looks up)* For this we're missing the party of the year?

JULIA: Where *is* he then?

JAMES: Darling, Peter is a genius at theatrics. You've heard of a late entrance? It's an old stunt. Believe me, I do it all the time.

JULIA: I hope you're right.
(GUS has entered with a pile of coats.) There you are, Fred.

GUS: It's Gus.

JULIA: I'm sorry. Gus. Who do all those coats belong to?

GUS: *La Cage Aux Folles.*

JULIA: I don't remember inviting *La Cage Aux Folles.*

GUS: Everybody's asking for you down there.

JULIA: We're just on our way down. *(Calling to JAMES)* James?
(But now it's JAMES who is transfixed. HE is reading the other side of PETER's note.)

GUS: They're all saying you've got a big, big hit, Mrs. Budder.

JULIA: From your lips to God's ears. Thank you, Gus. *(GUS goes.)* James?

JAMES: "P.S. The play never really had a chance without James Wicker in it. Of course, he was a son of a bitch not to have done it and I wish him and his fucking series a sudden and violent death. No hard feelings, Jim, you miserable no-talent fruit, but you will rot in hell for this. P.P.S. Believe it or not, I love you. The Nipper."
(There is a pause.)

JULIA: You call him The Nipper?

JAMES: Just a nickname I had for him.

JULIA: Had?

JAMES: Have, have!

JULIA: I'm sure he doesn't mean that side of the note either.

JAMES: "No hard feelings, you miserable no-talent fruit."

JULIA: You? No-talent? That's ridiculous.

JAMES: You certainly came off a hell of a lot better than I did.

(GUS enters with coats. JULIA takes galoshes and bag into bathroom.)

GUS: They're having the time of their lives down there. Lena Horne just finished singing *Stormy Weather*, and Beverly Sills burst into something from *Faust*. I was hoping maybe I could sing something tonight.

JULIA: Sing, dear? Sing what?

GUS: A song. You know, audition.

JULIA: I don't see why not. *(To JAMES)* I'll only be a moment.

JAMES: Julia!

JULIA: I only use Equity members when I entertain. I believe we of the theater should extend a helping hand whenever we can.

(SHE is heading towards the piano.)

What are you going to sing for us, Gus?

GUS: *Raindrops Keep Falling upon My Head*.

JULIA: One of my favorites. What key?

(Seating herself at the piano, SHE flashes GUS her most radiant smile and gives him a tonic chord for his song. HE has a big

booming voice. After a moment or two of this torture, JAMES *gets to his feet. The phone starts ringing.)*

My very most private number. It could only be Elliott. I won't be a moment.

(SHE goes to the phone. GUS continues to sing, turning all his attention to JAMES *now.)*

Darling, how are you? . . .

JAMES: *(To* GUS *as* HE *ushers him out of the room)* Wonderful, just wonderful. *(Towards the phone)* Your wife's got a big fat hit on her hands, Elliott!

JULIA: *(Into phone)* Jimmy Wicker. Darling, I've been talking to Howard and he thinks we should pull out of the resort in Santo Domingo while we're ahead and consider those condominiums in Nova Scotia . . . Mmmmmmm . . . Mmmmmmm . . . Mmmmmmm.

(JAMES has started browsing through a pile of play scripts that are stacked on a coffee table in front of him.)

JAMES: *(Reading aloud) Bluestocking* by Caroline Comstock.

(IRA DREW comes into the bedroom. HE *has a furtive air. There are dandruff flakes on the lapel of his ill-fitting tuxedo.)*

At rise: nothing. Ten seconds of this.

JULIA: That's exactly what I told him.

JAMES: The lights come up on a green chair. It is empty. A woman screams in the distance. [Or is it a woman?] We hear a flourish of wind. [Or is it wind?]

(IRA leans over JAMES.*)*

IRA: How do you like it so far?

(JAMES jumps at the intrusion.)

I'm sorry. I'm waiting for Mrs. Budder.

JAMES: I'm afraid this room's off limits.

IRA: I just need a quick word with her.

(HE gestures towards JAMES.*)*

And talk about killing two birds with one stone!

JAMES: I beg your pardon?

IRA: I gave you a wonderful notice once.

JAMES: You did?

IRA: That little Lorca play at the Theatre De Lys, remember?

JAMES: No, that was Gordon Small.

IRA: Gordon Small, of course. Wonderful actor.

JAMES: Wasn't he?

IRA: Wasn't? What do you mean, wasn't?

JAMES: Is. I meant is. At least I assume he's still around. Gordon hasn't worked much lately. Ever since the Theatre De Lys, in fact.

IRA: *Uncle Vanya* in Chicago?

JAMES: No, I don't think . . .

IRA: James Wacker, of course. *(Remembering his quote)* "James Wacker is a consummate actor. His Mercutio was a pip." I never forget what I write about anyone.

JAMES: Wicker.

IRA: Hmm?

JAMES: James Wicker.

IRA: I know that.

JAMES: You said Wacker.

IRA: No! *(Starting to laugh)* Wacker! *(It's growing.)* That's terrible. *(It's out of control already.)* Wacker!

JAMES: And you are?

IRA: I'm sorry. I just assumed. Ira Drew.

JAMES: *The* Ira Drew?

IRA: There's another?

(JAMES offers some Yummies to IRA.)

JULIA: Darling, this isn't going to affect our trip. Let me write it down or I'll forget. Golf clubs.

JAMES: Wasn't the play wonderful tonight?

IRA: You'll have to wait two weeks to find out what I thought *and* it'll cost you two-fifty.

JAMES: Two-fifty for a magazine!

IRA: Thirty-five dollars for an orchestra seat.

JAMES: *(Absolving himself)* I'm on television now. I'm free. Besides, critics don't pay for their tickets.

IRA: This one does. The League of Producers barred me from the press list. "Too vicious." I call them as I see them.

JAMES: You've always been very good to me.

IRA: Television? I wondered what happened to you.

JULIA: *(The house phone is buzzing her.)* They're calling me from downstairs. I'll have to get back to you . . .

JAMES: Her husband.

IRA: He invented toilet paper?

JAMES: Perfected it. Rich as Croesus.

IRA: I can see why.

JULIA: *(Still on the phone)* I love you, too. Stop, you're making me blush . . . I said stop, you're making me blush!
(SHE hangs up.)
That man! *(It's clear SHE adores him.)*

JAMES: This is Ira Drew, Julia.

JULIA: *(Brightly)* Hello!

JAMES: *The* Ira Drew.

JULIA: *(A merry laugh)* There's another? *(Into the house phone)* No, I didn't invite the cast of Annie. Tell them to go away. I'm sorry but they can't come in.
(SHE hangs up.)
More crashers. I'm sorry, Mr. Drew.

IRA: I'll come right to the point. I really shouldn't be up here with you at all.

JAMES: Excuse me, Julia, I'll be downstairs.

IRA: Please, stay. This concerns the both of you. You've been sent a new play to consider, Mrs. Budder, a certain *Bluestocking*.

JULIA: Yes, I have. It came this morning.

JAMES: I was just leafing through it.

IRA: *Bluestocking* is the best American play I've come across in a long time. It has humor, depth, wit, wisdom, compassion, truth, a small cast, and one set.

JULIA: It sounds like a producer's dream.

JAMES: Next thing you'll be telling us is you wrote it.

IRA: Caroline Comstock wrote *Bluestocking*! We've all heard the same sordid rumors about our relationship. I can't help them. But Caroline is only my protégée, nothing less and nothing more. I'm merely Svengali to her Trilby, Pygmalion to her Galatea, John Derek to her Bo.

JULIA: Why are you telling us this?

IRA: We need new faces in the theater. New voices, new visions. Caroline's day will come, Mrs. Budder. I'd like to see yours come with her.

JULIA: Thank you, but for tonight I'm concentrating on Peter Austin's day.

IRA: You haven't much time. Even as we speak, the Shuberts are dickering for an option. David Merrick is—
   (HE *turns suddenly as* GUS *enters with a new pile of coats.*)

GUS: *Cats* and *42nd Street* are here.
   (IRA *makes a "Sssshh" motion.* THEY *all look at* GUS. HE *dumps the coats on the bed.* THEY *continue to look at him.*)
   Don't pay me no mind, Miss Scarlett!
   (HE *goes, but not without some fanfare.*)

IRA: Can he be trusted?

JULIA: He's bonded, if that means anything.

IRA: No one must ever know of this meeting. It is highly unethical. Like a weekend in the Hamptons together, it would compromise the three of us.

JAMES: What did I do?

IRA: *Bluestocking* was written for you, Mr. Wicker.

JAMES: Two minutes ago you wondered what happened to me.

IRA: Wait'll I tell Miss Comstock I've found you. I place my reputation in your hands.
   (HE *is bowing out backwards.*)
   Thank you for your consideration, Mrs. Budder.

JULIA: Thank you for your inside lead, Mr. Drew.

JAMES: I'm always looking for the right vehicle!

IRA: It awaits you!
   (HE *is gone, falling downstairs.*)

JULIA: Mr. Drew, are you alright?

IRA: *(Offstage)* Fine.

JAMES: Certainly he's the last person I would have expected to see here tonight.

JULIA: I didn't invite him. He came with Lina Wertmuller.

JAMES: That's a fun couple!

(HE *puts down the play script.*)

"The American theater would be a better place today if Peter Austin's parents had smothered him in his crib."

JULIA: What a horrible thing to say.

JAMES: Ira Drew's review of *Flashes*. I just hope he doesn't run into Peter down there.

(PETER AUSTIN *runs into the bedroom.* HE *is in evening tails and outer coat.* GUS *is in pursuit.*)

JULIA: It's all right, Gus.

GUS: He ran right by me.

JULIA: It's the nipper.

GUS: Who?

JULIA: Mr. Austin wrote *The Golden Egg*.

GUS: Well why didn't he say so? Gus. Gus Washington, actor. (HE *goes.*)

PETER: I just hope the next young American playwright who has a play open on Broadway doesn't have the misfortune of walking into his opening-night party with Arthur Miller right behind him.

JULIA: Peter, what happened?

PETER: All my life I dreamed they'd yell "Author, Author!" when I got there. Instead what I got was "Arthur, Arthur!" He just won another Nobel Prize or something.

JAMES: Hello, Judas.

PETER: Is that who I think it is? You made it. You actually came.

JAMES: I wouldn't have missed this for anything.

PETER: Do you know who this is, Julia?

JULIA: Well of course I do.

JAMES: Then you're the first one this evening who does.

PETER: I love this man. I don't care who knows it. I love this person.

JAMES: Even though you wish him and his television series—

JULIA: James!

PETER: Maybe I can get through all this now. This means everything. Thanks, Jimmy.

(HE *hugs him.*)

JULIA: I wish I had my camera!

PETER: You look marvelous.

JAMES: Thank you.

PETER: Guess how many times I threw up today?

JULIA: I couldn't.

PETER: Actually leaned over the bowl and heaved my guts up?

JULIA: Is this a game?

PETER: Seven. Seven whole times. That's what this night means to me. Well ask James, Jimmy, Jim, Jimbo.

JAMES: Just be careful. This is a new tux.

PETER: Where are you staying?

JAMES: The Sherry.

JULIA: Peter, you had us all worried. Where have you been?

PETER: You promise not to laugh?

JULIA: Of course not.

PETER: I've been out there growing up.

JULIA: I'm going to cry.

PETER: No, I mean it.

JULIA: So do I. That's wonderful.

PETER: You know where I spent our opening? In that bar across the street.

JULIA: I didn't know there was a bar across the street.

PETER: From the theater.

JULIA: For a moment . . . ! My heart.

PETER: It felt like I'd written the longest first act in theater history.

JAMES: I know.

PETER: Thank God for Dolores Guber. She was in the original production of *Panama Hattie*. I told her I had a play opening. That play. "Welcome to the theater, kid," she said. I told her I was already in the theater. You know, off-Broadway, off-off. "They ain't theater," she said and nodded towards the Barrymore. "That's theater." And then it was intermission. I saw you, Jimmy, talking to Bob Fosse. He was bent over double. God, you are a funny man. I wanted to cross the street and join you. Instead I threw up. I walked over to St. Patrick's but it was closed so I just walked around the theater district. So many theaters dark. Marquees left up because nothing new has come in. It's scary. I felt such a responsibility. I saw that goddamn new hotel.

JAMES: Terrible, just terrible.

PETER: They tore down three theaters for that? *Streetcar* opened at the same theater we did tonight. December 3, 1947. My birthday. How could you tear that down? By now it was after the play and everyone was gone. Our marquee was still lit. I think that was the first time I really saw it. Before that I was always too nervous. *The Golden Egg*, a new play by Peter Austin. It's a beautiful marquee, Julia. Downtown we never had that. Don't believe anyone who says it isn't nice. And then someone inside turned the lights off and we went dark. It was like we never existed. It's only a play. I grabbed the first cab I saw, it was a lulu! Asked them to drop me off here, then go to the *Times* and wait for the review. This is where I want to be and the people I most want to be with, if not for the rest of my life, at least until the *Times* is out.

JULIA: Next play I promise you that turntable.

PETER: Next play I'm going to want two turntables.

JULIA: Done! That's the Peter I like to see.

JAMES: Are you grown up? Can we go down now?

JULIA: James . . .

JAMES: I cry at a red hat.

PETER: I wanted you up there so bad tonight.

JAMES: Jack's marvelous.

PETER: I know.

JAMES: Not that marvelous.

PETER: They're already talking about Redford for the film.

JAMES: What of?

(JULIA *is tiptoeing towards the bathroom.*)
Julia!

JULIA: I won't be a moment. (SHE *makes "reconciliation" gestures to* JAMES. PETER *doesn't see them.*)

PETER: I guess I have to go down there and take my bows.

JAMES: You deserve them. It's quite a party. It looks like all Broadway is down there.

PETER: What's left of it.

JAMES: The opening night of *Flashes* we were taking bows in that Spanish restaurant on Bleecker Street. What was it called?

PETER: I got so drunk. It's a video rental shop now.

JAMES: The Jai Alai Restaurant.

PETER: Opening night of *Flashes* really was more about you than me.

JAMES: The first hysteria maybe. It put us both on the map.

PETER: I wish it could have been the two of us again tonight.

JAMES So do I. Peter, I wish you the best possible success with this play.

PETER: You really liked it?

JAMES: Peter, I'm the last one to ask. I was a middle-aged, not Robert Redford-looking character actor, one of thousands in this city. I would have gone on having ten lines in each act in New York and forty lines in stock for the rest of my life. Maybe once, just once, I would have played Willy Loman or Falstaff in a city my friends and my agent wouldn't mind coming to. And I would have gone on thinking I was lucky. Then you sent me *Flashes*. Make no mistake: I knew I was very, very lucky.

PETER: Then I'm very glad I saw you do those ten lines in that awful play at the Cherry Lane.

JAMES: So am I. And it was fourteen lines. I was on a roll that season.

PETER: Jack was okay tonight?

JAMES: Jack was fine.

PETER: Now he was just "fine"!

(JULIA *opens the bathroom door.*)

JULIA: May I come out?

PETER: May we go down?

JAMES: Does anybody remember what food tastes like?

(VIRGINIA opens the door to the bedroom and comes in.)

VIRGINIA: There you are! Where the fuck have you been? All my friends want to meet you.

PETER: Look at that *faccia*. Is this a star or is this a star?

VIRGINIA: Was I good tonight?

PETER: You're always good. Tonight you were fantastic.

VIRGINIA: I didn't want to let you down.

PETER: You didn't. Other than . . .

VIRGINIA: What?

PETER: Nothing.

VIRGINIA: Tell me.

PETER: It's so small.

JULIA: When she dropped the bottle.

VIRGINIA: I didn't drop the fucking bottle. It fucking slipped. What?

PETER: You know that line in the second act?

VIRGINIA: What line?

PETER: Where you're supposed to say "It's about time" to Jack when he enters in the second scene.

VIRGINIA: It's one of my highlights. What's the matter? I said it, didn't I?

PETER: You said. "There you are."

VIRGINIA: So?

PETER: Instead of "It's about time." But no matter, no matter. I don't even know why I mentioned it. It's only a line.

VIRGINIA: So bring me up on Equity charges.

PETER: You asked me.

VIRGINIA: Please, I insist.

PETER: I'm sorry.

VIRGINIA: Playwrights!

PETER: Actors!

JULIA: The theater!

PETER: Is word perfect asking so much, Lord?

JAMES: Is a little nourishment?

VIRGINIA: I'm sorry Peter, tomorrow night it'll be "There you are."

PETER: "It's about time"!

(PETER *and* VIRGINIA *hug.)*

VIRGINIA: It doesn't get any better than this!

PETER: I hope not!

VIRGINIA: Hey, quit shaking!

PETER: An evening like this is every playwright's rite of passage. Look to your laurels, Mr. Miller, here comes the next generation!

JULIA: Bravo! Bravo!

(PETER *and* VIRGINIA *exit the bedroom.)*

JAMES: As Bette Davis once said, "Who do you have to fuck to get something to eat around here?"

JULIA: Me, darling!

(JULIA *and* JAMES *make ready to leave the bedroom as* FRANK *comes into the room.)*

FRANK: I should have played poker in Tribeca with Robert Wilson and Pina Bausch. If one more person tells me I am a genius I am going to freak out.

JULIA: But you are a genuis, darling.

FRANK: I am not.

JULIA: I'm sorry but you are. That's why we hired you.

FRANK: They only hired me because I always get good reviews.

JAMES: That's a pretty good reason.

JULIA: And you're from Chicago, darling. Let's not forget that.

FRANK: I was born in New Jersey.

JULIA: We don't talk about that. You came to us from Chicago.

FRANK: I don't know what I'm doing!

JULIA: You don't?

FRANK: You wait and see: I'll win a Tony for this.

JULIA: Well I certainly hope so.

JAMES: May I see your lighter?

FRANK: Why am I smoking? I don't smoke . . . I ate red meat tonight.

(HE *tosses* JAMES *his lighter.)*

JAMES: This is my lighter. Carol Burnett gave it to me.

FRANK: Prove it.

JAMES: Right there, the engraving. "All my love, Carol."

FRANK: Sorry. Carol Burnett gave it to me.

JAMES: Prove it.

FRANK: Right there, the engraving. "All my love, Carol."

(HE *pockets the lighter.)*

JULIA: Maybe it is his lighter, James.

JAMES: A while ago I caught him stealing this box.

JULIA: Please, don't handle that. It's extremely delicate.

FRANK: It really means that much to you, man? Here, you can have mine.

JAMES: I don't want yours.

FRANK: See? You admitted it.

(HE *tosses the lighter to* JAMES.)

JAMES: Can we go down now, Julia?

FRANK: I am in despair, people.

JULIA: What kind of despair, Frank?

JAMES: *(A whimper)* Oh my God!

FRANK: Deep despair. Life despair. Everything despair.

JULIA: This should be the biggest night of your life. A debut on Broadway at your age. How old are you?

JAMES: Julia, please.

FRANK: The emperor isn't wearing any clothes!

JAMES: *(Anticipating/mimicking* JULIA*)* What emperor, darling?

FRANK: This emperor. I'm a fake. My work's fake. I can't go on like this—the critics' darling—knowing that it's all a fake.

JULIA: Try to hold on just one more time.

FRANK: I've had fourteen hits in a row Off-Broadway and thirty-seven Obies. I want a flop. I need a flop. Somebody, tell me, please: when is it my turn? I'm no good. You've got to believe me. I'm no good.

JAMES: We believe you. Julia, now can we go down—?

FRANK: Hold me.

JULIA: We can't leave him like this.

FRANK: Do you know the only flops I've ever had? At drama school. Nobody liked my production of anything. My Art Deco *Three Sisters*. My spoken *Aida*. My gay *Godot*. But what got me expelled was my *Titus Andronicus*. I did the whole thing in mime. No dialogue. No poetry. No Shakespeare.

JULIA: What did it have?

FRANK: Blood bags. Every time somebody walked on stage: splat! They got hit with a big blood bag. God, it was gross.

JULIA: It sounds interesting.

FRANK: It was terrible. But at least everyone said it was terrible. I'm pulling the same stunts in New York and everybody says it's brilliant.

JULIA: It is brilliant.

FRANK: I hate it! God I miss Yale.

JAMES: I'm sure Yale misses you.

FRANK: *(Emptying his pockets)* I don't want these things. Honest I don't. Please, don't leave them around.

JULIA: Frank, that's my good pepper shaker!

JAMES: May I see that?

(JULIA *and* JAMES *are amazed at the size and diversity of* FRANK's *haul.*)

FRANK: You know what my analyst says? "Put it back, Frank." Seventy-five bucks an hour and that's all she says. "Put it back, Frank."

JULIA: *(Reading an engraving)* To Dr. Mildred Sturgeon, Ph.D. Who's Mildred?

FRANK: My fucking analyst! I wanna know why I pick it up in the first place.

JAMES: *(Reading from a cigarette case)* "Mary. You are the *Sound of Music*. All our love. Dick and Oscar." He's a syndicate. *(VIRGINIA comes into the bedroom.)*

VIRGINIA: That fucking Channel 7. That fucking faggot dyke hermaphrodite transsexual whatever the hell you call it they have for a critic.

JAMES: We missed Katie Kelly's review! *(To FRANK)* This is all your fault.

(HE turns on the television.)

I fly in six thousand miles for an opening night and I can't even get the goddamn reviews.

TV ANNOUNCER: In other news tonight, a Boeing 747 jet-liner filled to capacity—

(JAMES hits TV "muting" switch.)

JAMES: *(To FRANK)* I hope you're pleased with yourself.

VIRGINIA: I just told a roomful of people to shut the fuck up so they could hear Katie Kelly say "Virginia Noyes stinks."

JAMES: I'm sure she didn't say "Virginia Noyes stinks."

VIRGINIA: "Virginia Noyes stinks." You could hear a pin drop, she was smiling when she said it: "Virginia Noyes stinks."

FRANK: *(Going to comfort her)* Ginny.

VIRGINIA: You cast me!

FRANK: The best move I ever made with this play.

JULIA: Frank's right. You were wonderful, darling. No matter what happens with the critics, you must never forget that. You were wonderful.

VIRGINIA: Do I know you?

JULIA: It's Julia, darling, your producer.

VIRGINIA: Oh, yeah, right, hi, thanks. You want a hit? *(Handing JULIA a joint.)*

JULIA: Don't ask silly questions. Of course I want a hit. Everyone at this party does. What did she say about the play?

VIRGINIA: "Good solid theater."

JULIA: That's exactly what what's-his-name said.

VIRGINIA: Who?

JULIA: The one who reviews for Channel something-or-other-I-don't-know. Until tonight I never heard of these people.

(GUS *appears with a new load of yellow slickers.*)

JAMES: Don't tell me. *Singin' in the Rain.*

GUS: Is Felda Toeshoe anybody?

JULIA: Who?

GUS: That's what I thought.

JAMES: Everybody in the theater is somebody. I think that's probably the most pretentious thing I've ever said.

(PETER *comes into the bedroom.*)

PETER: They don't have a clue who I am down there. Colleen Dewhurst thought I was help and asked me to bring her a gin spritzer.

There he is! My genius director. I'm difficult to work with and you're close to impossible. It's a marriage made in Heaven and I'm sending you my next play.

FRANK: Next time I'll cut all the stage directions.

PETER: Next time I'll let you do all the rewrites. Why is that television not on? It's almost time. Has Buzz called?

(HE *is already dialing the number.*)

He should have some word on the *Times* by now. I guess you heard we've already gotten two raves?

JULIA: We did? That's wonderful. Who from?

PETER: Stewart Klein and Katie Kelly.

JULIA: They weren't raves, dear. They said we were "good solid theater."

PETER: That's pretty damn good, Julia. What do you want, blood?

JULIA: Buzz promised me the moon!

PETER: *(Into phone)* What are you telling this woman, Buzz?

VIRGINIA: Buzz Hepburn. The asshole press agent.

JULIA: He's at the top of his heap, Virginia.

VIRGINIA: Some heap.

PETER: *(Into phone)* Forget all that, Buzz. Any word on the *Times*? You're kidding! *(To the* OTHERS*)* He heard it's an out-and-out rave! He went crazy for us! *(Into phone)* You're sure? *(To* OTHERS*)* He bribed a copy boy. *(Into phone)* That's great, Buzz. *(To* JAMES*)* Channel 2 is coming up.

(JAMES *will get the television set ready.*)

He says it's going to be unanimous.

JULIA: You see, Virginia?

VIRGINIA: I hope he's right.

PETER: Thanks, Buzz, I really appreciate that.

(HE *hangs up.*)

He says this play is proof you can still write a serious play for Broadway and have a house in the Hamptons as well. Actually, I've got my eye on something in Nantucket. I've always felt very close to Melville.

(HE *shivers.*)

JULIA: What's the matter?

PETER: If we have a smash hit on our hands, I hope I can handle it.

(FRANK *makes a retching noise.*)

Better than you anyway. You know what I'm going to do with my first royalty check? Buy this one four hundred of his own Mark Cross pens.

(JAMES *has turned up the television sound.*)

JAMES: Channel 2. Here we go.

(JAMES *waves the remote control at* FRANK.*)

I'm hanging on to this.

TV: Hi, theater lovers. This is Kevin Kunst filling in for our regular critic who's out with a bug. That was no bug, he's gonna tell me. That was my wife.

(*There is much hilarity in the television studio; almost none in* JULIA*'s bedroom.*)

JULIA: What are we watching?

PETER: Channel 2, Good Ol' Boy News.

TV: It was quite a kick for me to cover a big-time Broadway opening. I was sitting next to award-winning director Bob Fosse. I asked him what he thought. "Forget what I thought," Mr. Fosse laughed. "Let me tell you what—"
(JAMES turns off the volume.)

JAMES: I'm sorry. I never did know how these things work.

PETER: Give me that.
(HE turns the sound back on. Again, there is much hilarity in the television studio.)

TV: . . . "Gobble, gobble!" Anyway, for what it's worth, I thought Peter Austin's new play was the kind of good old-fashioned play nobody writes anymore except Peter Austin. But what do I know?

PETER: Not very much. That is the face of an imbecile.

TV: This is Kevin Kunst. Channel 2, Good Ol' Boy News.

TV: In other news tonight, and this is just in, a packed Roosevelt Island Cable Car—
(PETER turns the sound down.)

PETER: I'd call that mixed.

JULIA: I'd call it lousy. What did I ever do to Kevin Kunst? Who is he? What is he? How dare he?

VIRGINIA: You want a downer?

PETER: God, I want a cigarette.

VIRGINIA: Do the wires.

FRANK: I still don't believe it and I've seen it a hundred times.

JAMES: What does he have in there?

VIRGINIA: Little wire staples. When he presses them, they send a message to the nerve ends and he doesn't want to smoke.

JULIA: Acupuncture sounds horrible.

VIRGINIA: It's fucking fabulous. I used it to get off drugs.
(The phone rings. PETER will answer it. GUS enters with more coats.)

JULIA: Now who?

GUS: *The Iceman Cometh* and *Mavens.*

JULIA: *Mavens?*

JAMES: A new musical that's opening next month. They start previews this weekend.

JULIA: They've got some nerve. Didn't *Iceman* close?

VIRGINIA: Yes, but nobody's told them yet.

PETER: Stop the presses! He's got new quotes. "Hats off and Hallelujah. Peter Austin has written the best American play since *The Man Who Had Three Arms*. Virginia Noyes lights up Broadway."

VIRGINIA: You bet your fucking A I do!

PETER: "Frank Finger's direction is superb, taut, and just plain perfect."

FRANK: That's it?

PETER: "Along with David Mamet, Sam Shepard, Michael Weller, Albert Innaurato, David Rabe, John Guare, Wendy Wasserstein, Tina Howe, Christopher Durang, Ted Talley, David Henry Hwang, Beth Henley, Lanford Wilson, Marsha Norman, A.R. Gurney, Jr., Wallace Shawn, Ntozake Shange and Hugh Golden . . ."

THE OTHERS: Who?

PETER: "Peter Austin is in that small handful of our more promising young American Dramatists."

JULIA: Amen.

PETER: The *Newark News*. Thanks, Buzz. How much longer before we get Rich? Very funny. Another half hour? (HE *hangs up.*) We're a smash in Newark.

JULIA: That was a wonderful review.

PETER: Not if you're David Mamet, John Guare, Sam . . .
(HE *sees a new picture on the television set.*)
Channel 7!
(HE *turns up the sound.*)

TV: For what it's worth, I'd call this the best American play of the season hands down.
(THEY *all cheer and hug.*)

VIRGINIA: Right on!

JULIA: I hope Elliott is watching. He had doubts.

JAMES: No!

JULIA: Real doubts.

TV: In the excellent cast, Jane Bergere is brilliant as the shepherdess.

PETER: What shepherdess?

VIRGINIA: Who the fuck is Jane Bergere?

TV: In short, at least in this workshop production, Robert Patrick's new play scores a clear home run. Back to you, Carmen.

TV: Two-time Academy Award winner singer/actress Barbra Streisand was found—

(PETER *turns off the sound.*)

JAMES: Something about Barbra!

PETER: Thank God we know the *Times* is a rave.

JAMES: Something happened to Barbra Streisand!

PETER: The television didn't like *Flashes* either.

JAMES: Doesn't anybody care?

PETER: At this point, five years ago, we were all suicidal.

JAMES: I'm still suicidal. Give me that.

(HE *takes the remote control.*)

PETER: I don't know about anyone else but I am going to have some of that gorgeous food I saw down there. Julia?

JULIA: I don't think so.

PETER: James?

JAMES: I want to find out what happened to Barbra.

PETER: Ginny? Frank?

VIRGINIA: Once was enough. If you see Paul Verrano, tell him I'm up here.

FRANK: Is that who you're with? He's gay.

VIRGINIA: I know. Who are you with?

FRANK: No one.

VIRGINIA: So look who's talking.

JAMES: I give up.

PETER: It can't be that important.

JAMES: Anything that happens to Barbara is important.

PETER: I want you to do me a favor down there. Ask Walter
  Kerr what he thought.

JAMES: Are you crazy?

PETER: I have a feeling he liked it.

JAMES: He never has before.

PETER: I had a mass said for them.

JAMES: Peter.

PETER: They know I had a mass said for them. I sent a mass
  card. *(PETER leaves.)*

JAMES: You know I wouldn't put it past him.
  *(There is the sound of window breaking from behind the closed
  drapes.)*
  What was that?

JULIA: It sounded like the window.
  *(JULIA, JAMES, FRANK, and VIRGINIA go to the window and
  pull back the drapes. There is a broken pane, shattered glass on
  the carpet, and a snowball.)*
  Do you see anyone?

JAMES: Across the street. *(Yelling at them)* What's the matter
  with you? Are you crazy? Look out! *(Another snowball is
  thrown.)* A snowball! This would never happen in California.

FRANK: Who are they? Street toughs?

JULIA: It's the cast of *Annie.*

JAMES: Are you sure?

JULIA: I'm a principal investor. *(There is a commotion from
  downstairs.)* Now what?

JAMES: It sounds like a brawl.

JULIA: All I did was produce a play on Broadway and give
  an opening night party!

JAMES: Welcome to the theater.

JULIA: What's happening down there?
  (JULIA and JAMES leave the bedroom.)

FRANK: You want to split?

VIRGINIA: If I had any sense I would.
  *(IRA DREW rushes in. HE is holding his mouth with a
  handkerchief.)*

IRA: Bathroom?

(FRANK *indicates the bathroom.* IRA *enters it.* HE *is promptly set upon by* TORCH.)

FRANK: Is that who I think it is?

VIRGINIA: If it is, score one for our side.

JULIA: Where is he? Where's Mr. Drew?

(*There is the sound of a gunshot from the bathroom.* JULIA *screams.* FRANK *and* VIRGINIA *jump.*)

FRANK: What the fuck was that?

JULIA: Noooooooooooooooooooooo!

(*The bathroom door opens.* IRA *comes out. His pants legs are in shreds.* HE *is still dabbing at his mouth with his handkerchief.* HE *carries a pistol.*)

IRA: I guess that's your dog.

JULIA: Murderer. Mur-der-er!

(SHE *hurls herself at* IRA *and beats him with her fists.*)

IRA: I didn't shoot him. He's perfectly all right.

JULIA: He'd better be. Torch! Darling Torch!

IRA: Darling? It's the last remaining Hound of the Baskervilles. Look at me.

FRANK: Is that thing real?

IRA: Don't worry. It's loaded with blanks.

(IRA *lets* FRANK *look at the pistol.*)

I had to start carrying it in self-defense.

(HE *takes the pistol back.*)

I'm Ira Drew. Good evening, Miss Noyes. I enjoyed your performance. I liked your work, too, Mr. Finger, but then I always do. *Titus Andronicus. Splat.*

FRANK: Looks like somebody decked you.

IRA: Your playwright.

FRANK: Peter took a swing at you?

IRA: Mr. Austin took several swings at me. The next thing I knew I was on the floor and Linda Hunt was kicking me.

FRANK: This I gotta see.

IRA: You're too late. (*But* FRANK *is gone.*) That's right. Mr. Finger adores violence.

VIRGINIA: I guess that's it for your review.

IRA: Nothing is going to affect my review. Critics can't afford to hold petty grudges. Your playwright's only human, the little shit.

VIRGINIA: You just said—

IRA: Just because I think someone's a little shit doesn't mean I'm going to give him a bad review. My sole responsibility as a critic is to objectively evaluate what the little shit's written.

VIRGINIA: In print you describe yourself as a Humanist.

IRA: I am a Humanist. I just happen not to like most people! (HE *laughs.* JULIA *comes out of the bathroom.*) How is he?

JULIA: He'll be right up to apologize.

IRA: I meant Grendel in the cave.

JULIA: He's fine. I don't understand. He's never turned on anyone before. I'm so disappointed in him tonight. Thank God you missed. I don't know what I would have done.

VIRGINIA: So what did you think of the play tonight?

JULIA: Mr. Drew doesn't have to answer that question.

VIRGINIA: Why not?

JULIA: He's a critic. We have to wait to read what he writes. It's very rude to ask.

IRA: If you'd rather wait for my piece . . . !

VIRGINIA: He was going to tell us.

IRA: Besides, waiting for the *Times*, that's what tonight's all about. Who cares what a nonentity like me thinks.

JULIA: You're not a nonentity and you're very well thought of.

IRA: Not well enough apparently for a performance scheduled to begin this evening at 6:45 sharp to begin at 6:45 sharp because the critic from the *Times* wasn't in his seat.

JULIA: Well, with this blizzard . . .

IRA: It snows for all of us, Mrs. Budder. Then, just as I'm lighting another cigarette and wondering whether John Simon minds being so unpopular, a stretch cab pulls up, the *Times* pops out, and there's a stampede towards the theater. By the time I get to my seat, the play's already begun. I don't want Mr. Rich's job. [I'll take his seat location.] I just want to finish my cigarette. I am sounding petty.

JULIA: Nonsense. It's good for a producer to hear these things—!

IRA: All right! I am sick and tired of half the audience, every time there is a laugh line, turning around in their seats to see if he is laughing. I have been reviewing plays for eighteen years and no one has ever, not once, turned around in their seat to see if I were laughing.

JULIA: That's the saddest thing I ever heard.

IRA: I saw you peeping at him through the side exit curtains tonight, Mrs. Budder.

JULIA: I wasn't peeping at him, Mr. Drew. I swear to God, I wasn't peeping.

IRA: Don't deny it, Mrs. Budder.

JULIA: All right, yes, I was!

IRA: What am I? The Invisible Man?

VIRGINIA: You're one of the most vicious critics in New York.

IRA: Throw that in my face. I love the theater; it's what people are doing to it I can't stand.

JULIA: It's not on purpose.

VIRGINIA: "She reminds me of nothing so much as a female impersonator in search of a female to impersonate."

JULIA: What a dreadful thing to say about anyone.

IRA: I said that about Norma Bird in *The Sea Gull* at the Provincetown Playhouse in 1968. It's curious you remember that.

VIRGINA: I was Norma Bird in *The Sea Gull* at the Provincetown Playhouse in 1968.

JULIA: You changed your name?

VIRGINIA: After his review I changed my face.

IRA: I'm sorry. I had no idea I'd—

VIRGINIA: Face it, you don't like anything!

IRA: That's not true and a lot of good it does me when I do. Who of you remembers my rave review of *Windswept?*

JULIA: *Windswept?*

IRA: I said it was the best American play since *Leaf People.*

JULIA: *Leaf People?*

(PETER *enters with* FRANK.)

PETER: I'm sorry, Mr. Drew. Deeply and truly and terribly sorry.

IRA: Just as you're entitled to writing your plays, I'm entitled to my opinion of them.

PETER: (As THEY *shake hands*) Fair enough.

(PETER *drops to his knees, still holding* IRA's *hand.*)

Hear a playwright's prayer, Oh Lord. Listen to the humble plea of thy humble servant, Peter, descendant of Aeschylus, Shakespeare, Molière, Ibsen, Chekhov, O'Neill, and Pinter.

FRANK: What the hell is he doing?

PETER: Bless me and my meager skills with which I've only tried to amuse, intrigue, provoke, stimulate, and move You and an audience while creating believable characters in true-to-life situations which somehow illuminate the human experience.

JULIA: (Touched) Oh, Peter!

PETER: Bless thy humble producer-servant Julia.

JULIA: (Sinking to her knees) How lovely!

PETER: Bless all producers who put our plays on and keep them running, even when it means enormous financial sacrifice.

JULIA: I don't care about that, Peter, you know I don't.

PETER: Bless her and forgive her her choice of press agent.

VIRGINIA: You hear that, Julia?

PETER: Bless thy humble actress-servant, Virginia, who gave the performance of a lifetime tonight.

JULIA: Get down, Virginia!

PETER: Bless her unique timing, her wonderful voice, her way with a prop.

VIRGINIA: It slipped, Peter.

PETER: Bless her for being almost letter perfect in her part.

VIRGINIA: Will you lay off?

PETER: Bless thy humble director-servant, Frank.

FRANK: *(Self-conscious)* Oh, Christ.

PETER: Bless him for returning my raincoat, which so mysteriously vanished the second day of rehearsal. Bless him for his unbroken string of successes. Bless all directors with an unbroken string of successes.

(JAMES enters.)

JAMES: The food is wonderful . . .

PETER: Bless my best friend, James, thy humble television series star-servant, who had to turn my play down and so we came up with Jack, for whom everyone says there is a definite Tony nomination, if not award, in this. Bless Jack and his Tony nomination, it not award. Also bless James's series, which is rumored to be going off the air.

JAMES: Where did you hear that?

VIRGINIA: Liz Smith, *Live at Five.*

JULIA: Quiet!

(JAMES has gotten to his knees during this. Only IRA is still standing. HE is clearly opposed to joining the others on the floor, but PETER is really putting him on the spot.)

PETER: Bless thy humble critic-servant, Ira. Bless him for writing the one and only pan of my first play, *Flashes*, which all the other critics loved and made me rich and famous, which made him look like something of a fool and which is why I hit him.

(IRA is about to protest.)

Bless this good man, Lord. Bless my . . . dare I say it? . . . my newest friend. Bless all critics who mean well and are only trying to uphold the standards of the theater without knowing how truly hard it is to write a play. Shower them with the same mercy they deny others. And

bless the theater in which we all serve. Bless this ancient
art which is so superior to the movies.

(At some point during this IRA *will put on his yarmulke.)*

JULIA: The theater, yes!

(GUS has come upstairs and entered the bedroom.)

GUS: Mrs. Budder.

JULIA: Get down, Gus!

GUS: *(Kneeling)* I'm also supposed to be getting Lauren
Bacall her coat.

PETER: Bless thy humble servant-servant . . . what's your
name, love?

GUS: Gus.

PETER: Gus, who is bringing Betty Bacall's coat down to her.
Bless Betty. Bless all those people down there whose
happiness and approval means so much to me. Bless Hal
and Judy and Steve, Josh and Nedda, Betty and Adolph,
even dear Rex and poor Sylvia.

IRA: Who is Sylvia? Damn it, I fell for it.

PETER: And finally, Lord, bless the taxi driver who dropped
me off here and who this very minute is waiting at the
Times with the meter running, ready to rush back here
with their review. . . .

*(An audible shiver of excitement runs through the kneeling
group.)*

Bless this driver. Bless their review.

JULIA: Amen!

PETER: *(Just as the others are about to get up)* Lord! In our hour
of greatest need, give us . . . you who have given me the
greatest gift of all, the gift to realize that no matter what
happens tonight, it's only a play . . . give us just one
more thing. It's not much. When you consider the problems you've unleashed on this world: wars and famines
and jet-plane crashes, surely you can give us a hit tonight.
If you can't give us unanimous raves, we'll settle for the
Times. The rest are negotiable. That is my prayer to you,
Lord. That is every playwright's prayer.

JULIA: Amen.

THE OTHERS: *(Muttered)* Amen.

PETER: Do you hear me, Lord, may I hope for some sign?

(The telephone begins to ring.)

GUS: That was quick.

(GUS picks up phone.)

Hello?

(To JAMES)

It's for you.

JAMES: Who on earth could that be? Hello?

IRA: You know, Mr. Austin, there was a genuine sincerity when you spoke.

PETER: That surprises you?

IRA: From the author of this evening's play, quite frankly, yes.

JULIA: I'm so glad to see you two getting along.

IRA: It's the funniest thing. I like you personally.

JULIA: We all do.

IRA: It's just your work I can't stand. Now you take someone like David Mamet, and I have the totally opposite reaction.

(PETER is upon him! In a flash, HE has hands around IRA'S throat and is trying to do him great harm. VIRGINIA and FRANK are taking coke.)

VIRGINIA: Hit it, hit it!

JULIA: Peter! Gentlemen! Stop that, please!

IRA: Help! Help!

(JAMES is having his own problems on the telephone.)

JAMES: Cancelled? My series has been cancelled?

JULIA: Will somebody do something?

(JULIA is turning in circles.)

FRANK: *(Holding the spoon for VIRGINIA)* Hit it, Ginny, hit it!

(EMMA is seen coming up the stairs. SHE is wearing a leather jacket, jeans, and a cloth cap. EMMA comes into the bedroom. This is what SHE sees: PETER standing and strangling IRA; JULIA running in hysterical circles; VIRGINIA and FRANK doing

coke; JAMES *in a state approaching catatonia.* EMMA *puts two fingers in her mouth and whistles. It is a loud whistle.* EVERYONE *stops what they are doing and looks at her.)*

EMMA: Hey you!

PETER: What?

EMMA: You know that paper you're waiting on?

ALL: *(Except* JAMES*)* Yes!

EMMA: The one with the review?

ALL: Yes!

EMMA: The *New York Times?*

ALL: Yes!!!

EMMA: They got it down there.

(Total chaos. EMMA *is knocked over in their surge to get downstairs and get that paper.)* What's wrong with these people? It's only a play! *(The curtain is falling.* JAMES *looks like something out of the Last Judgment. All the phones on* JULIA*'s desk have started ringing.* TORCH *is barking and tearing at the bathroom door. The Curtain is Down.)*

END OF ACT I

ACT II

AT RISE: *The same as Act I, a few moments later.* JAMES *is seated by the telephone, clutching his head in despair.* GUS *is looking through piles of coats.* EMMA *is brushing herself off.* TORCH *is still savaging the bathroom door. All the phones are ringing.*

GUS: *(To the phones)* Hold your horses!

EMMA: *(To* JAMES*)* All I said was "Here's your paper." What's the matter with those people?

JAMES: Do you mind? I have my own problems.

GUS: *(Snatching up the house phone)* Yes? . . . Tell Miss Bacall I'm looking for her coat!
    *(*HE *hangs up and continues to search.)*

EMMA: *(To* JAMES*)* I know you.

JAMES: Please.

EMMA: Don't worry. I'm cool. I've had celebrities up the kazoo in my back seat. I respect their privacy and I expect them to respect mine. "Top of the morning to you, Mrs. Onassis," and that's it until she gets out. Then it's "Have a good one, Mrs. O." I like 'em to know that I know but that's it. You dig? Now of course you take someone like Howard Cosell who's a real chatterbox and it's a whole other thing.

JAMES: I'll sell the house and do a new Neil Simon play. If Doc doesn't have a new play I'll go out with *Charley's Aunt* again.

GUS: *(Snatching up the phone again)* You're out of food down there? Call Chicken Delight! *(HE hangs up and continues to search.)*

EMMA: See, celebrities are just like anybody else. They just happen to be famous. I could be Lucille Ball, only I'm not. Big deal.

GUS: *(Snatching up an outside line this time)* Yeah? . . . Anybody here put in a call to Dinah Shore?

(JAMES breaks down and cries.)

EMMA: I'll talk to her.

GUS: Wrong number.

(HE hangs up.)

EMMA: Is it always like this around here?

GUS: I wouldn't know. I'm temporary.

EMMA: I'm Emma.

GUS: I'm Gus.

EMMA: Emma, Emma Bovary. It's a long story. We all have a cross to bear. Listen, it could have been Hitler, you know? Emma Hitler. Count your blessings, that's what I always say. What are we looking for?

GUS: Lauren Bacall's mink.

(EMMA will help him search for the coat.)

JAMES: Does anybody know if *The Mousetrap* has ever been done in America?

(PETER, JULIA, VIRGINIA, FRANK, and IRA tearing up the stairs. THEY have the New York Times, only it is in several sections. As they come pouring into the room, a desperate battle ensues. These people will stoop to anything to get their hands on that review. Think of children in a sandbox.)

PETER: Give me that.

IRA: Let go.

VIRGINIA: That's mine.

JULIA: It's my house.

IRA: Fight fair.

PETER: Go write your own review.

JAMES: I just want the television page.

PETER: It's my paper. I sent for it.

FRANK: Why didn't you get two?

PETER: I didn't know so many crazy people would be fighting over it.

FRANK: You're ripping it.

IRA: Give me that.

(THEY *rip the section in half.*)

FRANK: Now look what you've done.

(EMMA *steps forward.*)

EMMA: We're missing a mink up here.

PETER: You!

EMMA: Don't worry. I've stopped the meter.

PETER: Just tell me what he said.

EMMA: What who said?

PETER: The *Times*, the *Times*, the *Times*!!

EMMA: I don't read the *Times*, the *Times*, the *Times*!! What do I look like? I'm a *News* reader.

(SHE *has made the mistake of taking the* News *out of her back pocket.*)

PETER: (*Snatching it*) Give me that!

EMMA: (*Snatching it right back*) No!

PETER: Please!

EMMA: Well don't grab. (SHE *gives it to him.*) Here. Half an hour ago you were a nice young man.

PETER: (*Throwing the paper down*) Tell me about it. It's an early edition. There's no review.

JAMES: Doesn't anybody have the television page?

VIRGINIA: It's not here.

JULIA: It has to be here.

JAMES: Here it is! (EVERYONE *freezes.*) "ABC Announces Four Cancellations; *Out on a Limb* Among Them."

(*The frenzied search resumes as* JAMES *crosses to sit and read the television page.*)

EMMA: Aw! I liked that show.

FRANK: Wait. Listen to this. "For reasons of space, Frank Rich's review of last night's opening at the Barrymore appears today on page seventy-six under *Dogs, Cats, and other Pets*."

PETER: They buried us.

FRANK: Who has seventy-six? *(There is much rustling of newspaper.)*

IRA: I've got one through nine and then they're all in the thirties.

VIRGINIA: *(Struck by a news item)* Jesus! *(Again* THEY *all freeze.)*

ALL: What?

VIRGINIA: *The Fantasticks* is closing.

PETER: Fuck *The Fantasticks*.

JULIA: What page are we looking for?

ALL: *(Apoplectic)* Seventy-six!

JULIA: *(With great dignity.* SHE *is not to be shouted at like this. Ever.)* I produced this play and I can close it. *(*SHE *calmly checks her page numbers.)* Now let me see. Page seventy-four, Consumer Notes. Page seventy-five, Wine Talk.

PETER: It's Chinese torture.

JULIA: Will you people stop crowding me? Thank you. Here we are. Page seventy-six!

*(*THEY *descend on her, snatching the precious page.)* Be careful! *(*PETER *wins. The paper is his.)*

PETER: Now everybody sit down.

EMMA: Me, too?

PETER: Sit down and shut up. *(To* EMMA*)* You shouldn't even be here.

EMMA: I know. You want me to go . . . *(*SHE *sits.)*

PETER: No!!

JAMES: *(Throwing his section of the* Times *aside)* We never had a chance.

PETER: That goes for you, too.

JAMES: Not with our writers.

PETER: James.

JAMES: Not in our time slot.

PETER: Jimmy!

JAMES: Not with her for a co-star. (HE *has gone to the telephone.*)

PETER: What are you doing?

JAMES: *(Already dialing)* There are other things in the world besides your play.

PETER: Not for the next five minutes there are not.

JAMES: *(Into phone)* Hello, ABC? I represent eight hundred Italian Catholics in the Bronx and I want to protest the cancellation of— (PETER *breaks the connection.*)

PETER: This is my moment and you're not going to spoil it.

JAMES: You could stuff a moose with the egos in this room.

GUS: *(Taking this as a cue to sit)* Miss Bacall says she's not leaving till she gets her coat back. Neither is Leonard Bernstein.

JULIA: *(On the house phone)* I can't talk to you when you get like this, Betty. (SHE *hangs up.*)

PETER: May I have silence?

(The phones have begun to ring again. PETER *will take them all off the hook.)*

Until we finish, there will be no interruptions.

VIRGINIA: Don't be so dramatic, Peter.

PETER: Drama is my business, lady.

JAMES: You could have fooled me.

PETER: Who said that? Who said that?

JAMES: I did. God, I wish I did drugs.

PETER: *(All ready to read)* Ahem!

VIRGINIA: Will you just read it, Peter?

PETER: *(After taking a deep breath)* "*Golden Egg* opens at the Barrymore."

VIRGINIA: We know what the name of your play is.

PETER: And then there's a smaller headline: "Actor scores brilliant triumph." That'll be Jack.

VIRGINIA: I knew it, I knew it. That's the part.

PETER: "With *The Golden Egg*, which opened last night at the blah blah blah, Peter Austin makes his eagerly awaited Broadway debut."

JULIA: It's a rave! I knew it!

PETER: *(HE stops.)* I can't.

JULIA: Peter!

PETER: I'm sorry, everyone. I'm too nervous. You, the cab driver. What's your name?

EMMA: Emma.

PETER: You read it.

EMMA: Emma Bovary.

PETER: Skip it.

EMMA: *(Taking the paper from him)* You're right. I'm the only objective person here.

GUS: I'm objective.

EMMA: I'm more. Now everybody sit.

(PETER sits. EMMA reads the review.)

PETER: Well?

EMMA: I'm reading, I'm reading!

PETER: Out loud!

(HE grabs the paper from her.)

EMMA: What am I? A mind reader?

PETER: Here. What's your name. You read it.

(GUS takes the paper and begins to read very haltingly.)

GUS: "With *The Golden Egg*, which opened last night at the—

PETER: Oh, give me that! *(HE snatches it from him.)* Where was I . . . ? *(HE finds his place.)* ". . . Peter Austin makes his eagerly awaited Broadway debut. Would that he hadn't." *(HE looks up.)* It's going to be mixed. *(HE resumes.)* "This is the kind of play that gives playwriting a bad name and deals the theater, already a somewhat endangered species, something very close to a death blow." *(HE looks up.)* I don't think he liked it.

VIRGINIA: Peter.

PETER: I'm okay, Ginny, I'm okay. *(Resumes)* "It tarnishes the reputation of everyone connected with it, not permanently perhaps, but certainly within their lifetime."

JULIA: That sentence doesn't even make sense. What's more permanent than your lifetime?

PETER: "Even the usherettes and the concessionaires at the Barrymore should be walking with lowered heads today and for at least another season to come."

EMMA: When they go for the ushers! That's gotta be a first.

PETER: "Shame, ladies and gentlemen of the cloakroom, shame." *(HE looks up.)* I'm going to be sick.

EMMA: *(Her hand out for the paper)* You don't want me to . . . ?

PETER: I began and I'll finish it.

(Perhaps a wild howl escapes from him at this point, perhaps not.)

"Any play that calls itself *The Golden Egg* is just asking for it." The title is a metaphor, an ironic metaphor.

EMMA: I don't know what an ironic metaphor is. I just know a lousy title when I hear one.

PETER: Who is this person anyway?

EMMA: The salt of the earth. Now are you going to finish that? We're on pins and needles.

PETER: *(Resuming)* "With such a title, I must confess that I arrived at the playhouse with my critical hackles already up."

JULIA: He's admitting he was prejudiced.

PETER: "After ten minutes of Mr. Austin's play, they were so up the woman behind me complained she couldn't see. Lucky lady." *(HE looks up.)* You think this is easy? *(HE resumes.)* "If *The Golden Egg* is not the worst American play since *Pinched Nerve,* it is not for Mr. Austin's lack of trying. Better luck next time." Would you think any less of me if I burst into tears?

(HE lets the review fall as JULIA comforts him. IRA snatches it up.)

JULIA: My darling Peter.

IRA: "It is dismaying to remember that Mr. Austin . . ."

JULIA: Please, Mr. Drew!

PETER: It's all right, I can take it.

JULIA: You're only tormenting yourself.

PETER: Maybe I want to.

IRA: ". . . was the author of *Flashes*, which I praised to the skies along with my colleagues, with the single exception of Ira Drew, who I generally find the least perceptive and the most prejudiced of the New York critics." *(HE looks up.)* That's a little dig. *(HE resumes.)* "Were we all wrong? Was Mr. Drew a prophet crying in the wilderness? I think so now and my apologies to Mr. Drew . . ." *(HE looks up.)* He's trying to make it up to me now. Too late, Frankie. *(HE resumes.)* ". . . whom I still regard as the least perceptive, most prejudiced, physically unappetizing and generally creepy drama critic in New York." *(HE looks up.)* I knew Frank didn't like me but the *extent*.

JAMES: *(Reaching for the paper)* Are you going to finish the review or not?

IRA: *(Resuming in fury)* "The plot of Mr. Austin's debacle . . ."

JAMES: We know all that.

VIRGINIA: Get to the acting.

IRA: "I can be more cheerful about the acting."

VIRGINIA: I should hope so.

IRA: "But not much. Only Jack Nimble, as the unlucky Tamburini, a role that was clearly tailored for James Wacker—"

JAMES: Wicker!

IRA: It says Wacker. *(HE resumes.)* "—emerges with distinction. If there any justice in our theater, and I am becoming less and less convinced that there is—How can there be, when plays like this get produced?"

PETER: Leave me alone, goddammit!

IRA: "Then Mr. Nimble is a shoo-in for this season's Best Actor Tony Award."

JAMES: A what?

IRA: "As for Mr. Wicker—"

JAMES: What did I do?

IRA: They got it right this time. *(HE resumes.)* "—who is chiefly remembered hereabouts for his somewhat over-praised performance in Mr. Austin's *Flashes*—"

JAMES: For my what?

IRA: Somewhat overpraised performance. *(HE resumes.)* "Certainly I preferred his replacement, Charles Nelson Reilly, who brought a more masculine presence and yet strangely cutting sensitivity to the role . . ."

JAMES: A more what?

JULIA: *(Always helpful)* A more masculine presence and—

JAMES: Shut up, Julia. I heard what he said.

IRA: ". . . he should count himself lucky to be out of this turkey due to his commitments to his enormously popular television series (I must admit I'm mad for it but don't tell my colleagues) *Out on a Lamb.*"

JAMES: "Limb," dammit, "Limb."

IRA: It says "Lamb."

JAMES: Give me that! *(HE furiously snatches the paper.)*

VIRGINIA: That's funny, I thought I was the star of this thing.

JAMES: Don't worry, honey, he'll get to you. He went bananas tonight. *(HE reads.)* "Virginia Noyes, making one would have thought a welcome return to the New York stage after an ill-starred stint in Hollywood, wears out her welcome in her first speech."

VIRGINIA: I don't have a speech. I only have three lines.

JAMES: "She reminded this poor groundling of nothing so much as a female impersonator in search of a female impersonator to impersonate."

IRA: That's almost out-and-out plagiarism.

VIRGINIA: Jesus.

JAMES: "I hope by the time she reads this, she is headed back to Burbank. Bon voyage and good riddance, Miss Noyes." *(HE looks up.)* Why that's terrible, just terrible.

EMMA: I wouldn't be in the theater if you paid me.

JAMES: "The rest of the cast is outstanding."

JULIA: Now that's more like it.

JAMES: "Considering what these valiant troopers have been asked to perform, I'm only surprised they haven't marched on the producer's house and stoned it."

JULIA: He put them up to it.

JAMES: "As for the producer, one Julia Budder, and I urge you to remember that name, Julia Budder, remember it well, Julia Budder—"

JULIA: Stop, this is inhuman!

JAMES: "The *Playbill* tells us that this is her first independent production after many years as an extremely successful investor."

JULIA: I don't see what that has to do with the price of fish.

JAMES: "With the money she has made from these other shows, Mrs. Budder should have done something worthwhile: such as open a mental hospital in which to have her head examined.

JULIA: I have opened hospitals. I've done a lot for charity.

JAMES: "When one thinks of the plays Mrs. Budder could have produced, a Lanford Wilson—"

JULIA: I'm going to.

JAMES: "Or a Hugh Golden . . ."

JULIA: Who is he? I'll do him.

JAMES: ". . . instead of Mr. Austin's dreck, the mind boggles. *(HE looks up.)* Does anyone want to take over? *(HE resumes.)* "Not only was her decision to mount this play imbecilic, it was also immoral. What possessed you, Mrs. Budder?"

JULIA: What possessed any of us?

JAMES: "What possessed any of you? Have I left anyone out?"

FRANK: Everyone's favorite director.

JAMES: "Oh, yes, the direction of Frank Finger."

FRANK: Here it comes. I've been expecting this a long time.

JAMES: "Long the most brilliant of our younger directors [his production of *Titus Andronicus* at Yale has attained legendary status in certain circles; wretched me, I didn't see it], Mr. Finger again gives us a stunning production. This is a man who can do no wrong, and I am sure his wrong would be right."

FRANK: I never heard such bullshit.

VIRGINIA: You want to trade?

PETER: Congratulations, Frank.

JULIA: Bravo, Darling, Bravo.

JAMES: "I hope this review will not make you want to rush to the Barrymore Theatre."

IRA: Can't you just see the lines on 47th Street? *(HE laughs; quickly catches himself.)* I'm sorry.

JAMES: "Besides, I bet they're striking the scenery at the Barrymore this very moment."

JULIA: What does that mean? Striking?

EMMA: Taking it down.

JAMES: "Unless, of course, it hasn't already collapsed out of sheer embarrassment. Oh well, onwards and upwards with the Arts." *(Short pause)* That's it.
(HE lets the review drop to the floor and sits. No one moves. There is a long gloomy pause now.)

PETER: I think it's important that we all love one another very, very much right now.

VIRGINIA: He didn't even say I was pretty. I always got pretty at least before.

JAMES: *(HE will never really get over this.)* Charles Nelson Reilly?

IRA: Seeing you people like this, the genuine hurt . . . I'm sorry more critics can't share this experience with me.

JULIA: Oh, fuck off! I'm sorry, Mr. Drew, but please!

GUS: Down home we'd wipe a dude like that out. Your mama would pack a gun and go shoot the mother. How do you write something like that about somebody's child?
(There is a burst of applause from downstairs.)

PETER: Listen! You hear that?

VIRGINIA: *Popular Mechanics* just came in. I heard they loved us.

PETER: Besides, I knew he wouldn't like it. His best friend's wife's sister's niece is a Catholic. And anyway, I can think of lots of hit shows that made it without a good review from the *New York Times*.

EMMA: You can?

PETER: Will you stay out of this? It never fails. At every opening, some total stranger manages to penetrate the inner sanctum. Opening night of *Flashes* it was a chiropodist from Long Island. Everybody thought he was with somebody else. It turned out he hadn't even seen the show. Remember, Jimmy?

JAMES: Charles Nelson Reilly?

FRANK: For what it's worth, guys, I'm very proud I did this play.

PETER: Coming from you, that's worth a lot.

FRANK: This play threatens a lot of people.

JULIA: It does? Now you tell me.

JAMES: Dom De Luise I could accept but Charles Nelson Reilly?

VIRGINIA: Who was it who said, "Where else but in the theater do you get to rehearse and rehearse for weeks and weeks just to make a horse's ass of yourself?"

IRA: Did someone say that? That's very funny. *(HE stifles himself.)* But did you hear the one about the terrible actor who was playing Hamlet? He'd barely begun "To be or not to be" when the audience began booing, throwing things, the works. Finally, the actor stepped forward and said, "I didn't write this shit."

(This time he can't control himself. THE OTHERS *look at him with much loathing.)*

"I didn't write this shit."

(HE is writhing with laughter. Finally, he is aware of the silence in the room and that he is at the center of it.)

I'm sorry. But seriously, weren't you aware something like this might happen?

PETER: Nothing's happened! We got one lousy review. Big deal. We still have the other papers, the weeklies, the monthlies.

IRA: What about your preview audiences?

VIRGINIA: What about them? We had two and a half weeks of nurses, nuns, and nitwits.

JULIA: Don't be bitter, Virginia. It doesn't become you.

EMMA: Are you a straight play or a comedy?

VIRGINIA: Don't look at me.

PETER: We're a comedy with serious overtones.

EMMA: There's your trouble. People don't like overtones.

PETER: Don't be so literal. You haven't even seen the play. All I'm saying is: we don't need the critics. We'll run because we've got word of mouth.

VIRGINIA: We've got hoof and mouth!

JULIA: Virginia! I hate pessimism. I hate it in real life and I hate it in the theater. That's why I'm a producer.

FRANK: Don't let them do this to you, Ginny.

VIRGINIA: They ain't doing nothing. They tried that number on me out in Hollywood. "You're only as good as your last picture," my agent told me. "Bullshit," I told him. "Nothing's as bad as my last three pictures but especially me. Just get me a job." "Ginny, I can't get you arrested. Cool out for a couple of years. Get married again." Me, Miss Two-Time Tony Award Winner! Miss Hot Shit Herself! They wouldn't touch me with a twenty-foot pole. And people wonder why I bottomed out? It took seeing my face on the front page of the *National Enquirer* after marriage Number Three ended for it to suddenly hit me: what am I doing out there? Standing in the check-out line at the Arrow Market on Santa Monica wearing a dirty bathrobe and nothing else, that's where I remembered who I was! An actress, a fucking stage actress. Two days later, I packed everything I owned into my little red Mustang and burned rubber straight back to New York.

PETER: You did the right thing, Ginny.

VIRGINIA: I didn't let you down?

PETER: Are you crazy?

VIRGINIA: I gotta hear it. I gotta hear it a lot.

FRANK: Anytime.

VIRGINIA: Good thing I didn't know I'd already worn out my welcome on my first speech.

(SHE *goes.*)

JULIA: Virginia!

FRANK: I'll go.

(FRANK *goes.*)

PETER: You still want to be in show business, Gus?

GUS: Oh sure! Don't you?

EMMA: You're safer doing ninety miles an hour blindfolded on the Jersey Turnpike.

GUS: My teacher says we're acrobats of the gods, working without a net.

JULIA: Gus?

GUS: Yes, Mrs. Budder?

JULIA: The party.

GUS: I'm sorry, Mrs. Budder. I forget sometimes.

JULIA: We all do.

(GUS *goes.*)

EMMA: Can I get anyone anything?

PETER: Not for me.

EMMA: You could all use some food. Besides, I'm feeling a bit peckish myself. I hate sitting still. Always have. Maybe that's why I'm a cab driver. No, that's not why. I like people too much. I like listening to their problems. I'm not much of a talker myself. I get a kick out of gab. I hope I don't run into anyone I know down there. Look at me. They're your peers but my fares.

(EMMA *goes.*)

PETER: James?

JAMES: No.

PETER: For the last time: will you please go down there and ask Walter Kerr what he thought or not?

JAMES: You are asking this somewhat overpraised, ex-star of stage, screen, and now television to go down there into that den of success and Charles Nelson Reilly's and ask Walter Kerr what he thought of your play? Sure, I hope he peepee-cacas on it.

(JAMES *leaves to go downstairs.*)

PETER: No wonder we haven't heard any more from Buzz! (PETER *has noticed that all the telephones are still off the hook. During the following,* HE *will rush about the room putting the receivers back onto their cradles.*)

Just remember your promise to me, Julia. You'll put up a fight for this show.

JULIA: One good quote and I'll put up the biggest fight anybody ever saw.

PETER: You might be needing that blimp yet.

IRA: What blimp?

PETER: Our press agent hired the Goodyear blimp with quotes for the play.

IRA: What's he going to quote?

PETER: Our good reviews. And here they come!

(*Almost all the phones have started ringing again.* PETER *snatches one up.*)

Budder residence, Mission Control. This is the Playwright speaking. Who is this?

JULIA: I'm not at home to anyone but the Shubert Organization, TWA, a Mr. Yamamoto, or Gloria Vanderbilt.

PETER: It's Lanford Wilson.

JULIA: Darling Lance! (SHE *will pick up an extension.*)

PETER: "Darling Lance!"

IRA: Have you read Mr. Wilson's new play?

PETER: It's terrific. I hate it. (*To* JULIA) Would you mind not tying up the phones, Julia? I'm sure Buzz is trying to get through.

JULIA: (*Into phone*) Lanford, you're hysterical. I can't talk to you when you get like this. (*To* PETER) He's worried I'm not going to produce his play now.

PETER: *(Snatching up an extension)* She's sick of the Talleys. Everybody is.

(HE hangs up. EMMA returns with a heaping plate of food for PETER and the others.)

EMMA: I just had a run-in with one of your guests. I said "Listen, mister, I don't care if you're Ed Koch, I saw the shrimp first." *(SHE is offering PETER food.)* Here.

PETER: I can't.

EMMA: Eat.

PETER: I—

EMMA: Eat, I said! *(To IRA)* You too.

(JAMES enters.)

PETER: Did you see Walter Kerr?

JAMES: Yes.

PETER: What did he say?

JAMES: He's returning your Mass card. You got another "good solid theater." The *Wall Street Journal*.

(JAMES goes to the bathroom. TORCH goes into action. JAMES isn't having any, however.)

Watch it, Buster.

PETER: I'm sick of "good solid theater."

EMMA: What's wrong with it?

PETER: It's not enough anymore.

IRA: You actually sent Walter Kerr a Mass card? Now I've heard everything.

PETER: Put a bag over your head and I'd fuck you for a good review.

IRA: I can see that. But a Mass card?

JULIA: *(On the phone)* Now do some rewrites, Lanford! . . . Any rewrites. I don't want another tonight on my hands. *(SHE hangs up.)* He's so dear.

PETER: Dear? I'm dear. He's pushy.

EMMA: *(Answering another phone)* Hello? It's for you, Mrs. Budder.

JULIA: Who is it?

EMMA: It's a Hugh Golden.

JULIA: Who?

PETER: Hugh Golden. The *Times* wants you to produce his new play. What did they do? Run your number with that review? *(Snatching up extension)* You certainly didn't waste any time! She never hear of you either.

(HE slams down his extension. JULIA has already picked up hers.)

JULIA: Hello, Mr. Golden. This is a pleasure.

PETER: Where is Rita Chang when I need her? I want a cigarette. I need a cigarette. Somebody give me a cigarette.

IRA: *(Offering one)* Here you are.

PETER: Get away from me. That man is the devil.

IRA: I'm trying to understand what this experience must be like for you people.

PETER: I'll tell you in one word: not nice.

(We can almost see IRA count, start to correct PETER but think better of it. Almost.)

JULIA: *(Into phone)* Of course I'd be interested in reading your new play, Mr. Golden. You'll bicycle it over tonight?

PETER: I'm sure Buzz is trying to reach us, Julia.

JULIA: *(Into phone)* All right then, Hugh.

PETER: Hugh? It's Hugh already?

JULIA: *(Into phone)* Onwards and upward yourself! *(SHE hangs up.)* He sounds very talented.

PETER: At what?

IRA: He's no Caroline Comstock, Mrs. Budder.

PETER: *(Playwriting makes strange bedfellows.)* And Hugh! He's got her calling him Hugh!

JULIA: It's his name, darling.

EMMA: *(Taking another call)* Yes?

JULIA: I feel like a producer again. I've got the old adrenalin going.

EMMA: Neil Simon on three. Irene Fornes on six.

JULIA: *(SHE's on a winning streak.)* I'll have to get back to you, Doc. You, too, Irene. *(SHE hangs up.)* Playwrights! I am going to be the earth mother of the American theater, and you will all be my children. Come to me. Give me your plays! I want to spread theater. Increase and multiply it. The sky's the limit. Watch out, Broadway, here comes Julia Budder!

(EMMA *has answered the extension nearest her.*)

EMMA: Joe Papp on five.

JULIA: *(Scooping the phone up in one extravagant gesture from her last speech)* Joseph, darling, how are you?

PETER: It's like my play never happened. *(Furious at himself)* Why do I keep talking to you?

EMMA: Harold Pinter on two?

PETER: *(Snatching up extension)* She said American theater! *(HE hangs up.)*
Of all the chutzpah! (IRA *corrects his pronunciation.*)

JULIA: *(Whose spirits have visibly wilted)* How large a donation were you thinking of, Mr. Papp? Of course I support the Offenbach in the Park Festival next summer. Don't bite my head off. I just didn't expect you to ask me to put my money where my mouth is tonight.

IRA: That's the kind of behavior which has gotten him where he is today, which is almost nowhere.

JULIA: *(Hanging up)* I can never say no to that man. He wants thirty thousand dollars. Who is Offenbach?

(JULIA *will rip a check out of her ledger-sized checkbook.*)

PETER: A dead French composer. I am a living American playwright. Why don't you give me thirty thousand dollars?

JULIA: I'm trying to give you a hit.

PETER: Do you have to do that now?

JULIA: It's just money. Besides, he's on his way over for it.

PETER: How? On his dog sled! All the reviews aren't in yet, Julia.

JULIA: How many *p*s in Papp?

PETER: Four. I'm still here, people. My play isn't over. I sense an avalanche. I feel an abandonment. I smell a stampede.

(PETER *is pacing in furious circles. No one pays him any mind.*)

GUS: *(Entering)* Can you come downstairs, Mrs. Budder? They're running out of everything!

IRA: Mrs. Budder, about *Bluestocking* . . . !

EMMA: Where do you keep your vacuum cleaner, lady?

JULIA: I don't know.

EMMA: I hate a room to get like this.

(JAMES comes out of the bathroom.)

JAMES: Bye-bye, Torch. Night-night. *(To the OTHERS)* It's amazing what a little Valium will do.

JULIA: James!

JAMES: Kidding! That dog just needs a strong authority figure.

EMMA: You all do. *(To JULIA)* You think it's downstairs?

(JULIA goes, followed by IRA and EMMA. PETER will look up a telephone number in his pocket diary and dial it during the following.)

PETER: Do they know what I turned down to write this play? The financial sacrifices I made? The screenplay for *Annie*. A mini-series on the life of Henry Winkler. He's had a very interesting life. A pilot for Mary Lou Retton. A chance to work with Franco Zeffirelli on the history of civilization. Don't tell me I didn't pay my dues to write this play. *(Into phone)* Hello! Did I wake you? Good. This is James Wicker.

JAMES: What are you doing?

PETER: I just read your review of the new Peter Austin play and I think you're full of shit.

(HE hangs up.)

I guess that's telling him.

JAMES: Who was that?

PETER: Frank Rich.

JAMES: Frank Rich?

PETER: You see what they're driving me to?

JAMES: Frank Rich?

PETER: You're not listening to me.

JAMES: Frank Rich. You listen to me. You call him right back and tell him that wasn't me.

PETER: I love you. You're my best friend. I don't want to do these things.

JAMES: I love you, too, and I don't want you doing them. Dial.

PETER: If it means that much to you!

JAMES: Of course it means that much to me.

(PETER *is looking up the number again.* EMMA *appears pushing the vacuum cleaner.*)

EMMA: It was right across the hall.

PETER: Where's your famous sense of humor?

JAMES: I never had one. Ever. It was all a lie. Hurry up. Before he reviews me again. What are you doing with his number anyway?

PETER: I have all the critics' numbers.

JAMES: And they have yours! *(To* EMMA*)* He called Frank Rich and said it was me!

EMMA: You see an outlet?

PETER: *(Into phone)* Hello, Mr. Rich? That wasn't James Wicker who just woke you up and said you were full of shit.

JAMES: Thank you, God. It was Charles Nelson Reilly.

PETER: It was Lanford Wilson.

(HE *hangs up.*)

If I weren't a playwright, I'd be a very nice person.

JAMES: Grow up, Peter. Face facts. Your play is a flop. *(Realizes what he's said)* I mean—!

PETER: You've been waiting to use that word all evening.

JAMES: That's not true.

PETER: You're actually frothing at the mouth. Look at you. There's foam on your lips. Say it again. Say flop.

JAMES: This is ridiculous.

(*At some point in what follows,* EMMA *will turn off the vacuum and listen.*)

PETER: Say it.

JAMES: I don't have to say it.

PETER: Oh, a new tack! *(To* EMMA*)* He's not saying flop. He's implying it.

JAMES: So are a lot of other people.

EMMA: You want me to leave?

PETER: No! God, if that isn't the ugliest word in the English language, Emma—flop!—I'd like to know what is.

JAMES: How about wishing someone and his fucking series a sudden and violent death?

PETER: I was hysterical when I wrote that note.

JAMES: Not half as hysterical as I was when Julia showed it to me.

PETER: "Love" was the operative word, don't you know that yet?

JAMES: I'm sorry, but I fail to see any love in "you miserable, no-talent fruit."

PETER: First chance you get and you bring the conversation right back to yourself. You can't stand someone else being in the spotlight for a change.

JAMES: Considering the spotlight you're under tonight, not really.

PETER: Considering the state of your career, I don't blame you.

EMMA: Grown men!

JAMES: I never believed you when you said you liked my series.

PETER: I never even watched it.

JAMES: I wish I could say the same about your play.

PETER: You didn't like it?

JAMES: I turned it down, didn't I? When have I ever turned anything down? I do *Love Boat*.

PETER: To think I made you a star.

JAMES: To think you what?

PETER: You heard me.

JAMES: Made me a star?

PETER: *Flashes* would have made anyone I let play it.

JAMES: I thought you wrote it for me.

PETER: I did. Only real stars wanted to do it.

JAMES: Name one.

PETER: I can name twenty.

JAMES: Why didn't you go with one of them?

PETER: It was your play.

JAMES: After I got through with it, it was. I should have gotten author's royalties.

PETER: And I was thinking of reviving it with you.

JAMES: Revive it with someone with a more masculine presence who cuts deeper.

PETER: You know something? He did.

JAMES: Funny it closed three weeks after I left and he went in.

PETER: If you'll remember, there was a big strike on at the time.

JAMES: United Parcel for Christ's sake. Next thing you'll be telling us is this one flopped because it opened on Flag Day.

PETER: You realize this is a wrap for our friendship?

JAMES: Total.

PETER: Good. *(To* EMMA*)* You're my witness.

EMMA: If I had a best friend, I'd cherish him.

PETER & JAMES: So would I!

*(*EMMA *turns the vacuum back on as* JULIA *and* IRA *return.)*

JAMES: I spilled the beans, Julia. He's all yours.

JULIA: What happened?

PETER: Something that should have happened five years ago.

JAMES: Ten!

JULIA: Emma! I have someone for that!

EMMA: *(Turning off the vacuum to hear)* What?

JULIA: Not now!

IRA: If I could just read you the one passage from the second act—

JULIA: You either! *(To* PETER*)* What about the rest of the reviews?

PETER: *(Shaking his head, looking at his watch)* Any minute now.

JULIA: Have the Shuberts called yet?

PETER: Those vultures.

JULIA: They want me to keep us open until someone called Charo is ready to come in.

JAMES: What's she coming in in?

JULIA: Some little Lorca play.

PETER: Close this play, Julia—!

JULIA: Who said anything—!

PETER: It's crossed your mind. Don't deny it.

JULIA: Well of course it's crossed it. No one's that stupid.

(FRANK *comes into the room with* VIRGINIA *and* GUS.)

VIRGINIA: Are we gonna run?

PETER: We're still waiting for the rest of the reviews.

VIRGINIA: *El Diario* loved us. They gave us two ears and the tail.

PETER: Are you okay?

VIRGINIA: Is there a choice?

(*The phone rings.* PETER *darts for it.*)

PETER: Buzz? (*Handing the phone to* JULIA) It's the Shuberts.

JULIA: Thank God, maybe they can help us. (SHE *takes the phone.*) Bernie, darling. (*On the phone*) We're in an absolute state of shock. Do you think we could find a way to lower our weekly operating costs? Maybe we could persuade the *Times* to lower their advertising rates? (SHE *covers phone*) He's laughing. (*Into phone*) Then what about all those stagehands who just stand around staring at a disc? It doesn't even move. And who are those men playing poker in the basement? But we're not a musical.

EMMA: You don't wanna go messing with the unions.

JULIA: What you're telling me, Bernie, is that no one at the Barrymore will take a salary cut. I thought they liked Peter's play. I don't see how asking the playwright to waive his royalties will solve our problems.

PETER: I already am. Thanks a lot, Bernie.

JULIA: Well, if your hands are tied, Bernie, what about mine? . . . Of course I don't want that on my conscience.

(SHE *hangs up.*)

PETER: What?

JULIA: If I close tonight, they'll give the Barrymore to *Leather Maidens of Amsterdam.*

IRA: It's a Dutch porno film. I mean, I heard it's a Dutch porno film.

PETER: What happened to Charo?

JULIA: She's closing in Baltimore.

PETER: She gets to go out of town and I don't. It's not fair.

JULIA: The thought of that beautiful theater being turned into a house of pornographic film.

JAMES: Terrible. Just terrible.

EMMA: *Amen.* New York without a theater district might as well be Newark.

GUS: Heck, they can't tear any more theaters down. I haven't made my Broadway debut yet.

PETER: I'd hate to be in your shoes, Julia.

JULIA: They're your shoes, too. They're everybody's.

(*The phone rings.* EMMA *answers it.*)

PETER: That'll be Buzz.

EMMA: Hello?

(THEY *all seem to sense that this is "it."*)

JULIA: All we need is one strong quote and I'll run this play forever.

PETER: The rest of this season will do.

EMMA: It's your press agent with the rest of the reviews.

(EMMA *is holding the phone out.*)

JULIA: (*Shaking her head*) All right. Here we go. I'm too nervous, James.

(JAMES *reluctantly starts for the phone.*)

PETER: The moment he's been waiting for.

JAMES: That's not true.

JULIA: He doesn't mean that.

(JAMES *takes the phone.* JULIA, PETER, VIRGINIA, *and* FRANK *hold hands.*)

JAMES: *(Into phone)* Listen, Buzz, I hope you've got some good news for us . . . Jimmy Wicker . . .

EMMA: I take shorthand. You want me to . . . ?
(JULIA nods. EMMA takes up pencil and paper.)

JAMES: That review in the *Times* was a shaft out of left field. *You* were double-crossed? How do you think they felt? Okay, let's go.
(HE will listen and repeat the following.)
"In the final analysis, Mr. Austin's new play falls just short enough of the mark to fail utterly, however honorably." The *Daily News*.

PETER: I love you, too.

JAMES: "If and when the great American play is written, and I sometimes wish our playwrights would forget all about even trying to, Peter Austin could be its author, but not with this one."

FRANK: You hear that?

VIRGINIA: A review like that would keep me going for at least the rest of my life.

JAMES: "Virginia Noyes is a luminescent actress."

VIRGINIA: That sounds good.

FRANK: It is good.

JAMES: "Frank Finger's direction . . ."

FRANK: We know. Look, I don't enjoy this.

JAMES: ". . . escapes me, the play, and the production."

FRANK: Escapes who?

JAMES: "Long the most overrated talent in the American theater . . ."

FRANK: Is he talking about me?

JAMES: "Mr. Finger is one emperor who isn't wearing any clothes."

FRANK: He took the words right out of my mouth.

JAMES: "Clive Barnes. The *New York Post*."

JULIA: Congratulations, Frank.

FRANK: Thanks.

VIRGINIA: Are you okay?

FRANK: I'm fine. So. Here I am. Here we are. Fuck. Hell, he's right, the little Cockney limey. Give them a Green Card and they think they own the world. I got what I wanted. I'm not angry. I'm happy. You want to see anger? That's anger. You want to see happy? That's happy. *(They're the same.)* Who does he think he is anyway? My father? Oh, wow! Get in touch with this. You're having a breakthrough. Father! Critics! Good boy! Bad Boy! Spank! Ouch! Hug! Oo! Puppets! Basement! Daddy! Yes!

(HE is having a breakthrough: psychic fireworks abound. Finally, he grows still.)

I had a breakthrough. Thank God I've got Mildred tomorrow. Here. *(HE unloads more purloined goods.)* Thank you, Clive.

VIRGINIA: You okay now?

FRANK: Terrific.

(THEY hug. FRANK laughs easily. Do we sense a new FRANK after this catharsis?)

JAMES: Yes, we're still here, Buzz. You've made one person happy.

PETER: What about the weeklies?

JAMES: *(Quoting BUZZ)* *Time* doesn't review shows that already closed.

PETER: We haven't closed!

JAMES: *Newsweek* left after the first act. *New York* left during the first act.

PETER: Get Brendan Gill in the *New Yorker*. He's always been a big fan of mine.

JAMES: He's coming the second night, if there is one.

(THEY all look at JULIA. SHE shakes her head and weeps.)

Should we cancel the blimp? *(JULIA sobs.)* I guess that's the ball game, Buzz.

JULIA: Tell him I'm very disappointed in his services.

JAMES: *(Hanging up)* He just told me he quit.

PETER: I wish I were dead.

JULIA: Gus, I want you to go downstairs and ask everyone to leave. Tell them the party's over.

GUS: Okay. I'll tell most of 'em, but I ain't telling that Bacall woman nothing. For what it's worth, you people: I'm sorry.

JULIA: Thank you.

GUS: It was just getting to be my turn to sing. (HE *goes.*)

PETER: I'll tell you one thing, Mr. Drew. God punishes people who get their plays done on Broadway. He punishes them good.

IRA: That's why He invented regional theater.

PETER: Don't give me regional theater. I'll tell you what regional theater is: plays that couldn't get produced in New York with actors who couldn't get a job in New York performed for audiences who wish they still lived in New York. This is my regional theater. Right here.

JULIA: Peter!

PETER: I still wish I was dead.

EMMA: I just hope all you nice people have the good sense not to brood over this and get on with the next one. You heard him: onwards and upwards.

JULIA: Thank you, Emma.

EMMA: See, if this was nuclear physics I'd keep my big mouth shut, but I know something about show business. The original Harvey was a giraffe. Making him a rabbit happened in my cab.

JULIA: I can't deal with a remark like that.

JAMES: When I'd get discouraged, my father used to say, "It's only a play, Jimbo, it's only a play." Only he said it in Italian. "Non c'e che una commedia, Jimbo, c'e che una commedia." He never saw me make it.

JULIA: Mine used to say, "It's only money, angel. Your money. And don't you forget it."

(GUS *returns.*)

GUS: It's breaking up down there. I didn't have to ask. Everybody's real disappointed. The cast was wondering if there's going to be a second night.

JULIA: That's up to Peter.

PETER: What'd be the point?

(HE *turns away.*)

GUS: They said to thank you for being the nicest producer they've ever worked with.

(HE *gathers more coats to take down and goes. The phone has started to ring. No one has the heart to answer it this time.*)

PETER: No more calls.

EMMA: Hello? (*To* PETER) It's for you.

PETER: Who is it?

EMMA: Steubenville, Ohio.

(PETER *walks to the phone. It is the longest mile.*)

PETER: Hi, Dad. How are you feeling? . . . Hi, Mom . . . Pretty good. Not great but . . . No, not as good as *Flashes*. Listen, can I get back to you when we have all the reviews? I don't want to tie this . . . I love you, too.

(HE *hangs up. He is crying. A wild howl escapes him. He breaks down.*)

FRANK: Hey, c'mon, man, don't. I hate emotion.

(*This time* HE *has heard himself.*) I mean—! Wow!

(*Now it is* JULIA *who breaks down and sobs.*)

JULIA: It's all my fault. That turntable did matter. I'll never forgive myself.

(*The tears are contagious. Now it is* VIRGINIA *who breaks down and sobs.*)

VIRGINIA: It's my fault. I wore out my fucking welcome. I dropped the fucking bottle, it didn't slip.

JAMES: He's right. The play never had a chance without me. I would have been marvelous.

PETER: It's all my fault. I wrote it. Will any of you ever forgive me?

FRANK: Hey, c'mon, you people. It's only a play. We did our best. Oh shit, this is worse than Yale!

(HE, *too, breaks down and cries and joins the others in a tearful huddle of mutual comforting and stroking.*)

EMMA: Papa! *(SHE, too, has broken down.)* He wanted to see Finland before he died. Was that asking so very much?
(THE OTHERS open their arms to her. The stage is awash in tears, real tears. Even TORCH joins in with a heart-rending whine from the bathroom.)

JULIA: Torch!
(GUS has returned for more coats. Instead, HE breaks down when he sees the wailing group and joins them, sobbing his heart out).
It wasn't your fault, Gus.

GUS: I know.

JULIA: Then why are you crying?

GUS: I'm a nice person.

JAMES: *(To THE OTHERS)* A play of Peter's did make me a star. I've never been able to admit that.

PETER: James could have saved my ass tonight. Like he did in *Flashes*. I've never been able to admit that.

JAMES: Here's to our next one.

PETER: After tonight, who'd want to produce it?

JULIA: I certainly would. Why do you think I produced this one?

PETER: I don't know. A tax loss?

JULIA: Peter!

PETER: You really liked it?

JULIA: And I thought a lot of other people would, too. Well I was wrong. Of course there were things wrong with your play. I wish I could have helped you fix them. I wish I had your genius for the moments that did work. We just didn't have quite enough of them. But the ones we did have were splendid. The sight of Virginia in the last act: the way that Frank had her standing, her hair, the costume, the lighting, your beautiful words . . . you could hear a pin drop.
(We see FRANK "frame" VIRGINIA with his hands as if HE were directing the moment JULIA is describing.)

VIRGINIA: "I would dream of Persia and flying carpets and every far-off place I'd ever read of. I could dream of them under my quilt with the calico patches."

EMMA: Sounds like I missed something.

JULIA: You did, Emma. And I produced it. Anyone can come up with a tax loss. It takes a very special maniac to produce a play.

(There is a final cadenza of tears and sniffles from the surrogate "family" on the sofa. Only IRA has been excluded from this grouping.)

IRA: I just don't understand you people. One minute you're at each other's throats, the next you're sticking up for one another like you're in some kind of club.

JAMES: We are.

IRA: I'm in the theater, too, you know.

VIRGINIA: On the outside looking in, baby, on the outside looking in.

IRA: I'm sorry, but I feel in.

OTHERS: You ain't.

(And now it is IRA's turn to break down and sob. At once, HE is the center of their attention as their cares and woes are temporarily forgotten.)

IRA: I can't live with it anymore! I've got to tell someone. I am Caroline Comstock.

VIRGINIA: Who?

IRA: My nom de plume. I didn't want to unduly influence anyone because of my position as a critic. I won't call *Bluestocking* a masterpiece. Let's just say it's the best American play in years. On top of everything else, it only has one set and two characters.

JULIA: You already mentioned that.

IRA: In this day and age, it bears repeating. I felt such a pang of envy when that curtain rose this evening. It's as if that set had been designed for *Bluestocking*.

PETER: They all want to be playwrights. It's a noble profession. Well, dream on, Mr. Drew. I'm not anymore.

JULIA: Don't say that.

PETER: I wrote my first play in high school. The life of George Greshwin. I got all my information from the back of record jackets. In the first scene, young George got thrown out of a music publisher's office. The secretary consoled him and shyly confessed she was a budding lyricist. "What's your name?" George asked her. "Ira," my first heroine said. I think my career has been downhill ever since. I love you all very much, I'm taking the next plane to California. Where do we go from here?

EMMA: The Brasserie's open all night.

PETER: The salt of the earth is finally making sense. You're on and it's on me.

GUS: I'd better get the rest of these coats downstairs.

(GUS exits.)

JULIA: The thought of that beautiful theater dark even one night, or a pornographic film place, or worse, demolished!

VIRGINIA: You've offered *Bluestocking* to Meryl What's-Her-Name, right?

IRA: Meryl Streep for *Bluestocking*! Don't make me laugh.

(But we can see that the idea has enormous appeal for him.)

JAMES: Who's it for? Two men, I guess? More gay theater.

IRA: It's for one man, one woman. Both fiercely heterosexual.

JULIA: Elliott would like that. He's bullish in that department.

IRA: Actually, Miss Noyes, you'd be wonderful for the role of Cubby.

VIRGINIA: Who?

IRA: Cubby. Cubby Blunt. She's sort of an Everywoman figure. Down to earth, basic, warm, very vital.

PETER: Ginny? Frank? Julia? Let's go. James?

JAMES: What about the man's role?

IRA: His name is Fred Brown.

JAMES: Fred Brown.

IRA: But that could be changed. Along with the title.

EMMA: Now you're talking. I hate *Bluestocking*. How about *Clap of Doom?* I've always thought that would make a great title for something. *Clap of Doom.*

(SHE will leave PETER to join THE OTHERS over by IRA.)

IRA: Actually, George is sort of an Everyman figure, too.

JAMES: Who's George?

IRA: Fred is. I just changed it.

VIRGINIA: I thought I was the Everyman figure in this play.

IRA: You both are. George, or maybe it's Fred, after all, Fred is good, it's strong.

JAMES: I like Tucker.

IRA: Tucker is marvelous. Anyway, Tucker, Fred is down to earth, great humor, lots of warmth.

JULIA: Just like you, James.

JAMES: Virile?

IRA: Extremely. You'd be perfect for it.

JULIA: You say *Bluestocking* could be done on Peter's disc?

PETER: Julia!

JULIA: I just wondered.

IRA: With only the slightest of modification.

FRANK: You mind if I take a look at this?
    (HE *will take the script of* Bluestocking *and study it.*)

VIRGINIA: Can you imagine me going from one play right into another? There must be a name for something like that.

IRA: *Coup du théâtre.*

VIRGINIA: *Coup du fucking fabulous.*

JAMES: What about me going from a cancelled series right into the lead of a Broadway show? There must be a name for something like that, too.

PETER: What do you people think you're doing?

JAMES: *(His bubble burst)* He's right. You'd think we were doing this *Bluestocking.* Sorry to get your hopes up.

FRANK: *(Suddenly)* He's right! It could be done on our set.

JULIA: But the Shuberts will want us out of there long before we could be ready to open this one.

FRANK: Wrong again. We could preview tomorrow.

VIRGINIA: Tomorrow? You know me and lines, Frank.

FRANK: Dig this for a concept: two actors, a bare disc.

JULIA: I'm getting goosebumps. Go on.

FRANK: That's it.

JULIA: I like it.

FRANK: Somebody . . .

(GUS *enters.*)

GUS: That's it.

FRANK: . . . a black mute—puts a script in their hands and pushes them on. Instant theater.

VIRGINIA: I buy it.

JAMES: I love it.

JULIA: It's brilliant, Frank. What do you think, Emma?

EMMA: That sounds interesting.

IRA: But that's exactly the idea behind *Bluestocking*. The play is set in a rehearsal situation. The two actors are meant to be carrying their scripts. It's part of my concept.

FRANK: Your concept? Who's directing this show anyway? Let him direct it for you, Julia.

JULIA: Mr. Drew didn't mean it like that. (*To* FRANK) Frank, we could preview tomorrow, you say?

FRANK: Preview?! (THEIR *spirits all collapse.*) We could open. No rehearsals, no rewrites, no previews. (*There is a great renewal of the spirit.*) The whole risk with a project like this, Julia, is the actors getting stale.

JAMES: I don't get stale. I ripen.

PETER: What the hell is going on here?

GUS: Don't say nothing, but I think we're doing another play.

JULIA: All I'm thinking, Peter, is that with *Bluestocking*, Virginia, Frank, and now James will be right back to work, Gus will get to Broadway, and the Ethel Barrymore will be blazing anew with us tomorrow night at eight.

FRANK: We need more scripts.

IRA: They're right downstairs!

(HE *dashes out of the room.*)

JULIA: That reminds me, Gus, there should be a new script down there. It was just bicycled over.

GUS: Okay, but that's it. I'm in rehearsal.

(HE *goes.*)

PETER: What do you think you're doing?

JULIA: Oh, pshaw, Peter. If you had something ready, we'd be doing yours.

PETER: Plays don't pop up like toast.

JULIA: They should! Next time, I think you should write a love story.

PETER: This one was a love story, only nobody noticed. James?

JAMES: You know there's no one I'd rather do than you.

PETER: Then don't do this to me.

JAMES: It's only a play.

PETER: Somebody else's play.

JAMES: You can't write every play.

PETER: I can want to. Virginia . . . ?

VIRGINIA: The sooner you get back up on that high wire, Peter, the better.

(IRA returns with a briefcase full of scripts.)

IRA: Sorry I took so long.

PETER: You're too late. She's doing Hugh Golden.

JAMES: I have a hunch about this script!

VIRGINIA: I want a phone in my dressing room, Julia.

EMMA: *(Who has answered the phone)* The Shubert Organization again. They have to know.

JULIA: Put them on hold, Emma. James . . . ?

JAMES: I'm in.

JULIA: Virginia?

VIRGINIA: Me, too.

JULIA: Frank? Frank? Frank?!

FRANK: I am in rehearsal, Julia!

JULIA: Hello, Bernie. Tell your Leather Maidens they can't have the Barrymore. We're staying. We're holding back the night. We're putting out fingers in the dyke. Budder's back in business.

(SHE hangs up.)

EMMA: *(Holding out another phone)* It's your press agent.

JULIA: He quit.

EMMA: He hears you're producing a new play.

VIRGINIA: Over my dead body.

JULIA: Mine, too, Virginia. *(Into phone)* Buzz off, you asshole.
(SHE *slams the phone down.*)
Now let's get crackin'.
(GUS *returns with a script for* JULIA.)

GUS: What did I miss?

PETER: Frank changed his concept. He's going with Whoopi Goldberg.

GUS: No fair. She's already been to Broadway.

VIRGINIA: I'm going to wear my hair in tight little curls.

JAMES: I see this guy in a plaid jumpsuit.

EMMA: Hey, you got a thunderstorm here.

IRA: I know that!

EMMA: That's something people go for in a play: special effects.

IRA: There's a typhoon in the second act.

EMMA: I'll tell you something else they go for: intermissions.

JULIA: *(Clutching the script to her bosom)* Little Epiphanies by Hubert A. Golden III. I am the luckiest woman in the world!

IRA: You're not going to read Mr. Golden's play tonight?

JULIA: You playwrights are all alike. A producer even looks at another script and you feel abandoned.

FRANK: People, we have an opening. Can we get started?

VIRGINIA: In front of him?

IRA: I don't mind.

VIRGINIA: You will.

JULIA: This is exciting.

IRA: Too exciting. I'm going to throw up.

JULIA: Nonsense. Now come and sit here by me. *(To* GUS*)* Congratulations, Gus.

GUS: *(Looking at his script)* When do I come in?

JAMES: What did I miss? I was counting my lines.

PETER: I thought you all loved me.

JULIA: We do, darling, we just love the theater more.

FRANK: "*Bluestocking*, a new play in four acts by Caroline Comstock."

IRA: Do you know how long I've waited to hear that? Eleven years.

JULIA: That's the second saddest thing I've ever heard.

PETER: Mr. Drew?

IRA: Please, we're working.

PETER: Good luck.

FRANK: "At rise, nothing." *(To* CAST*)* Let's make that something.

IRA: But—! It has to be nothing . . .

FRANK: If he keeps this up, I'm gonna want him barred, Julia.

EMMA: I thought of something else people want in a play. Life! Lots and lots of life.

PETER: Thanks, I'll try to remember that.

FRANK: What do all these dots mean?

IRA: Hesitations, pauses.

JAMES: I don't do hesitations.

IRA: Pinter uses dots.

FRANK: Fuck Pinter.

(HE rips pages from IRA's *script.* JAMES, VIRGINIA, *and* GUS *follow suit.* IRA *apologizes.)*

JULIA: I hope you're taking this all in, Emma. It's the real thing.

EMMA: I never knew it was like this.

JULIA: Wait! It gets better.

PETER: *(HE sees his next marquee.)* "*It's Only a Play*, a new play by Peter Austin."

FRANK: Lights up. "A woman screams in the distance."

(VIRGINIA screams.)

"Or is it a woman?" "Or is it a woman?"

(JAMES screams.)

"An ineffable sound."

GUS: Me?

FRANK: No, Julia.

(JULIA screams.)

Yes, you!
(GUS *screams. A star is born!*)
Where have you been all my life?
(HE gives GUS a big kiss.)
VIRGINIA: *(To JAMES, low)* We got our hands full with this one.
EMMA: *(To JULIA)* The kid's good.
GUS: Thank you.
FRANK: May we continue? Virginia, you'll be downstage right in a spot. James, downstage left.
(The lights begin to fade on the grouping as they continue to rehearse.)
PETER: *(Beginning to create)* "The curtain rises. An opening-night party is in progress."
(The lights are beginning to fade on him, too. The lights fade to black.)

THE PLAY IS OVER

(IMPORTANT NOTE: *The first curtain call is taken by* TORCH. HE *comes out of the bathroom.* HE *is an adorable beagle.)*

0586